Inside China's Automobile Factories

In *Inside China's Automobile Factories*, Lu Zhang explores the current conditions, subjectivity, and collective actions of auto-workers in the world's largest and fastest-growing automobile manufacturing nation. Based on years of fieldwork and extensive interviews conducted at seven large auto factories in various regions of China, Zhang provides an inside look at the daily factory life of autoworkers and a deeper understanding of the roots of rising labor unrest in the auto industry. Combining original empirical data and sophisticated analysis that moves from the shop floor to national political economy and global industry dynamics, the book develops a multilayered framework for understanding how labor relations in the auto industry and broader social economy can be expected to develop in China in the coming decades.

Lu Zhang is an assistant professor of sociology at Temple University. Her research concentrates on globalization, labor and labor movements, and the political economy of development in East Asia, particularly China. Her work has been published in *International Labor and Working Class History* and the *International Journal of Automotive Technology and Management*. She has contributed to five books: *China & Global Governance: The Dragon's Learning Curve* (2015); *Workers in Hard Times: A Long View of Economic Crises* (2014); *From Iron Rice Bowl to Informalization: Markets, Workers, and the State in a Changing China* (2011); *Globalization and Beyond: New Examinations of Global Power and Its Alternatives* (2011); and, *China and the Transformation of Global Capitalism* (2009). She received the Thomas A. Kochan and Stephen R. Sleigh Best Dissertation Award from the Labor and Employment Relations Association, and the Best Dissertation Prize from the journal *Labor History*. She is currently researching capital relocation strategy and labor politics in China and Vietnam.

Inside China's Automobile Factories

The Politics of Labor and Worker Resistance

LU ZHANG

Temple University

CAMBRIDGE
UNIVERSITY PRESS

32 Avenue of the Americas, New York, NY 10013-2473, USA

Cambridge University Press is part of the University of Cambridge.

It furthers the University's mission by disseminating knowledge in the pursuit of education, learning, and research at the highest international levels of excellence.

www.cambridge.org
Information on this title: www.cambridge.org/9781107030855

© Cambridge University Press 2015

First published 2015

A catalog record for this publication is available from the British Library.

Library of Congress Cataloging-in-Publication Data
Zhang, Lu.
Inside China's automobile factories : the politics of labor and worker resistance / Lu Zhang.
    pages   cm
ISBN 978-1-107-03085-5 (Hardback)
1. Automobile industry workers–China.   2. Automobile industry and trade–China.
3. Automobile factories–China.   4. Labor relations–China.   5. Labor markets–China.
6. Political economy–China.   I. Title.
HD8039.A82C69 2014
331.7′6292220951–dc23   2014014325

ISBN 978-1-107-03085-5 Hardback

Inside China's Automobile Factories

The Politics of Labor and Worker Resistance

LU ZHANG

Temple University

CAMBRIDGE
UNIVERSITY PRESS

32 Avenue of the Americas, New York, NY 10013-2473, USA

Cambridge University Press is part of the University of Cambridge.

It furthers the University's mission by disseminating knowledge in the pursuit of education, learning, and research at the highest international levels of excellence.

www.cambridge.org
Information on this title: www.cambridge.org/9781107030855

© Cambridge University Press 2015

First published 2015

A catalog record for this publication is available from the British Library.

Library of Congress Cataloging-in-Publication Data
Zhang, Lu.
Inside China's automobile factories : the politics of labor and worker resistance / Lu Zhang.
    pages   cm
ISBN 978-1-107-03085-5 (Hardback)
1. Automobile industry workers–China.   2. Automobile industry and trade–China.
3. Automobile factories–China.   4. Labor relations–China.   5. Labor markets–China.
6. Political economy–China.   I. Title.
HD8039.A82C69 2014
331.7′6292220951–dc23   2014014325

ISBN 978-1-107-03085-5 Hardback

To Giovanni (1937–2009)

Contents

Figures

Tables

Acknowledgements

The origins of this book can be traced back to a conference paper presented ten years ago with Beverly Silver at the "AUTO21 Conference: Workers and Labor Markets in the Global Automobile Industry" at McMaster University. The paper was entitled "From Detroit to Shanghai? Patterns of Capital Relocation and Labor Militancy in the World Automobile Industry from the 1930s to the Present." It was an initial effort to explore labor relations in the fast-growing automobile industry in China, and to identify similarities and differences between key features of the ongoing Chinese transformation and previous phases of capital relocation and labor militancy. In subsequent years, the probing yet unanswered questions raised in the paper ultimately prompted me to write a dissertation, and now this book, on labor politics and worker resistance in the Chinese automobile industry.

This decade-long endeavor would not have been possible without the generous support of so many people and institutions in so many ways. First and foremost, I owe a great debt to my interviewees – the autoworkers, managers, and union leaders – who opened up to me and took the time to share with me their stories, thoughts, and feelings. Their testimony served as the foundation of this book. Although they will remain anonymous in the interest of confidentiality, their trust, honesty, openness, and support are deeply appreciated. I am also thankful for the cooperation of management and unions of the automobile enterprises that granted me access to conduct fieldwork in the factories. The identities of the companies and the factories will remain undisclosed to protect confidentiality.

As is typical of books that begin as dissertations, I am immensely indebted to my dissertation advisors. Beverly Silver, my committee chair, has been an inspiring and supportive mentor throughout. From kindling the inception of this project, to helping refine the theoretical and analytical framework along the way, to providing invaluably rich "food for thought" – including both theoretical and practical advice – during my time conducting fieldwork in China, to carefully reading and revising the entire manuscript at various stages, her passion, insight, commitment, and support have seen me through every phase of this project. It is to Beverly that I owe the greatest intellectual debt, not to mention the deepest personal appreciation. Joel Andreas has offered unfailing support throughout my graduate studies at Johns Hopkins and beyond, always making himself available, reading multiple drafts of the dissertation, prospectus, and related proposals and articles throughout the long writing process. His stimulating questions and incisive and constructive critiques have always encouraged me to push the project further in terms of its depth, clarity, and intellectual rigor. Melvin Kohn has been supportive and positive throughout. From his insights on the research design at the early stage of this project, to his feedback on the methodological and comparative issues following my dissertation defense and during the revision process, Mel always has prodded me to frame my analysis more vigorously, broadly, and comparatively. I am very grateful to Kellee Tsai and William T. Rowe, each of whom served on my committee and provided me with insightful and constructive interdisciplinary comments. I appreciate their willingness to be readily available in the face of unexpected schedule changes and to offer engaged commentary within a very short time. Their thoughtful comments pushed me to think more expansively in terms of how my work relates to other works and disciplines, and to make connections that I otherwise would not have been able to make myself. I simply could not have asked for a better committee.

I want to extend my deep appreciation to those who have supported me with intellectual advice, inspiration, encouragement, and practical help at the various stages of this project. Yuan Shen, Ching Kwan Lee, Jianzhong Dai, Tongqing Feng, Gaochao He, and Wei Zhao provided me with useful advice on conducting fieldwork in factories in China, as well as comments on some central issues at the early stage. Cathy Walker introduced me to one of my case companies, and has remained supportive throughout. Ellen David Friedman brought me into close contact with some labor activists and progressive local union officials in China. Her work and commitment to labor movements and worker empowerment in both China and the U.S. has been a source of inspiration for me. Liu Jinyun introduced me to several labor law scholars and labor arbitrators who shared with me their experiences and insights on the legislation and practice of labor laws in China. Xin Xu helped me with logistics – from renting apartments to making local contacts – while I was doing fieldwork in China, which made my life in the field much easier.

While working on this book, I have received helpful comments, suggestions, and support from numerous individuals. Nelson Lichtenstein and Mary Gallagher read the entire manuscript and provided me with detailed and insightful comments and interdisciplinary perspectives that helped improve the final version of the manuscript in notable ways. For their time and valuable comments on various chapters and articles related to this book, I wish to thank Rina Agarwala, Tim Bartley, Anita Chan, Peter Coclanis, Leon Fink, Mark Frazier, John French, Jane Gordon, Burak Gruel, Kevan Harris, Phillip Hough, Ho-fung Hung, Ulrich Jürgens, Rachael Kamel, Scott Kennedy, Margaret Keck, Dustin Kidd, Sarosh Kuruvilla, Byoung-Hoon Lee, Joseph Tse-Hei Lee, Mary Nolan, Stephen Philion, Kristin Plys, Ben Scully, Mark Selden, Adam Joseph Shellhorse, Renqiu Yu, Xiaodan Zhang, and Guanghuai Zheng. I am also grateful for the helpful comments I received from the participants of the book workshop at the Johns Hopkins University and the Political Theory Workshop at Temple University. I had the opportunity to present the manuscript at talks held at the University of Michigan and Brown University, and I am grateful to the audiences for their interest and stimulating questions. I would also like to thank Joel Andreas and Phillip Hough for suggesting the title for the book.

Since arriving at Temple University as an assistant professor, I have been very fortunate to be immersed in a supportive and vibrant intellectual community. I especially want to thank Julia Ericksen, Rosario Espinal, Sherri Grasmuck, Robert Kaufman, Dustin Kidd, Judith Levine, and Anne Shlay for their encouragement and useful advice as I have navigated the book-publishing process.

I am grateful to several institutions for the generous funding I have received in support of this study. Research for the project was supported by the Social Science Research Council International Dissertation Field Research Fellowship, with funds provided by the Andrew W. Mellon Foundation, the National Science Foundation Dissertation Improvement Grant, Small Grants Awards from the China and Inner Asia Council of the Association for Asian Studies, various scholarships and research travel fellowships from The Graduate School at the Johns Hopkins University, as well as the Faculty Summer Research Award and Grant-in-Aid for Research Award at Temple University. I want to extend my special thanks to the librarians, Ellen Keith and Yuan Zeng at Hopkins and Gregory McKinney at Temple, for their excellent research assistance.

My editor at Cambridge University Press, Robert Dreesen, has offered guidance and support throughout the process of developing my initial manuscript into the present book. I appreciate his belief in the project from an early stage. I would also like to thank Elizabeth Janetschek for her superb editorial assistance; Chloe Harries and Britto Fleming Joe for keeping the project on track; and Noam Rifkind for his meticulous copyediting; thanks also to Eric Crawford, for working his illustration magic with the map, diagrams, and figures in the book, and to Robert Swanson, for his excellent indexing.

I am extremely fortunate to have been supported by many close and devoted friends. Nicole Aschoff, Astra Bonini, Ling Chen, Rachel Core, Kevan Harris, Lingli Huang, Yao Li, Bei Liu, Lily Liu, Yingyi Ma, Daniel Pasciuti, Ben Scully, Juan Wang, Weidong Wang, Yin Yue, Jin Zeng, and Shaohua Zhan have always been supportive and made my life at Hopkins very enjoyable. My special thanks go to Adam, who has been there for me along the way, through all of the ups and downs – whether spending hours reading through multiple drafts with an editor's eye or consoling me in the face of various setbacks with his humor and enthusiasm. His unfailing love and support have helped me through the many days and nights spent writing this book.

Finally, I come to the most personal source of gratitude. My parents have always believed in me and have unconditionally supported my academic pursuit. They taught me to embrace life with love, sympathy, curiosity, and generosity. I could not be more grateful to my parents for their unfailing love and support.

I dedicated this book to Giovanni Arrighi (1937–2009), my lifetime mentor. As an inspiring, dedicated, passionate, and beloved teacher, thinker, scholar, and fighter, Giovanni taught us to strive for perfection in research and writing, to remain humble and respectful to the people, to struggle for the cause we believe in, and to keep smiles and a sense of humor to live a good life and get through the tough times. He has been a continuous source of encouragement and inspiration for both my intellectual and personal development. It is to Giovanni that I dedicate this work.

Abbreviations

ACFTU	The All-China Federation of Trade Unions
AMC	American Motors Corporation
BAIC	Beijing Automobile Industry Corporation
CATRC	China Automotive Technology and Research Center
CBN	China Business News
CCP	The Chinese Communist Party
CCAG	China Changan Automobile Group (Chang'an)
CHERY	Chery Automobile Co., Ltd. (Chery)
CNHTC	China National Heavy Duty Truck Group Corp., Ltd
DFM	Dongfeng Motor Corporation (Dongfeng)
EPC	Enterprise Party Committee
FAW	First Automobile Works
FAW-VW	First Automobile Works-Volkswagen
FDI	Foreign direct investment
FESCO	Foreign Enterprises Service Corporation
GAIG	Guangzhou Automobile Industry Group Co., Ltd.
GM	General Motors
HRM	Human resource management
ILM	Internal labor markets
JIT	Just In Time
JV	Joint venture
LCL	Labor Contract Law
LDMAC	Labor Dispute Mediation and Arbitration Committee
MNC	Multinational corporation
MOHRSS	Ministry of Human Resources and Social Security
NBS	National Bureau of Statistics
NPC	National People's Congress
PCM	Product cycle model
PLA	People's Liberation Army
R&D	Research and Design
RMB	Renminbi (Chinese currency)
SAIC	Shanghai Automotive Industry Corporation (Group)

SASAC	State Assets Supervision and Administration Commission of the State Council
SOE	State-owned enterprise
SDRC	State Development and Reform Commission
SPC	State Planning Commission
SVW	Shanghai Volkswagen
TAW	Temporary agency work
TPS	Toyota Production System
TQM	Total Quality Management
UAW	United Auto Workers
VQC	Vocational qualification certificate
VTE	Vocational and technical education
VW	Volkswagen
WTO	World Trade Organization

I

Introduction

In mid-June of 2004, when I arrived in China to begin my fieldwork at a state-owned truck maker, the first thing I heard from workers was about a wildcat strike that had just happened at the factory a week before my arrival. Over 300 temporary workers at the assembly shop stayed in their dorms and refused to go to work during a night shift to protest the delay of their monthly pay. Workers spoke in amusement about how managers rushed around trying to find workers and how the seemingly never-ending assembly lines suddenly stood still. The whole assembly shop was shut down. With the support of formal (regular) workers, production ceased for 15 hours before striking workers received their delayed pay and agreed to return to work.[1]

In June 2006, a wildcat sit-down strike hit another automobile factory where I was conducting fieldwork, a Sino-US joint venture (JV). Around 400 regular day-shift workers in the general assembly shop went to work as usual, but stood by the line and refused to work when the line started running at 8:00 a.m. Workers at the press, body, and paint shops soon followed suit, bringing the entire plant to a standstill. At the same time, leaflets stating workers' demand for a 500 *yuan* wage hike – a roughly 25 percent raise – were quickly distributed throughout the factory. June is one of the busiest months of production, and the factory in question produces several top-selling compact car models. The last thing management wanted was an interruption in production. After a ten-hour stoppage, management agreed to raise workers' wages by 300 *yuan* – 15 percent – if they would return to work immediately. Without any support or representation from the official union to negotiate with management, the striking workers decided to accept the 300 *yuan* offer and production resumed.[2]

The vignettes described above are just two examples of many incidents of autoworker unrest that took place during my twenty months of fieldwork at

---

[1] The author's field notes, June 2004. For details about this strike, see Chapter 6.
[2] The author's field notes, September 2006. For details about this strike, see Chapter 5.

seven large auto assembly factories in China between 2004 and 2011. Over the course of my fieldwork, I documented various hidden and open forms of worker resistance, including wildcat strikes, sabotage, slowdowns, pilferage, effort bargaining, filing labor dispute cases, and collective acts of defiance. Particularly noteworthy was the increasing activism among temporary workers, whose numbers had grown to account for between one-third and two-thirds of the total production workforce in major automobile assembly factories in China.

Between June 2004, when I began my fieldwork, and May 2010 – when a major wave of auto strikes broke out that made international headlines – the autoworker unrest I observed went largely unreported in the newspapers and unrecognized in the social scientific literature on labor in China. Indeed, most people would not have expected me to find labor unrest in China's booming auto industry when I started my fieldwork in 2004. Chinese autoworkers, especially those working in large assembly factories, were seen as enjoying relatively high wages and generous benefits compared to workers in most other manufacturing sectors. It was widely thought that autoworkers were satisfied with their material gains and would remain quiescent. Moreover, the predominant view in the literature was that Chinese workers, even if they had grievances, would not risk open protests given the lack of independent trade unions and what many presumed to be a virtually inexhaustible supply of migrant labor from the countryside ready to take up jobs in manufacturing.

So when a wave of auto manufacturing strikes hit national and international newspaper headlines in the summer of 2010, many were caught by surprise.[3] The historic events unfolded when a nineteen-day strike at Honda Auto Parts Manufacturing Co., Ltd., in Foshan, Guangdong Province (a transmission plant that provides 80 percent of the automatic transmissions for Honda's assembly plants in China), led to the shutdown of the Japanese automaker's four China-based assembly plants and brought Honda production in China to a dead halt. At the peak of the strike, over 1,800 workers walked out, demanding not only a significant pay increase but also the ability to elect their own union officials at the factory union – a branch of the state-controlled All-China Federation of Trade Unions (ACFTU), the only legal trade union in China.

Like the autoworker unrest I observed during my fieldwork, the Honda strike was organized and fought by the workers themselves. The factory union did not support or represent them in negotiations. The workers elected their own delegation of representatives from each department to negotiate with management. When faced with management efforts to divide the workers by

---

[3] At least twelve strikes were reported to have taken place in the automobile industry in China between May and July, 2010. See Carter (2010) for a detailed timeline of the 2010 auto strike wave.

proposing unequal wage increases between regular workers and student intern workers, the workers maintained their solidarity and insisted on the same monthly salary increase for all workers without distinction. The striking workers also reached out to independent labor experts for help in negotiating with management, and appealed to the media and the general public through "open letters" and online postings to gain broad public support.

Eventually, management was forced to agree to a 35-percent pay increase for all workers to end the strike. The strike's success in winning concessions from employers inspired a wave of strikes in a dozen other auto plants, as well as in other manufacturing sectors. By the end of 2010, almost every province and municipality in China had increased its monthly minimum wage by an average of 23 percent (China Labour Bulletin 2011). The Honda strike received extensive media coverage and wide publicity from within and outside China.[4] For the first time, it brought public attention to the militancy and grievances of the 3 million autoworkers in China who for years had been "manufacturing" the country's auto industry miracle, but whose concerns had been unduly neglected until the 2010 strike wave.[5]

Achieving a better understanding of Chinese autoworkers' current conditions, subjectivity and collective actions is important not only because of the pivotal role they have played in the post-2010 wave of labor unrest in China, but also because of the crucial position they occupy in the world automobile industry. The Chinese automobile industry has grown at an exponential level over the past two decades: annual output increased seventeen-fold, from 1,296,778 units in 1993 to 22,116,800 in 2013, making China the world's largest vehicle manufacturing nation, accounting for about a quarter of total global automobile production. The startling growth in production has gone hand in hand with the rapid expansion of China's domestic auto market. Since 2009, China has become the world's largest auto market; over 21 million vehicles were sold in 2013 alone.[6] Joint ventures between multinational corporations and Chinese state-owned enterprises (SOEs) have played a crucial role in fueling the expansion. By the early 2000s, all of the world auto giants had established JVs with Chinese SOEs to manufacture and sell vehicles in China. Especially in the wake of the 2008 global economic

[4] As many have noted, official tolerance toward the media report to such a degree reflected the tacit support by the central government in favor of the striking workers' demands for wage increases. Among the substantial volume of Chinese media reports, see, e.g., Cheng and Li (2010); Guo (2010); Ni (2010), Zhang (2010), Zheng (2010), Zhou (2010), Zhou and Liu (2010). From the extensive English-language coverage, see in particular, Barboza (2010); *Bloomberg* (2010); Bradsher (2010a, 2010b, 2010c); Bradsher and Barboza (2010); Carter (2010); Meyerson (2010); Pierson (2010); Shirouzu (2010); *The New York Times* (2010); Wang and Rabinovitch (2010); Wasserstrom (2010); Wong (2010); Zhang (2010).

[5] In 2010, approximately 3.37 million people worked in the automobile industry (CEIN, 2012: 29), of which 2.2 million were regularly employed in automobile manufacturing (CATRC 2011: 483).

[6] *Chinese Automotive Industry Yearbook*. 2011, pp.1, 9, 468; China Association of Automobile Manufacturers (CAAM), January 2014.

crisis, China emerged as the primary profit generator for automobile multi-nationals such as General Motors (GM), Volkswagen (VW), and Nissan. The weight of China – and hence of Chinese autoworkers – in the global auto industry cannot be exaggerated.

Despite the extensive interest in China's fast-growing auto industry, and unlike their well-studied counterparts in the US and many other countries, there has been little written about Chinese autoworkers. Thus far, there have been several English-language books published on the Chinese auto industry (for instance, Anderson 2012; Chin 2010; Harwit 1995; Thun 2006). But they focus on the automobile industry itself or on the Chinese government's strategies for developing the industry. None deals with labor issues or tells the stories of workers. These workers and their factory lives are the focus of this book.

ETHNOGRAPHY INSIDE CHINA'S AUTOMOBILE FACTORIES

The book's findings are based primarily on my twenty months of ethnographic research inside seven large automobile assembly factories in six cities in China during multiple field trips conducted between 2004 and 2011. The core of the book provides an in-depth analysis of the transformation of the Chinese auto assembly industry and its labor force over the past two decades, an intimate portrait of the work regime and factory social order therein, and a detailed account of social composition, wages, job security, the nature and extent of grievances and bargaining power, as well as collective actions of Chinese autoworkers. I also devote much attention to the status, aspirations, and social consciousness of both formal workers and the various types of temporary workers employed in great numbers in China's major auto assembly factories.

Given the lack of available information, it seemed that the best way to find out the condition of autoworkers in China would be to go inside the factories and examine the situation there in order to produce this first industrial ethnography of Chinese autoworkers. Gaining access to China's large automobile factories is not easy. It often requires a combination of persistent effort, personal connections, and good fortune. I began my fieldwork in June 2004, by getting access to a state-owned truck maker located in my hometown. A close relative of mine, who was a good friend of a senior manager at the plant, helped me to secure access to the factory. I was introduced to management as "a Chinese graduate student who is studying in the United States and is doing fieldwork for her dissertation on human capital and management in the Chinese automobile industry." With hindsight, I realize the fact that I was introduced by a senior manager, combined with the stated purpose of my research, led to the expectation among managers that my research would produce a positive outcome and be a potential benefit to the factory. Although this perception facilitated my access to and interviews with managers, and allowed me to be present inside the factory with ease, it also caused suspicion among workers such that it took me some time to gain their trust, as I will discuss below.

My initial request to work on the line with ordinary workers was immediately turned down by management, out of consideration for my safety and the high physical demands involved in automobile production (my small size and identity as a female researcher seemed to further justify such concerns). Instead, I was assigned to the factory Party Committee Office to help in collecting shop-floor material and editing factory newsletters aimed at promoting the deeds of "model workers" and "advanced production teams" to boost worker morale. This position allowed me to hang around shop floors freely and talk to workers when they were not working. At the beginning, workers were both suspicious and curious about my presence on the shop floor. They either refrained from talking to me or asked me a lot of questions about myself and my dissertation project before I could even ask them any questions. I had to constantly explain my research goals and reassure workers that I was neither hired nor paid by management. I could tell that the workers were amazed and puzzled by the fact that I – a young, female, graduate student who grew up locally and went abroad to pursue a Ph.D. in sociology – would choose to spend months in the factory, trying to write about Chinese autoworkers and their everyday work life. As time went by, some workers began talking to me. As one worker later told me, they started to see me as "a sincere and hard-working student who'd like to listen to their trivial stories and complaints for hours with great interest." I gradually gained workers' trust. At the same time, by relying on semi-structured interview techniques with a sympathetic and patient ear, I was able to establish a rapport with workers and get them to open up and to share with me their stories, aspirations, and emotions.

For about two months – June 2004 and September 2006 – I went to work at this state-owned truck factory every day, starting from the 7:30 a.m. pre-shift work group meeting and getting off at 6:00 p.m. with the day-shift workers. I observed how production was organized, what the working conditions were, how people interacted with one another, and what kinds of exchanges took place on a daily basis. I ate in the factory cafeteria with workers, and visited workers' dormitories and homes after work. I rarely used a tape recorder since I noticed it tended to make people feel uncomfortable and self-conscious while talking to me, except for formal speeches given by factory leaders on a few occasions. I wrote down the daily work routines that I considered meaningful (while observing them or immediately afterward), such as pre-shift work group meetings held by team leaders and workers' conversations during work breaks and lunch time. I also collected relevant factory files, including statistics on production and employees, work rules and regulations, and internal newsletters and references.

In early August 2004, a new opportunity arose. I attended a two-week-long training workshop for model team leaders organized by the truck factory's parent auto group – one of China's largest auto groups – for its various subsidiary companies. I went as a newsletter editor of the factory Party Committee Office, along with select team leaders from the factory. During the workshop, I got a chance to meet and interview several managers and team leaders from a Sino-German JV that was part of the same parent auto group. They were surprisingly open with me. In retrospect, I realize that being able to attend the workshop as a representative from the truck factory made it much easier for me to be received as an "insider" of the same auto group. In addition, it appeared that my personal experience and the idea of writing a book about managers and workers in the Chinese auto industry impressed and interested my interviewees.

This connection opened the door for me to begin field research at a Sino-German auto assembly factory. In August 2004 and October 2006, with the assistance of a senior production manager and a party committee leader whom I had met at the workshop, I was able to spend six weeks in one of the JV's assembly plants. My request to work on the line was rejected outright, for the same reason given at the state-owned truck factory. Instead, I was assigned a position as a liaison between the factory Party Committee Office and Party branches of various workshops, a position that afforded me plenty of freedom to hang around on shop floors. At the same time, several of my worker friends at the state-owned truck factory informed their friends and former classmates at the Sino-German assembler to "take good care of me" (many of the workers graduated from the same automotive junior college affiliated with the auto group). This informal "introduction" proved to be extremely helpful in establishing trust and gaining support for my fieldwork among workers at this second site. During the time I was present, the plant operated two shifts of ten hours each, with two days off every month. The line ran very fast, and it was very difficult to talk to the workers at work. Many workers sacrificed their limited and precious spare time to talk to me, and patiently answered my questions for hours after work. Some workers also invited me to their homes, and to after-work social gatherings. At the same time, plant managers were eager to tell me their views, and curious to know my findings and hear my observations on the shop floor, but they did not put explicit pressure on me to report about my findings and interviews with workers. In retrospect, I can only speculate that it could be due, in part, to the fact that I was introduced by higher-level company managers, and therefore it would be considered inappropriate for plant managers to ask me to report to them.

Being present inside the factory every day certainly enriched my knowledge and understanding of the complexity and nuances of life in the factory. It also enabled me to contextualize what people said in their interviews, and to identify and evaluate the nature and extent of workers' grievances, as well as the hidden and open forms of worker resistance on the shop floor. More importantly, I was able to document stories and incidents that would not be otherwise available to an outside researcher.

From these two factories – one SOE and one JV – I gradually gained access to an additional five major automobile assemblers through personal

TABLE I.I. *General information on the auto assemblers selected for the study,* *2006*

Name	Number of Employees[a]	Annual Output (1000s)	Ranking (Sales)	Main Product	Ownership Type	Found Year
USA-1[b]	5,535	413	1	Passenger Car	Sino-US	1997
USA-2[b]	3,096	87	1	Passenger Car	Sino-US	2003
GER-1	11,587	352	2	Passenger Car	Sino-German	1985
GER-2	9,284	351	3	Passenger Car	Sino-German	1991
SOE-1	13,100	300	4	Passenger Car	State-owned	1997
SOE-2	3,170	70	N/A	Truck	State-owned	1993
JAP-1	5,620	260	6	Passenger Car	Sino-Japanese	1998

Notes: [a] Number of employees includes active, formal employees listed on the books of the enterprises. It does not include temporary workers. See the discussion in Chapter 2.
[b] USA-1 and USA-2 belong to the same Sino-US JV. USA-1 hosts the central offices of the JV.
Sources: The author's field data; CATRC, various years.

connections, persistent effort, and good luck.[7] I managed to get into a variety of enterprises with respect to ownership type, geographic location, market position, and the country of origin of a JV's foreign partner. I conducted fieldwork at both the firm and the factory levels. Having access to this range of factories has allowed me to put together a fuller picture of labor and labor politics in the Chinese automobile assembly industry.

A few basic facts about my cases are presented in Table 1.1. Since I agreed to keep the names of the companies and factories confidential, I use pseudonyms to refer to the case enterprises. But when publicly available information is cited, the real names of the companies involved are used.

I do not claim that my cases are representative of the entire Chinese automobile assembly industry, nor do I intend to make generalizations about Chinese autoworkers as a whole.[8] I am confident, however, that the cases capture important characteristics across assembly enterprises, as well as illustrating the range of diversity within the industry.

As can be seen from Table 1.1, a key characteristic of the factories where I did my fieldwork was that they are all major auto assemblers with high output volume and a large number of employees. Except for the state-owned truck

[7] Unlike the case at the first two factories discussed, management of the other five assemblers only granted me access for interviewing but not to make daily observations inside factories.
[8] In fact, auto assembly workers are generally better off than auto parts workers in China. While this book focuses on assembly workers, it makes comparative reference to parts workers when sufficient information is available (see, in particular, Chapters 2 and 3).

maker, SOE-2,[9] they all held competitive market positions as of 2006; five of them were among the top six passenger-car producers in China.

Large assembly enterprises such as these are typical of the post-1980 Chinese automobile industry. The central government's policy in regard to the auto assembly sector in the reform era has favored the creation of large automobile groups, as well as the concentration of production in specific geographical areas (see Chapter 2). In 2012, the top ten automobile groups accounted for 87.3 percent of total vehicle sales in China (CAAM 2013).

Moreover, the dominant ownership structures – JVs and SOEs – are well represented among my cases.[10] As can be seen from Table 1.1, two of my cases are SOEs; the remaining five are JVs between Chinese state-owned auto groups and multinational corporations – two from the United States, two from Germany, and one from Japan.[11]

Finally, as shown in the map (Figure 1.1), my seven cases cover diverse geographical regions, including five of the six major automobile production bases in China.[12] They also include both older factories and relatively newly-established ones.

Overall, I managed to spend at least two months at each factory, visiting production lines, collecting company files and internal newsletters and periodicals, and conducting extensive interviews with a total of 120 formal (regular) workers, 80 temporary and student workers, 48 managers, and 30 factory Party and union cadres. I also interviewed 41 local government and trade union officials, labor dispute arbitrators, labor scholars, and automotive-industry experts in order to understand the state's role in the automobile industry and labor relations.[13] This in-depth fieldwork provides the basis for the book's narrative.

---

[9] The truck maker SOE-2 is a key subsidiary of one of China's largest auto groups. While its production and sales have fluctuated in recent years, it remains among China's top truck makers.

[10] The Chinese government does not allow foreign companies to set up wholly foreign-owned auto assembly plants in China, but it places no restrictions on ownership stakes in the auto-parts sector.

[11] There is a third ownership type, which is important but less prominent than JVs and SOEs: domestic private enterprises. I do not include private-owned domestic automakers in this study due to a lack of accessibility. While JVs and SOEs are the dominant ownership types, domestic private automakers such as Geely and BYD have grown rapidly in recent years in China. It is therefore important to incorporate this type of automaker into future research.

[12] The five major automobile production bases (by region) covered by this study are: Northeast region (Changchun), the Yangtze River Delta (Shanghai), Central region (Wuhu), the Pearl River Delta (Guangzhou), and the Bohai Sea surrounding areas (Qingdao and Yantai). The production base that is not covered in this study is the more recently developed Southwest region (e.g., Chengdu and Chongqing). For discussion on the six major automobile production bases, see *China Automotive Industry Yearbook* (2011: 134–137).

[13] For discussion on my research strategies in conducting interviews, see Methodological Appendix; for a breakdown of information about the interviewee sample, see Interviewee Index.

FIGURE 1.1. Map of the research fieldwork sites

This book, however, goes beyond a detailed ethnographic study. By combining empirical material with a multilayered analysis that moves from the shop floor to the national political economy and global industry dynamics, I attempt to develop a theoretical framework for understanding how labor relations in the automobile industry and broader social economy can be expected to develop in China in the coming decades.

THE POTENTIAL OF "CELLULAR" ACTIVISM

Since the 2010 auto strike wave, there has been growing awareness of labor unrest in China. The strikes clearly show that workers in China are no longer just passive victims of repression and exploitation. Rather, they are willing and able to organize to push for higher pay and better working conditions through concerted collective actions. But still the dominant view in the literature is that labor unrest in China is localized and apolitical, and thus not very effective in generating meaningful change. Sociologist Ching Kwan Lee (2007), for example, unequivocally concluded that labor protests in China are localized and "cellular"; and that unless Chinese workers can form their own independent trade unions, unless they can transform their "cellular" activism into cross-plant and cross-regional coalitions targeting the authoritarian regime, their struggles are unlikely to generate significant political and social change.

This book represents a departure from this line of argument. My study shows that even though labor unrest in China has not led to the formation of independent trade unions or competitive political parties that challenge the authoritarian party-state at the national level, widespread grassroots protests have succeeded in winning substantial wage increases and improved conditions for workers on the shop floor. Moreover, rising labor unrest, despite being localized and apolitical, has pressured the central government toward introducing new national labor laws and policy changes that extend new rights and improve conditions for workers, as part of its effort to stabilize labor relations and maintain social stability.

This should not come as a surprise. Indeed, as has been widely argued with regard to the US labor movement and elsewhere, institutionalized trade unionism has neither been a precondition for, nor a guarantee of, effective working-class mobilization (Kimeldorf 1999; Lichtenstein 2002; Martin 2008; Moody 1997). Rather, major advances for workers have often come as an outcome of a major wave of grassroots mobilizations and rank-and-file struggles without prior formal organization in parties and unions. Formal organization is an outcome of the struggles rather than vice-versa (Arrighi and Silver 1984; Clawson 2003; Friedman 2008; Levi 2003; Milkman 2006; Silver 2005). Similarly, this book finds that widespread grassroots labor unrest in China has been leading to meaningful improvements in conditions of work and life for the working class.

AUTOWORKERS AND WORKPLACE BARGAINING POWER

Historically, autoworkers have been especially successful in translating localized struggles into major victories vis-à-vis both their immediate employers and the state. As sociologist Beverly Silver (2003) explicated, autoworkers have had – and continue to have – strong *workplace bargaining power*, derived from their strategic location within the production process.[14] More specifically, because of the scale and capital intensity of automobile production, as well as the complexity of the division of labor, localized stoppages by a small group of workers are able to disrupt the output of an entire plant or even an entire corporation, and thereby cause large losses for capital.

At the same time, the nature of assembly line production in the auto industry tends to create strong grievances among workers – for instance, over the monotony of work, intense production pace, and management's arbitrary exercise of authority – despite the fact that autoworkers' wages are relatively high. These grievances combined with strong workplace bargaining power have produced major waves of autoworker unrest across countries throughout the

[14] Building on Erik Olin Wright's (2000: 962) distinction between associational and structural power, Silver distinguishes three types of workers' bargaining power: workplace bargaining power, derived from "the strategic location of a particular group of workers within a key industrial sector"; marketplace bargaining power, resulting from tight labor markets; and associational power, stemming from self-organization into trade unions, political parties and other forms of collective organization (Silver 2003: 13).

twentieth century, from the United States in the 1930s, to Western Europe in the 1960s, to Brazil, South Africa, and South Korea in the 1970s and 1980s. During previous waves of autoworker unrest, rank-and-file workers were able to utilize their workplace bargaining power to carry out plant-based, sit-down strikes that not only won significant concessions from their employers but also played an important role in broader labor movements that succeeded in transforming relations within the factory and society.[15]

Silver identified a recurrent historical pattern, whereby the geographical relocation of automobile production has created and strengthened new working-classes and labor movements in each new site chosen for rapid industrial expansion.[16] With China becoming the new epicenter of global automobile production at the dawn of the twenty-first century, Silver predicted that China would become the epicenter of a new wave of autoworker labor unrest (2003: 65). Indeed, as I will argue in this book, a similar combination of strong workplace bargaining power and major grievances among autoworkers is evident, and has been contributing to rising labor unrest in the Chinese automobile industry.

But where is this unrest heading? And how will labor relations in the Chinese automobile industry unfold in the coming decade? In answering these questions, I identify the processes at work in the Chinese automobile industry today that are similar to those observed elsewhere, while I also point to important dynamics that are specific to the Chinese case.

Among the similar processes at work is a fundamental underlying contradiction between legitimacy and profitability that has characterized capitalist development – more specifically, efforts to resolve a crisis of profitability tend to create or exacerbate a crisis of social legitimacy (and vice-versa).[17] Moreover, in China, as elsewhere, firms and the state have attempted to overcome this contradiction by drawing boundaries within the labor force. Automakers throughout the world have been creating divisions within their workforces – for instance, treating one group better than the other in terms of job security, pay and other conditions. As I will argue throughout the book, however, this boundary-drawing process generates new worker grievances and resistance.

Among the important elements specific to the Chinese case is China's condition as a state-led, late-industrializing nation with strong revolutionary and state-socialist legacies. In the context of rapid capitalist development and

---

[15] A case in point is the 1930s and 1940s upsurge of labor militancy among U.S. autoworkers that eventually forced hostile employers and the government to accept unionization and construct systems of labor protection, culminating in a labor-capital-state accord in the post-New Deal era.

[16] For a detailed discussion on the dynamics of labor unrest in the world automobile industry in the twentieth century, see Silver (2003), Chapter 2.

[17] For elaboration on the topic of capitalism's inherent contradiction between crises of profitability and crisis of legitimacy, see Silver (2003); see also, e.g., Habermas (1975); Harvey (1989, 1999); O'Conner (1973).

the associated commodification of labor, these revolutionary and socialist legacies are giving rise to an even more acute contradiction between pursuing profitability and maintaining legitimacy with labor. As we shall see, the case of the Chinese automobile industry exemplifies this acute tension.

THE ARGUMENT IN BRIEF

In the following pages, we will see that massive foreign investment and the increased scale and concentration of automobile production in China over the past two decades have created and strengthened a new generation of autoworkers with growing workplace bargaining power. At the same time, China entered the global competition in the mass production of automobiles at a late stage of the automobile "product cycle" (Vernon 1966), when competition is high and profit margins become much thinner. The state-led industrial restructuring and increased competition since the late 1990s has driven automakers in China to prioritize profitability and to move toward a leaner and meaner work regime. As a result, despite their relatively high wages, the new generation of autoworkers expressed strong grievances rooted, among other places, in the increased intensity of work, reduced job security, stagnant wages, the arbitrary exercise of managerial authority, the lack of advancement opportunities, and the inferior status of blue-collar workers in a hierarchical factory social order.

On the other hand, designated as one of China's pillar industries of strategic importance, the automobile industry has been under strong central state intervention, including the monitoring of industrial relations through cadre-managerial personnel systems at large SOEs and JVs. Management is responsible for simultaneously increasing profitability while maintaining its legitimacy with labor – that is, maintaining peaceful and cooperative labor relations. These contradictory pressures have driven major automakers in China to follow a policy of *labor force dualism* that draws boundaries between formal (regular) workers and temporary workers. I use the term labor force dualism to refer to a labor control mechanism that deploys formal and temporary workers side by side on production lines, having them perform similar or identical tasks but subjecting them to differential treatment. Formal workers enjoy higher wages, more generous benefits, and relatively secure employment as part of management efforts to gain cooperation from a "core" segment of workers; conversely, temporary workers have lower wages, fewer benefits, and little job security as management attempts to lower costs and increase profitability. Among the key findings of this book is the fact that China's market-oriented reforms have not produced a generalized "despotic factory regime," as many scholars have argued.[18] Instead, a dual labor regime

---

[18] Built on Michael Burawoy's (1983, 1985) notion of "hegemonic" and "despotic" factory regimes, some scholars argue that China's market-oriented economic reform without accompanying political reform only creates the conditions for a despotic factory regime. It is the

characterized by widespread labor force dualism has *re-emerged* as a central component of labor relations in many large, capital-intensive enterprises since the early- and mid-2000s.[19]

Labor force dualism was introduced as a solution to the contradiction between legitimacy (worker cooperation) and profitability (lowering costs). However, it carries notable unintended consequences. On the one hand, it has detached formal workers from temporary workers, and has kept the former relatively quiet so far, despite their serious grievances. On the other hand, a new generation of temporary workers, who are increasingly urban and better educated, have been radicalized and actively protest against unequal treatment at work. One of the main theses of this book is that management-constructed divisions among workers have become at once a continuous source of irritation and an impetus for the temporary workers to rebel.[20] This is the paradox of labor force dualism. The key question concerning the outcome then becomes whether formal and temporary workers are able to make common cause, or whether they end up fighting against each other. As we will see in subsequent chapters, this outcome is conditioned in large measure on how management and the state respond. Thus, I am also telling the story of how the ongoing transformation of China's auto industry is tied to the efforts of management and the state to resolve the profitability-legitimacy contradiction.

Furthermore, by situating autoworker resistance within the broader national context of rising labor unrest caused by intensified commodification of labor since the mid-1990s, my study shows how Beijing's top concerns with maintaining social stability and political legitimacy have led to the passage of three new labor laws in 2007. The new labor laws – most notably, the Labor Contract Law (LCL) – expand legal protections and rights for workers in an effort to stabilize labor relations and pacify disgruntled workers. While compromise in the law-making process has led to entrenched dualism and inequality between formal and temporary workers, the ongoing battle over amendments to the LCL suggests that Chinese labor politics is not a settled fact; rather, it is a *dynamic* process. The Communist Party's official adherence to its "mass line" and the "legitimate rights and interests of workers," while spearheading marketization and commodification of labor, has recurrently

Chinese state's pro-capital policy and its failure to protect the vulnerable in the marketplace that subjects Chinese workers to the despotic factory regimes. See, for example, Chan (2001), Chan and Zhu (2003), Lee (1999), O'Leary (1998).

[19] As will be discussed in Chapter 3, a dual labor system has been a persistent feature of the Chinese labor system throughout the history of People's Republic of China (PRC). But the boundaries between workers who are included and protected within the system and those who are excluded have been constantly evolving.

[20] To the extent that labor dualism and inequality exist and are ubiquitous between assembly workers and parts workers in the Chinese automobile industry (see, Chapters 2 and 3), it is no surprise that the main source of militancy is found among temporary workers in the assembly plants, as well as among parts workers in the lower tiers of the subcontracting system.

incited contestation, negotiation, and compromise among the state policy elites, capitalists/employers, and workers. This book is therefore also about the social-political contradictions of the development of capitalism – that is, the move toward commodification of labor and its countermovement – in post-socialist China.

To understand the acuteness of this contradiction and how it plays out in the Chinese case, however, requires an elaboration of how the specific industrial dynamics, national context, and historical legacies – notably, China's revolutionary and state-socialist legacies – have shaped labor politics in particular ways.

UNEVEN CONTRADICTION AND LABOR POLITICS

Industrial dynamics

Existing studies have suggested that state-led late-industrializers tend to confront more acute profitability pressures and labor-capital (state) conflicts when undergoing rapid, concentrated industrialization (Bergquist 1986; Deyo 1989; Humphrey 1982; Koo 2001; Seidman 1994). This is the case in part because workers concentrated in capital-intensive, dynamic industries gain strong workplace bargaining power when their industries are growing, and when employers' and states' dependence on their labor-power and cooperation in production is high. They are likely to exert this bargaining power to demand higher pay and better working conditions. At the same time, according to the product cycle model (PCM), as a product moves from the early "innovative" stage to the "maturity" and "standardization" stages, competition grows, as does the pressure to cut costs. As such, there is a decline in the industry's profitability as it progresses through its life cycle. Thus, newly innovated products typically are produced in high-income countries, while production facilities are dispersed to lower-wage sites as products reach the stage of maturity and standardization (Vernon 1966). This tendency implies that early "innovators" are better positioned to accrue high profitability that might allow them to redistribute wealth relatively more generously to their working class. By contrast, latecomers, including China, have to contend with more intense competition and profitability pressures at a late stage of the product cycle. That means they may have less room for an expensive social contract to gain workers' cooperation. As a result, late-industrializers tend to confront more acute profitability-legitimacy contradictions of capitalist development (Arrighi 1990a; Seidman 1994; Silver 2003).

Yet the PCM cannot fully explain the ongoing dynamics of the Chinese automobile industry, as it fails to accommodate the complexity of location-specific advantages of production (Dunning 1981), market dynamics possibly independent from product cycles (Taylor 1986), and state policies in promoting innovations and modifying product cycles. Whether and to what extent the Chinese automobile industry is able to move up in the global value-added hierarchy, as I speculate in the conclusion, will have important implications for the possible concessions workers might be able to gain from their employers, and therefore may have a far-reaching impact on labor relations throughout the industry.[21]

Contradictory state and regime legitimacy

My study also suggests that countries with strong revolutionary and state-socialist legacies, including China, tend to face a more acute legitimacy problem when undergoing capitalist development and commodification of labor.[22] To elucidate this point, an articulation of the nature of the Chinese state and the logic of its legitimation is in order.

More than three decades since its departure from Maoist state socialism, China is still a Leninist Party-state led by the Chinese Communist Party (CCP). Under Mao, the Chinese working class was proclaimed the "master of the country." The interests of the Party-state, workers, and their work units (*danwei*) were said to be concordant. There was no such thing as labor-capital relations, and industrial relations were essentially determined by the paternalistic Party-state (Taylor, Chang, and Li 2003). Workers' dependence on the state to provide employment, wages and welfare benefits through their work units was the foundation of their political acquiescence and of the regime's legitimacy under state socialism (Walder 1986).[23] This implicit political-economic bargaining between a communist regime and its working populace is known as the "socialist social contract."[24]

With China's transition from state socialism to a market economy, the socialist social contract of permanent employment has been replaced by a market-driven labor contract system in which labor becomes a commodity that can be bought and sold according to legal labor contracts on an open labor market. The

---

[21] This perspective concurs with the global commodity/value-chain analysis, which has explicitly argued that developing countries or regions can attain more desirable developmental outcomes – including labor rights and working conditions – through active state policies and concerted effort at upgrading within particular commodity/value chains. See, e.g., Bair (2009); Gereffi and Korzeniewicz (1994).

[22] Another immediate case in point is Vietnam, which shares with China an authoritarian, Communist Party-governed political system with mass revolutionary and socialist legacies. Both countries have been carrying out market-oriented economic reforms that have encouraged domestic and foreign capital investments and development; both countries have witnessed rising labor unrest during market transitions in recent years. Notably, both countries have recently passed or revised labor laws – China passed three new labor laws in 2007; Vietnam revised its Labor Code in 2008 – in order to stabilize labor relations and pacify disgruntled workers in response to widespread labor unrest. For discussion on China, see Silver and Zhang (2009); on Vietnam, see Kerkvliet (2011).

[23] This is not to say that the CCP enjoyed unchallenged legitimacy in Mao's China. As Teets, Rosen, and Gries have pointed out, "Legitimacy, in Mao's China and today, is never a state possession; instead, state and social actors continuously contest it" (2010: 17).

[24] For detailed discussions on the socialist social contract, see Bunce (1999); Cook (1993); Gallagher (2005a); Lee (2007); Ludlam (1991); Tang and Parish (2000).

legitimacy of the CCP in the post-Mao era is often said to be built on two pillars – sustaining economic growth and maintaining social stability. Although there is no doubt that Beijing's priorities for the past thirty years have skewed heavily toward supporting rapid economic growth and those interests that most directly help achieve this goal – that is, those of managers/capitalists – it is important to recognize the centrality of maintaining stability as the fundamental logic of the CCP's claims to political legitimacy. That is to say, the Party's pursuit of economic growth is not the goal, but a means through which to strengthen the regime's legitimacy and to maintain its monopoly of political power.[25] As Vivienne Shue put it, the legitimacy of the Chinese central state in the reform era lies in "its political capacity to preserve a peaceful and stable social order under which, among other good things, the economy can be expected to grow" – that is, "the conditions of *stability*" (2010: 46).[26] In other words, the impetus for China's economic reforms and marketization in the 1990s largely came from the belief of CCP top officials that market-oriented economic reforms are tactically necessary to create the conditions for more effective state guidance of the economy and to strengthen the state's power, rather than in pursuit of a liberal capitalist economy *per se* (cf. Arrighi 2007). Thus the nature of the Chinese party-state and its relationships with labor and capitalists in the reform era cannot be taken as a given, or defined in a simple, static, and monolithic way.[27] Indeed, China scholars have identified various contradictions and divisions within the Chinese state. These include conflicts between the central government and local governments, competing factions within the CCP leadership, and divisions among various state agencies and bureaucracies at the same administrative level.[28] This study explicates a key contradiction faced by the central state (and state-appointed managers) – the need to strike a balance between increasing profitability and maintaining legitimacy with labor.[29]

[25] This emphasis on the centrality of building regime legitimacy in relation to promoting economic development in post-Mao China parallels the developmental states in East Asia; see, e.g., Castells 1992.

[26] The centrality of stability was highlighted in a recent speech by China's new Party Secretary, Xi Jinping, in which he stated that "stability is the prerequisite for reform" (Xinhua 2013).

[27] This understanding of the state is in line with the theoretical insights into the "relative autonomy of the state" (see, e.g., Poulantzas 1975; Skocpol 1979; and, Therborn 1978). As Theda Skocpol aptly put it, "state rulers may have to be free of control by specific dominant-class groups and personnel if they are to be able to implement policies that serve the fundamental interest of an entire dominant class. That interest is, of course, its need to preserve the class structure and mode of production as a whole." (1979: 27)

[28] On the conflicts between the central and local governments under fiscal and administrative decentralization, see, among others, Landry (2008); Lee (2007); O'Brien (1996); O'Brien and Li (2006). On the factions within the Party leadership, see Li (2012). On the divisions among state agencies and bureaucracies, see Chen (2012); Gallagher and Dong (2011). For a useful discussion on studying local and administrative variations and divisions of the Chinese state, see Perry (1994c).

[29] Ching Kwan Lee, for example, describes a tension between the local governments' pro-capital drive for accumulation and the central government's concern with legitimacy (2007: 18–19).

Revolutionary and State-Socialist legacies

A directly related point is that legacies of mass revolution and state-socialism matter, and they continue to influence subsequent development trajectories, labor politics, state-society relations, public sentiments and popular protest in China in profound ways.[30] For one thing, despite workers' deep cynicism, the Communist Party's official ideology and its public commitment to "safeguarding the legitimate rights and interests of workers," provide Chinese workers with ready-made languages and legitimate claims on the basis of an ideology that the state could not rebut (Eyferth 2006; cf. O'Brien 1996; O'Brien and Li 2006; Perry 2007; Straughn 2005).

Furthermore, the CCP's continuing adherence to its revolutionary tradition of the "mass line" allows it to be more responsive to popular demands in comparison to most other authoritarian regimes. The mass line is the political, organizational, and leadership method of the CCP that "incorporate[s] both [the] vanguard role of the party and a strong participatory role for the populace" (Lieberthal 2004: 64). Unlike the insurrectionist aspects of the Russian Bolshevik party, the Chinese communists had to struggle for nearly three decades to win the support of the peasantry before they won power in 1949. In the course of the protracted struggle, they "developed a philosophy of responding to popular needs within the confines of a single party" (Hutton and Desai 2007: 3). As Fairbank pointed out, Mao's "From the masses, to the masses" was indeed "a sort of democracy suited to Chinese tradition, where the upper-class official had governed best when he had the true interests of the local people at heart and so governed on their behalf" (1992: 319). As I will show in later chapters, the participatory, egalitarian, and anti-bureaucratic experiments of democratic management in Chinese factories motivated by the Maoist mass line still have an impact on workers' formulating of grievances and the "evaluative norms" of managers at some SOEs and JVs in the reform era.[31]

At the same time, the official promotion of the populist mass line and mass mobilization throughout the history of the People's Republic of China (PRC) has emboldened active masses "with a self-confidence and combativeness with few parallels elsewhere" (Amin 2005, cited in Arrighi 2007: 376).[32] China's

---

This framing leaves out the important question about the nature of the *central* state, and its relationships with labor and capital in its own right. After all, in China, it is the central state that makes the rules specifying "who can do what to whom" (Piven and Cloward 2000: 416).

[30] On the enduring, albeit evolving, influence of China's revolutionary and state-socialist legacies, see, e.g., Arrighi (2007); Heilmann and Perry (2011); Perry (2006, 2007, 2010); Wright (2010).

[31] For discussion on "evaluative norms" and other mechanisms for eliciting labor effort, see Burawoy and Wright (1990: 252).

[32] Elizabeth Perry's (2006) compelling study of worker militias in modern China provides further evidence for the relative militancy of the Chinese working class emboldened by the mass line and continuing mass mobilization under the PRC when compared to their counterparts in the former Soviet Union.

long history of mass rebellions, and the CCP's own revolutionary road to power, have taught the Party's ruling elites that large-scale worker and peasant discontent can seriously jeopardize the regime, and that repression alone will not suffice.[33] Thus, the threat of mass disruption and social turmoil is very tangible to the CCP leadership when faced with mounting labor and social unrest incited by the social contradictions of capitalist development. This pressure from below, coupled with Beijing's reorientation of its development strategy to rebalance the economy and promote domestic consumption, has been the main force propelling the central government to pass new pro-labor laws and to reform social policies since the mid-2000s (see Chapter 7).

Legitimacy leverage

Based on the above discussion, I conceptualize *legitimacy leverage* as a specific type of workers' bargaining power in contemporary China (in addition to other types of bargaining power, noted in footnote 15, this chapter). Legitimacy leverage is essentially an ideological power. It is based on the idea and belief in workers' own power, and their willingness to struggle for change – what Piven and Cloward (2000) have called the "idea of power." It leverages the "credible threat" of the "disruptive power" of workers – on the streets as well as through strikes – and the CCP's top concerns with maintaining social stability and political legitimacy.[34] In this regard, legitimacy leverage is directly related to, and in effect reflects, workers' own *perceived* structural power. Legitimacy leverage appeals to the Party-state's official ideology and its public commitment to the legitimate rights and interests of workers. And yet it turns the dominant ideology into a counter-hegemonic weapon to advance workers' demands. As James Scott aptly put it (1985: 338):

[T]he very process of attempting to legitimate a social order by idealizing it *always* provides its subjects with the means, the symbolic tools, the very ideas for a critique that operates entirely within the hegemony... The most common form of class struggle arises from the failure of a dominant ideology to live up to the implicit promises it necessarily makes. The dominant ideology can be turned against its privileged beneficiaries not only because subordinate groups develop their own interpretations, understandings, and readings of its ambiguous terms, but also because of the promises that the dominant classes must make to propagate it in the first place.

---

[33] As Elizabeth Perry vividly describes, "China lays claim to one of the oldest and most robust traditions of protest of any country in the world. Passed down through such media as folk stories, legends, and local operas, familiar repertoires of popular resistance were for centuries a major means of alerting an authoritarian political system to the grievances of ordinary people." (2010: 24)

[34] The idea of the credible threat of disruptive power is borrowed from Piven and Cloward (1977). As Margaret Levi succinctly summarized, "the credible threat of disruption, on the streets as well as through strikes, is an important weapon in the labor repertoire, especially when there is ... governmental and employer hostility to unions and to labor rights" (2003: 59).

As should be clear, legitimacy leverage is not simply a tactic of framing, although framing and claims are certainly indispensable to such a leverage that is operated within the boundaries of official ideologies, rhetoric, and laws.[35] Rather, workers' legitimacy leverage can be exploited and translated into concrete bargaining power on the shop floor to win concessions from management and elicit pro-labor responses from the central government. For instance, my fieldwork found in many large auto assembly SOEs and JVs, management actively utilized certain socialist organizational legacies to advance its legitimacy and control, such as promoting enterprise paternalism, using campaign-style production mobilization, and mediating shop-floor conflicts through "heart-to-heart talks" (*tanxin*) and "thought work" (*sixiang gongzuo*) by factory Party committees and unions. Such rhetoric and strategies proved effective in eliciting workers' cooperation and facilitating profit-making while defusing direct labor-management conflicts. On the other hand, I also found important cases in which workers were able to turn the same rhetoric and ideology used by management and the state into legitimacy leverage, to negotiate and constrain management decisions that would have adversely affected workers. There is indeed a tacit bargaining between managers and workers around workers' legitimacy leverage that allows workers to wring specific concessions from management – even though conventional collective bargaining has been missing in China. The process is complex: as we shall see, some types of workers are more able to exert legitimacy leverage – such as those in large SOEs and JVs, where the central state plays a more interventionist role; some types of workers (such as veteran workers in early-built factories) are more likely to draw on socialist rhetoric than others.

Ironically, the lack of independent trade unions for effective labor representation and collective bargaining in the workplace often drives Chinese workers to turn directly to wildcat strikes or street protests in order to solicit government intervention for fast redress. As a result, labor-capital conflicts in the workplace can be easily escalated to social conflicts concerning social justice and regime legitimacy in the eyes of workers. This might explain why widespread, localized, and "apolitical" labor unrest in China can command direct central state intervention through labor legislation and social policy change in response to workers' grievances and demands.[36] Chinese workers are indeed "bargaining without union" (Zhang 2005); they are making use of their

[35] In this regard, legitimacy leverage resembles certain aspects of "rightful resistance" as Kevin O' Brien and Lianjiang Li (2006) have described. But unlike "rightful resistance," which emphasizes the "political opportunity structure" that produces protests and shapes the way protesters make claims (O' Brien 1996: 33), workers' legitimacy leverage has its own structural sources located in the workplace that can be translated into a concrete form of bargaining power.

[36] Certainly, the party-state is not hesitant to resort to repression when it senses any threat to its political power. However, outright repression is less likely when protesters' demands are considered legitimate and apolitical, and when protests remain localized, as repression under those circumstances is seen to carry the risk of further alienating the public and delegitimizing the regime.

legitimacy leverage arising from the state's concern with maintaining stability and political legitimacy to wring concessions from their employers. The idea that *legitimacy leverage* has become an important source of workers' bargaining power in contemporary China is an important theme of this book.

THE OUTLINE OF THE BOOK

Given this book's focus on the current conditions, subjectivity, and collective actions of Chinese autoworkers, the discussion presented in the core chapters proceeds through the four levels of working-class formation distinguished by Ira Katznelson (1986: 14–21): (1) "the structure of capitalist economic development" as seen from the transformation of the Chinese automobile industry and its labor force; (2) "ways of life," as seen from the organization of labor markets and factory settings in which workers exist, work, make decisions, act, and interact with one another; (3) "formed groups" with shared dispositions, as seen from group characteristics, aspirations, and grievances of formal workers and temporary workers, respectively; and, (4) collective actions of formal and temporary workers respectively. Analyses at levels (2), (3), and (4) are "experience-near," while level (1) is "experience distant" (structural). A parallel theme woven throughout this book is a multi-layered analysis of how shop-floor, national and global processes interact in complex ways to produce the specific labor relations in the Chinese automobile industry.

Chapter 2 sets up the broad sectoral context at the "experience-distant" level within which individual automobile firms operate. It traces the automotive industrial policy and development strategy of the central government since the 1950s, with a focus on the reform era. It documents how profound structural change in the Chinese system since the mid-1990s – including the deepening of SOE and labor reforms, and the government's industrial policy changes designed to prepare the auto industry to meet the challenge of China's WTO accession – has transformed the auto industry from a highly protected, monopolistic sector to a more open and competitive sector. The structural change and increased competition at the industry level have driven major automakers in China toward a leaner and more flexible workplace, including the introduction of labor force dualism and the use of a large number of temporary workers on assembly lines. The chapter discusses the transformation of production workforces and the rise of labor force dualism in the Chinese auto assembly industry.

Chapters 3 and 4 move from the "experience-distant" (structural) level of working-class formation to the first of the "experience-near" levels – that is, "ways of life," as seen from the organization of labor markets and factory settings. Chapter 3 looks into the labor market and social composition in the automobile industry, examining the supply and demand of formal and temporary workers respectively – who they are, how they are recruited, what are their wage and benefit conditions, and what criteria employers use to draw

boundaries between the two groups. The chapter first outlines the transformation of the Chinese labor system under market reform and lays out the various
institutional arrangements that provide auto manufacturers with various types
of workers. It also traces the evolution of labor force dualism from the Mao
Zedong era to the present day, showing how the Chinese state has recurrently
created boundaries and inequalities among its working population. My analysis
highlights the simultaneous dynamics of "flexibilization" and "dualization" in
the transformation of the Chinese labor system under market reform. It also
documents the re-composition of temporary workers, who have become
increasingly urban and better educated. This has blurred the existing boundaries between formal and temporary workers based on their urban-rural household registration (*hukou*) status, contributing to rising labor activism among
the new temporary workers. The chapter also investigates wage conditions and
demystifies the popular assumption that auto assembly workers are "affluent
workers, contented workers."

Chapter 4 examines the organization of production, working conditions,
and factory social order – that is, the factory settings under which managers,
different groups of workers, and factory Party and union cadres make their
decisions, act and interact with one another. I find that a leaner and more
efficient Taylorist/Fordist mass-production system has become generalized
in the Chinese auto assembly sector. The work regime under this system is
inherently exhausting and authoritarian, which is one of the main sources of
workers' grievances. The chapter also examines the cadre-managerial personnel
system, the role of enterprise unions, human resource management (HRM)
practices, factory hierarchy, and the operation of internal labor markets and
the structural opportunities for a blue-collar worker to move up in a large
automobile factory. My evidence shows that the hierarchical factory social
order and the institutionalized inferior status of blue-collar workers is another
main source of workers' discontent.

Chapters 5 and 6 take us onto the shop floor and present the comparative
ethnography of the two worlds of autoworkers under labor force dualism.
Chapter 5 investigates the contradictory dispositions of the "core" segment
of formal workers and their compliance with, and resistance to management
labor control. I find that, on the one hand, formal workers still enjoy higher-
than-average wages and relatively secure employment – given that the buffer
of a large number of temporary workers provides them with some sense of
job security and protection. Moreover, management's control over formal
workers is more sophisticated and hegemonic in nature. As a result, most
formal workers tend to resort to individual coping strategies when faced with
a leaner and meaner workplace and management arbitrary decisions. On the
other hand, intense competition in the auto industry has driven management
to reduce the protections and privileges of formal workers. As a result, there
have been declining consent and growing resistance among formal workers.
I argue that the current state of formal workers can best be understood as a
process of negotiated compliance, not consent. It is changeable and depends

on whether management will seek to entrench labor force dualism, or further reduce the privileges of formal workers.

Chapter 6 takes a close look at the "flexible" segment of temporary workers and their struggles against unequal treatment and arbitrary management control. The narrative centers on the paradox of labor force dualism as a mechanism of labor control and the dynamic relations between formal and temporary workers. The chapter explicates how temporary workers' changing social composition, growing workplace bargaining power and intense grievances as second-class workers have contributed to their rising labor activism. It analyzes the patterns, organizing strategies, outcomes, potentials and limits of temporary workers' struggles by comparing two wildcat strikes carried out by temporary workers. My evidence shows a detached (rather than antagonistic) and fluid relationship between formal and temporary workers that is conditioned by managerial strategy. The chapter also discusses management and union responses to temporary workers' resistance, and the limits of those strategies in solving the labor control problem. The paradox of labor force dualism reflects the underlying contradiction between profitability and legitimacy at the factory level.

Chapter 7 shifts the angle of analysis from the "contested terrain" of the shop floor to the broader national political dynamics, examining how the central state's labor laws and policies, concerned with maintaining "social harmony and stability," have been influenced by and have influenced labor unrest. It investigates the driving forces and the law-making process of the LCL, and discusses the impact of the LCL on management decisions and labor practice at the firm level. My analysis shows that the state deliberately draws boundaries among its working population in an effort to strike a balance: promising more protections for formal/regular workers as a way to shore up its legitimacy while excluding others in order to promote flexibility and profitability. However, the countermovement in the subsequent amendments to the LCL in response to popular pressure reflects the unresolved profitability-legitimacy contradiction faced by the party-state. Struggles for inclusion by the excluded workers can periodically propel the state to redraw boundaries and expand protection and labor rights to some of the formerly excluded.

The concluding chapter recaps the main themes of the book and discusses the possible future scenarios of labor relations in the Chinese automobile industry. I conclude by discussing the key insights and broader implications of this study of Chinese autoworkers for rethinking the role, strategy, and potential of labor and labor movements within and outside China for transformation from below.

2

Industrial restructuring and labor force transformation in the Chinese automobile industry

> Competition... is sure to increase as ambitious newcomers keep chipping away at the early leaders. China used to be an easy game. Not anymore.
> ———*Business Week*, May 9, 2005

> After all, the car business in China is a government controlled game. And the government wants big firms. To achieve large scales and high volumes in a short time, we rely not only on highly advanced machinery, but also on our hard-working workers – our comparative advantage.
> ———Interview with a manager at SOE-1, 2005

This chapter sets up the broad sectoral context within which individual automobile firms operate and their managers and workers act and interact on a day-to-day basis. The chapter starts with a brief review of the pre-reform development of the Chinese automobile industry and its organization and labor practices under state socialism, in particular the socialist egalitarianism and democratic management practices on the shop floor. These legacies have had an abiding influence on management decision-making, workers' formulations of legitimacy leverage, and shop-floor labor relations in the reform era, as will be discussed in later chapters.

The second section traces the development strategy and industrial policy of the central government in regard to the automobile industry in the post-Mao reform era. It presents an analysis of how the auto assembly sector was transformed from a highly protected industry in the 1980s and early 1990s, to a more open and competitive sector through industrial restructuring and massive foreign investment since the late 1990s. The growing competition at the industrial level drove major automakers in China to move toward a leaner and more flexible workplace and labor practice.

The third section investigates the workforce transformation and the rise of labor force dualism in the auto assembly sector in the reform era. It analyzes how the contradictory pressures of increasing profitability while seeking to maintain a peaceful and cooperative workforce have driven large state-owned automakers and Sino-foreign JVs to follow a policy of labor force dualism that draws boundaries between formal and temporary workers. The final section highlights labor force dualism as a key mechanism for understanding the labor politics in the Chinese automobile industry.

PRE-REFORM DEVELOPMENT AND SOCIALIST LEGACY IN THE CHINESE AUTOMOBILE INDUSTRY

China's leadership has long desired to develop a strong, independent motor vehicle industry since the early days of the People's Republic. In the pre-reform era, and under a centrally planned system, automobile production was mainly geared toward agriculture, capital goods production, and military purposes. It focused on truck manufacturing, self-sufficiency and geographical dispersion in production. The influence of the Soviet Union was strong. The establishment of First Automobile Works (FAW) in the early 1950s, China's first automobile manufacturer, almost completely followed the guidance of Soviet advisors (Harwit 1995: 26–37). Besides using Soviet technology, FAW also adopted the Soviet industrial model, characterized by the vertical division of labor and Taylorist scientific management. Under this system, all manufacturing operations, from manufacturing the most rudimentary components to the final assembly of motor vehicles, were carried out in one gigantic, all-encompassing enterprise such as FAW (Hiraoka 2001: 499). Those factories built later, such as the Second Auto Works – known today as Dongfeng Motor Corporation (DMC) – followed the same production model.

On the other hand, industrial relations in the early 1950s were generally inspired by the Maoist mass line, and the experiences of the masses were considered to be the best sources for improving production capacity. The early 1950s were marked by an emphasis on worker innovation in the production process. With the arrival of Soviet advisors in the mid-1950s, however, the focus shifted to the adoption of the Soviet industrial model and worker input was discouraged, as it was thought to interfere with the utilization of Soviet techniques. But the emphasis soon shifted back toward a reliance on Chinese workers' own innovation and experiences during the period of the "Great Leap Forward" (1958–1960) (Harwit 1995: 18–20).

Thus from the beginning, instead of adopting the Soviet "one-man rule" management hierarchy, FAW followed Mao's mass line and encouraged workers to participate in management tasks and managers to participate in actual production. Workers were organized into work groups (*ban zu*) to carry out daily production, and they were encouraged to learn multiple skills and to make rationalization suggestions to improve the production process. Some workers were sent to colleges to receive formal education in engineering and technology, and later returned to the factory to work as engineers and technicians. The popular slogan in the factory at that time urged workers to become "the master of the machine."[1] The "FAW experience" was later incorporated into the "An Gang Constitution"[2] (*an'gang xianfa*), endorsed by Chairman Mao in March 1960. The essence of the An Gang Constitution can be summarized as "two participations, one reform, and triple combinations" (*liangcan yigai sanjiehe*): workers participating in management and managers participating in production ("two participations"); reforming rules and regulations that inhibit the "two participations" ("one reform"); and realizing "the combination of technical theory with production practice through the leadership of the masses, technical staff, and managerial cadres" ("triple combination").[3] It marked a clear departure from the Soviet "one-man rule" and Taylorist production system by emphasizing the experience and participation of workers.[4]

Although workers' participation in management and managers' participation in production during the Mao years neither changed the factory hierarchy nor challenged the conventional division of labor among managers, technicians, and workers, it did raise workers' awareness of workplace democracy and of the divisions between cadres and workers, and between mental and manual workers (Zhang 2005).[5] Moreover, it established a set of "evaluative norms" of good or bad managers, with whom workers would either voluntarily cooperate or withdraw work efforts (Burawoy and Wright 1990: 252). For instance, the idea that workers should be able to have a say in their workplace, and that factory managers and cadres should listen to the "opinions of the masses," was still held among the interviewed workers. Workers were also very critical of the large discrepancy in earnings between workers and managers, whereas "in the past a skilled worker could earn as much as a shop manager."[6] Some of these socialist organizational legacies and evaluative norms, as I will show in the following chapters, continue to affect labor-management relations and shop-floor cultures in Chinese automobile factories (especially in early-built factories), including both SOEs and Sino-foreign JVs.

During the Cultural Revolution in the late 1960s, and throughout the 1970s, the government aimed to develop a self-sufficient automobile industry with

---

[1] Interview F2, GER-2, August 2004.

[2] "Constitution" in this context means rules and principles.

[3] See Andors (1977), Hoffmann (1974; 1977), Zhang (2005: 88–100) for more detailed discussions about democratic management in the Mao era.

[4] The Chinese intellectual, Cui Zhiyuan, has argued that China's "An'gang Constitution" can be viewed as the earliest experiment of Post-Fordism, in that it challenged the rigidities and vertical hierarchy of Fordism and aimed at promoting a committed and democratic workplace (Cui 1996).

[5] Even under Maoist Socialism, workers' democratic participation was limited in its effectiveness and scope. Workers could criticize cadres, and could weigh in with their opinions about basic leadership changes and some not-so-contentious issues at the plant level, but everything was controlled and led by the Communist Party. There was no autonomous worker organization except, in a limited way, during the Cultural Revolution. I thank Joel Andreas for this point on labor relations during the Mao era. On the Party's control in Chinese factories under Mao, see Walder (1986).

[6] Interview F10, GER-2, October 2006.

production bases in each province and to avoid any dependence on foreign technology. They believed that China should develop its own models that were suited to local conditions. In the 1960s, significant foreign investment in the automobile industry was precluded, as was the importation of completed vehicles and technologies. In the early 1970s, there was renewed interest in foreign technology. Chinese automobile manufacturers were able to participate in the exchange of technical experts with Japanese automakers in the mid-1970s (Harwit 1995: 25). One such noteworthy episode was the FAW's experiment with the Toyota Production System (TPS; *fengtian shengchan fangshi*) in the early 1980s, initiated after a FAW delegation visited Toyota's Japanese factories in the late 1970s. Lean production principles and practices, such as *kaizen* (the continuous improvement of all aspects of production) and quality circles, were introduced to FAW in the early 1980s. With the government as the sole customer, however, there was little need to consider production costs or worry about profitability. Until the mid-1990s, it remained more of a formality than a serious effort at promoting lean production.[7]

In sum, three decades of intermittent development of the automobile industry in the pre-reform era left an industry with a mushroom-like proliferation of vehicle factories that were "small, but complete" (*xiao er quan*) in almost every province, with outdated technology and low-quality products, isolated from global automobile production and markets. Yet those early decades also produced an experienced workforce with autonomous workplace consciousness. At the beginning of the economic reform era, there were 56 automobile assembly manufacturers, 129 repair plants, 24 motorcycle makers, 33 motor engine manufacturers, and 2,076 parts producers in China. The 56 state-owned auto assembly plants produced 222,288 units per year, and only 5,418 of these were sedans, based primarily on Eastern European designs from the 1950s.[8] Labor productivity was relatively low. In 1981, 904,000 Chinese autoworkers produced 176,000 four-wheeled vehicles. By contrast, 683,000 Japanese autoworkers manufactured over 11 million four-wheeled vehicles in 1980 (Marukawa 1995:333). It was in direct response to this industrial backwardness that the Chinese leadership formed its new development strategy and industrial policy for the automobile industry in the reform era. This is the topic to which we now turn.

THE DEVELOPMENT AND RESTRUCTURING OF THE CHINESE
AUTOMOBILE INDUSTRY IN THE REFORM ERA

Development strategy and industrial policy of the central government

The automobile industry was designated one of China's seven "pillar industries" of strategic importance by the State Council in the Seventh, Eighth

---

[7] Interview F15, GER-2, October 2006.
[8] Ministry of Machinery Industry (1994): 63, 73; as cited in Thun (2006): 54–5.

and Ninth Five-Year Plans (1986–1990, 1991–1995, 1996–2000), and was declared as a "leading industry" in the Tenth and Eleventh Five-Year Plans (2001–2005, 2006–2010).

The development strategy for the industry in the reform era was a complete departure from previous industrial development strategies and policies. There have been two consistent objectives in the central government's automotive industry policy throughout the reform era: consolidating the automotive sector to achieve optimum economic scales and efficiency[9] by supporting a handful of large auto groups;[10] and, encouraging large state-owned auto groups to enter into JVs with foreign partners to realize rapid transfers of technology and management skills as well as to advance independent R&D capacity. The Chinese government hopes eventually that China can develop its own "national champions" that can compete globally (Thun 2004; 2006).

These two objectives were specified through a series of industrial policies issued by the central government. In 1986, the central government designated the sector as a pillar industry of the national economy, and the emphasis shifted from truck manufacturing to passenger car production. Development efforts for passenger vehicles focused on three JVs with local governments – VW in Shanghai; American Motors Corporation (AMC), and then Chrysler, in Beijing; and, Peugeot in Guangzhou – and two with centrally controlled enterprises – VW with FAW, and Citroen with Dongfeng (Thun 2004: 459). The objectives for the industry were formalized in the 1994 "Automotive Industry Policy Statement," issued by the State Planning Commission (SPC). It clearly defined the development of passenger car production as the priority of the industry, and that the technological capabilities of the industry were to be upgraded through linkages to international auto companies (SPC 1994). The 2004 "Automotive Industry Development Policy" reiterated the objective of creating internationally competitive auto industry groups by 2010, while acknowledging the importance of strategic partnerships with global firms (SDRC 2004). The "Plan on Adjusting and Revitalizing the Auto Industry," issued in March 2009, continued to push for consolidation of the industry by reducing the number of major domestic automakers from 14 to 10. The central government aimed to create 2–3 giant automakers with annual sales and production capacity of 2 million units, and another 4–5 large enterprises, each capable of manufacturing 1 million vehicles annually by 2010.[11]

---

[9] According to Chinese auto industry experts, the minimum efficient scale of auto assembly production is 1 million units of a given model annually; the optimum efficient scale is 2 million. Interview No. 24, Shanghai, December 2006. By 2011, four Chinese automakers had surpassed the 2 million optimum efficient scale benchmark, and five had exceeded the 1 million minimum efficient scale threshold.

[10] China's large domestic automakers are generally known as the "Big Four" – FAW, DFM, SAIC, CCAG – and the "Small Four" – BAIC, GAIG, Chery, and CNHTC (*zhong qi*). See the List of Abbreviations for the full names of the automobile enterprises.

[11] The General Office of the State Council released its *Plan on Adjusting and Revitalizing the Auto Industry* (*qiche chanye tiaozheng zhenxing guihua*) on March 20, 2009. Under this plan, the

Despite the central government's efforts to consolidate the auto industry through its support for large automakers, there was a continued proliferation of small and inefficient auto assembly plants in almost every province (Harwit 2001: 661). The number of auto assemblers peaked at 124 in 1992, and that number remained high, at 115 as of 2011 (CATRC 2012: 468). Many of these companies had limited annual output of a few thousand or just a few hundred units and operated under the protection of local governments (Harwit 2001: 661). Fiscal decentralization in the reform era often led to contradictory interests between the central and local governments. Local governments remain keen on investing in the auto sector because of its long industrial supply chain and close linkages with many other industries, which can play a significant role in spurring local economies and creating jobs. As such, the desire of local officials to develop a local automobile industry and local protectionism persisted throughout the reform era. Not surprisingly, there is intense competition among local governments to attract new auto investments, typically bent to investors' demands.

To overcome local protectionism and to implement the desired industrial policy, the central government had to rely on the other two major actors – foreign automakers and the major domestic auto groups. A state-led "triple alliance" was forged with the establishment of centrally sanctioned JVs between foreign automakers and large state-owned auto groups.

State-led "Triple alliance" and hegemonic labor regime, 1980s–mid-1990s

The original notion of "triple alliance" comes from Peter Evans' (1979) classic work on the alliance of multinational, state, and local capital in Brazil. Eric Thun (2004: 455) applied this term to describe the relationship between the central state and foreign and domestic capital in the Chinese automobile industry. I emphasize that it is a *state-led* "triple alliance" – that is, the central state plays the dominant role in forging alliances between foreign direct investment (FDI) and large Chinese auto groups, which are owned or controlled by the state. The emphasis on the leading role of the state in developing pillar industries and nurturing large-scale enterprises is not foreign to students of East Asian developmental states. Yet unlike Japan and South Korea – which supported indigenous automobile manufacturers to compete head-to-head with leading foreign firms in the global market from the outset – the Chinese government chose to utilize FDI through the creation of JVs with large,

government set up a $1.5 billion fund to help China's automakers develop new-energy vehicles. It also offered nearly $1 billion in subsidies to support vehicle purchases in rural areas, and cut the sales tax on vehicles with smaller engines in half, from 10 to 5 percent. The government also sought to increase the market share of Chinese-brand passenger vehicles to 40 percent, a 6 percent increase from 34 percent in 2008. This plan was part of a larger government stimulus package for 10 key industries, including the automotive industry, announced in early 2009.

domestic auto groups at a very early stage to foster the development of China's auto industry.[12] But the central government's use of FDI was extremely cautious: foreign automakers are not allowed to build wholly-owned assembly plants, nor are they able to own a majority stake in assembly JVs. Moreover, the creation of new auto assembly JVs must get the approval of the central government, and it is the central government that often takes the lead on behalf of Chinese automakers in negotiating the terms of the deal and the models to be produced at newly established JVs.[13] Meanwhile, to protect domestic auto enterprises from direct international competition, the Chinese government imposed strict licensing requirements and heavy tariffs on imported vehicles and components.[14] Moreover, by controlling personnel decisions of senior management at the large state-owned auto groups – which appointed general managers and other senior Chinese managers at subsidiary JVs – the central government has been able to ensure that Chinese managers at JVs carry out the economic, political, and social agenda that is concordant with the goals of the party-state. Given this cadre-management personnel system at large JVs, it is not surprising to find notable "SOE characteristics" at China's large auto JVs, as we will see in the subsequent chapters.

The second main actor under the state-led triple alliance was automobile multinationals. A significant feature of the development of China's automobile industry was that the take-off and rapid growth of the industry in the reform era had been largely fueled by foreign investment through JVs with multinationals. During the 1990s, China received more foreign investment than any other developing country, and much of this foreign investment was in the automotive industry. By 2001, more than 800 Chinese companies in vehicle-related industries (including component manufacturers) had received FDI, and the total planned investment was valued at $233 billion. Cumulative "actually used FDI" in the automotive industry reached $45.4 billion in 2000, accounting for 13 percent of total realized FDI in China (Nag, Banerjee, and Chatterjee 2007).[15] There were two major waves of foreign investment in the Chinese auto assembly sector. The first wave, from 1984 to 1996, was pioneered by AMC/

---

[12] In the Japanese and Korean auto industries, foreign trade liberalization was introduced at a much more mature state of development than that in China. One reason for the difference, according to Thun (2004: 475), was that the conditions that proved favorable to the Japanese and Korean automakers no longer existed. China would be helped neither by a 1970s-style oil shock that boosted the demand for fuel-efficient cars – which had helped Japan to get ahead – nor by a favorable exchange rate as had helped South Korean automakers break into low-end European and North American markets. For more detailed comparisons, see Beeson (2009).

[13] Those automotive JV projects often include terms such as taking care of redundant workers from the Chinese partners, providing jobs for local peasants whose land will be used to build new factories, and other social and political considerations. Interview S2, GER-1, July 2004.

[14] China agreed to lower the tariffs on imported vehicles and components from 80–100 percent to 25 percent by July 1, 2006, as a condition for its WTO accession. See Table 2.1 for the changes in the Chinese auto industry before and after the WTO accession.

[15] The term "actually used FDI," means that FDI has been realized or utilized, as opposed to merely contracted or pledged FDI. See Buckley et al. (2007): 722.

Chrysler and VW in 1984 and 1985, respectively, followed by Peugeot (1985), Citroen (1992), and Daihatsu (1996). During this time period, due to tight state control and a relatively small domestic private auto market, foreign firms – with the exception of VW – were not profitable. Peugeot pulled out of the Chinese market, only to re-enter in 2003.

The second and more intensive wave of FDI started from 1997, when automobile multinationals were lured to China by its fast-growing domestic auto market and the prospect of easier access with reduced tariff and non-tariff barriers as part of China's preparation for the WTO agreement. Led by GM (1997) and Honda (1998), and followed by Kia (1999), Toyota (2000), Ford (2001), and Hyundai (2002), among others,[16] all the world's major automakers came to China and established JVs with one or two Chinese partners by the early 2000s. The JVs claimed a 97 percent share of China's passenger car market in 2000, while the domestic carmakers only had 3 percent market share. This JV domination has declined since 2004, as China's indigenous automakers such as Chery Automobile Co. (Chery), Geely, and BYD have grown rapidly. But Sino-foreign JVs still claimed a 74 percent share of China's auto market as of 2008 (CATRC 2001–2009; Liu 2009).

Relying on FDI to propel economic growth is considered one of the defining features of the Chinese economy in the reform era. Yet it should be emphasized that FDI in the Chinese automobile assembly sector has been the "market-seeking" kind. In other words, it is not merely driven by cost-cutting motives, as commonly seen in the labor-intensive export industries. Although cost is certainly important in the highly competitive automobile manufacturing sector, big auto multinationals invest in China mainly because they want to access the 1.3 billion consumers, and the only way to do so is to get Chinese government permission to establish JVs with local Chinese firms. This unique "market leverage" of the Chinese central government has endowed it with great bargaining power over foreign capital in negotiating contract terms.[17] Moreover, each Chinese auto enterprise is encouraged to have at least two simultaneous JV agreements with rival foreign competitors.[18] This arrangement enables the Chinese partner to learn "best practices" from both competitors, and to position itself as the only one in the three-player network to have access to all other parties (Shenkar 2006: 66). Thus, unlike other late-developers, the Chinese state tends to have more leverage to negotiate its position in the

[16] Others include Nissan (2003), BMW (2003), Peugeot (which returned to China in 2003), and DaimlerChrysler (2004). See Clifford, Joas, and Leung (2009).
[17] For a more general discussion on "market-seeking" FDI in China, and on the Chinese development model, see Arrighi (2007): Chapter 12.
[18] For instance, China's top four automakers each have at least two major foreign partners: SAIC has partnered with VW and GM; FAW with VW, Toyota and Madza; DFM with PSA, Nissan, Kia and Honda; and CCAG with Suzuki, Ford, Mazda, and PSA.

international division of labor, which may enable it to jump up in the global value-added hierarchy. We will return to this point in Chapter 8.

Some scholars go further, arguing that the market-oriented FDI in capital- and technology-intensive sectors is one of the main reasons for the high wages, better working conditions, and hegemonic labor relations at China's large automobile JVs. This is in contrast with FDI focused on cost-cutting, as is seen in labor-intensive, export-oriented sectors in low-wage countries.[19] As I will discuss below, it is overly simplistic to make a general linkage between different types of FDI and different labor regimes – after all, the bottom line for any type of FDI is to maximize investment returns and profitability. It is true though that market-seeking FDI tends to be more embedded in the local context and is thus more subject to state regulations and local labor politics.

The third main actor in the state-led triple alliance is a handful of centrally supported, large, state-owned auto groups. It is important to understand the pyramid-shaped hierarchy in China's auto assembly sector, in which every individual firm is positioned in a certain tier and receives different resources and support from the central government. In the top tier are the four largest state-owned auto groups, the so-called "Big Four" – Shanghai Automotive Industry Corporation (SAIC), FAW, DFM, and Chang'an Motors (CCAG).[20] They have always received strong government support and favorable treatment, such as preferred financing, support for R&D, priority in setting up JVs, and preference in sales outlets and parts subsidiaries. They are large and powerful SOEs with dozens of subsidiaries. In the second tier are the leading regional auto groups, known as "Small Four" – Beijing Automobile Industry Corporation (BAIC), Guangzhou Automobile Industry Group (GAIG), Chery, and China National Heavy Duty Truck Group Corporation (CNHTC). They also receive preferential treatment from the government in the form of policies and material support, especially from local governments. Moreover, by partnering large SOEs in the top two tiers with foreign auto multinationals, the central government also granted a select few SOEs dramatic advantages over other domestic auto firms. It is expected that many other smaller and less efficient domestic vehicle manufacturers will be weeded out through competition over time (Thun 2004: 469).

To be sure, until the early 1990s, most state-owned automobile enterprises were protected by the government from global competition with high tariff and nontariff barriers, and their primary goal was to "employ a lot of people and make as many vehicles as possible. Quality and efficiency were secondary" (Treece 1997: 1). Many state-owned automobile factories had low production

---

[19] See, for example, Chin (2003): 187–96.
[20] FAW, DFM, and CCAG are centrally-controlled key SOEs. SAIC is a key SOE under the supervision of Shanghai State Assets Supervision and Administration Commission of the State Council (SASAC).

volumes, weak technology, and a large number of redundant workers. For instance, SOE-2, an old state-owned truck manufacturer, produced only 4,770 trucks per year while it had over 5,000 state workers before it was acquired by FAW in 1993.[21] Until the early 1990s, most state-owned automobile enterprises still enjoyed soft budget constraints,[22] especially under local government protectionism.

Thus far, we have examined the overall industrial structure and the three main actors under the state-led triple alliance – central government, foreign multinationals, and large state-owned auto groups – in the auto assembly sector during the first stage of development in the reform era. Until the mid-1990s, the auto assembly sector was still a state-controlled and protected sector, dominated by a few centrally selected JVs and large SOEs. They were able to enjoy extremely high profits thanks to government protection, with soft budget constraints and high tariffs. Their main customers were government officials and state enterprise managers, who did not care much about prices. Especially for a few successful JVs, as one industry analyst observed, up until the early 2000s, equivalent models were 150 percent more expensive in China than in the United States and Europe, which allowed JVs in China to enjoy "levels of profitability not seen anywhere else" (Gao 2002: 148).

The windfall profits that accrued to Chinese automakers in the 1990s did not come from "innovation."[23] In fact, most of the cars made by the JVs in China in the 1990s relied on technology imported from foreign partners. The high level of profitability enjoyed by a few large automakers during this time period came from government protection and the environment of "controlled competition" under the state-led triple alliance.[24] Thus, once the central government decided to cut back the nontariff protection measures in the auto sector, we could expect a dramatic increase in competition and decline in profitability. This is exactly what has happened since the mid-1990s, as we will see below.

Nevertheless, the high levels of profitability allowed large auto JVs and their Chinese parent SOEs to provide their workforce with high wages, generous benefits, and stable employment. For instance, Shanghai Volkswagen (SVW) – one of the most successful JVs between SAIC and VW – dominated China's domestic passenger car market for nearly 20 years. Despite producing outdated

---

[21] The author's field notes, June 2004.

[22] A soft budget constraint refers to a loss-making company continuing to receive financing, especially prevalent in a socialist planned economy. For an informative discussion on the soft and hard budget constraints faced by different types of Chinese firms under economic reform, see Naughton (2007): 308–10.

[23] Here I am referring to Joseph Schumpeter's argument that the "spectacular prizes" accrue to the innovator of new products or techniques (1954: 73).

[24] Margaret Pearson (2003) has pointed out that in China's key sectors, such as the automobile industry, the central government tends to adopt a strategy of "controlled competition," to promote competition between several dominant "national champions" of large enterprise groups.

models and lagging behind international standards,[25] SVW enjoyed enormous profits – in 1996, the sale price of the SVW Santana, a 1970s VW model, was 66 percent higher in China than in other countries.[26]

Accordingly, workers at the auto assembly JVs were known for their high wages – 2–3 times higher than the wages of SOE workers and local average wages – and comprehensive benefits packages that were considered "even better than government officials'."[27] Indeed, Chinese regulations stipulate that the wage level at JVs is to be set at 120 percent to 150 percent of that of SOEs in the same line of business and the same locality. The rationale for giving higher wages to workers in JVs is that greater skills are generally required in the JVs (Tsang 1994: 8). It was also common for major auto JVs to provide their employees with a wide range of social welfare benefits that were typical under the socialist *danwei* system – benefits that were comparable or even better than those enjoyed by workers at the JVs' state-owned Chinese parent companies. For example, until the mid-1990s, Beijing Jeep Corporation – the first Sino-foreign JV established between Beijing Automotive and Chrysler – still provided its employees with subsidized housing, free lunch, health insurance and schooling for their elementary school-age children, under pressure from its Chinese state-owned parent company. The tab for these benefits roughly equaled a worker's monthly pay, about $200.[28] Also, it was rare for JVs to lay off workers during this time period. My interviews with workers at GER-1 confirmed that workers were never worried about losing their job until 2004 – the year when the company encountered its first market downturn since it was established.[29]

As for workers at state-owned automobile factories, while they earned on average much less than their counterparts at large JVs – about half or less, depending on the region – they at least had guaranteed employment and received full social welfare benefits until the early 1990s.

In sum, the evidence from the existing literature and from my interviews with veteran managers and workers suggests that factory regimes in the auto assembly sector until the early to mid-1990s can be characterized as "hegemonic," based on secure employment and a full range of social welfare benefits. Workers at large JVs were especially privileged, enjoying higher wages and more generous benefits than workers at state-owned auto enterprises and in other manufacturing sectors.

However, as China moved swiftly toward a more open economy in preparation for its WTO accession, the central government gradually reduced its

---

[25] The VW Santana produced by SVW, is a 1970s-era model that has long been out of production elsewhere. But it had remained China's best-selling car until the early 2000s even without a facelift for more than 15 years.

[26] The differences in sales price were calculated based on an exchange rate of 8.3 Chinese *yuan* to 1 US dollar (Xia, Shi, and Zhang, 2002: 232). According to the company's annual report, with total production of only 230,000 cars in 1998 and 1999, SVW earned a net profit of 6 billion yuan ($723 million).

[27] Interview S6, GER-1, July 2004.   [28] See Chin (2003): Chapter 4.

[29] Interview S5, GER-1, July 2004.

protections for the auto sector. A large scale restructuring and intense competition in the auto assembly sector loomed ahead. As will be discussed in the following sections, the changing automotive industry policy and the dramatic increase in competition quickly drove down prices and profit margins in the auto assembly sector. The crisis of profitability, in turn, led to changing workplace and labor practices, as well as the transformation of the automobile industry workforce since the mid-1990s.

Industrial restructuring and intensified competition, mid-1990s to present

Intensive restructuring in the Chinese automobile industry started in the mid-1990s. The sector saw waves of mergers and reorganizations, enterprise restructurings, and mass layoffs. In retrospect, the auto sector restructuring was part and parcel of the broader SOE reforms undertaken as China accelerated its move toward a market economy in the mid-1990s.

A new wave of SOE reforms began in the mid-1990s. A milestone was the adoption of the Company Law in 1994. The Company Law provided a framework for corporatizing traditional SOEs into legal corporations suited to a market economy, including the options of share-holding systems and bankruptcy (Naughton 2007: 301). In 1997, faced with large and unsustainable financial losses at SOEs that threatened the solvency of the banking system, the Chinese government moved ahead with a more aggressive SOE restructuring policy, called "grasping the large, and letting the small go" (*zhuada fangxiao*). With "grasping the large," the central government aimed to reorganize and restructure the large, typically centrally-controlled SOEs into even larger and hopefully more competitive enterprises, while keeping control in the hands of the state. With "letting the small go," the center gave authority to local governments to restructure their own small and medium SOEs, in particular through privatization and bankruptcy.

The extensive restructuring of the auto sector was carried out in this broad context, but the pressure on the central government to push it through in a relatively short time came from China's pending WTO accession. In 1994, as China began preparing for entry to the WTO, the auto industry was perceived as one of the most vulnerable sectors to the global challenge. This was not surprising given that the industry had long been protected by high tariff and nontariff barriers, and was dominated by a select few centrally supported, inefficient SOEs and their foreign partners. As seen in Table 2.1, with China's WTO accession, there was a dramatic reduction in tariff and nontariff barriers to imports. There were worries that the auto sector might not be able to survive the intense global competition of a post-WTO world. At the same time, the central government would not allow the auto sector to fail: total sales in the auto sector reached about $38 billion in 1999 – nearly 4 percent of the country's GDP. As of 1998, seven million people, or about 3.3 percent of the total Chinese urban workforce, were working in occupations related to the automobile industry (Harwit 2001: 661). There was an urgent need for

TABLE 2.1. *Changes in the Chinese auto industry before and after WTO accession*

	Before entry into WTO	After entry into WTO
Tariffs	200% in 1980s; 80–100% in 1990s	25% by July 1, 2006
Import quotas	30,000 vehicles a year allowed from foreign carmakers	Quota increased 20% a year, phased out by July 1, 2006
Local content	40% in first year of production, increasing to 60%, 80% in second and third years, respectively	No local-content ratio requirement
Foreign participation in sales, distribution	Limited to wholesaling through joint ventures; prohibited from consolidating sales organizations of imports, joint ventures	Will be allowed to own vehicle wholesale, retail organizations; integrated sales organizations permitted by 2006
Auto financing for Chinese domestic customers	Foreign, nonbank financial institutions prohibited from providing financing	Foreign, nonbank financing permitted in selected cities prior to gradual national rollout

Source: Gao (2002: 148).

all automakers in China to restructure and to prepare for the "bloody competition" in a post-WTO world in the mid-1990s.

Thus, the restructuring of the auto sector was carried out in a pro-active manner to prepare for the challenges following China's WTO accession. The 1994 Automotive Industry Policy called for the rationalization of the auto assembly sector through mergers and reorganization (*jianbing chongzu*), with large enterprises taking over smaller ones. A "leaning-out" industrial policy was introduced to bring labor productivity in line with the standards set by "international market rule" (Treece 1997). Between 1994 and 2000, the major domestic auto groups carried out a series of enterprise reforms and restructurings through mergers, acquisitions, downsizings, organizational streamlining, the shifting of primary products and markets, and by reaching out to foreign partners to establish new JVs. For instance, SOE-2, an old state-owned truck maker established in 1968, was acquired by FAW in 1993. It managed to push through two major enterprise reforms, in 1993 and 2000, reducing its total number of employees from over 5,000 to about 3,000. The sum result of early retirements, reassignments, and new hires of young workers was a dramatic decline in the average age of production workers to under 29 years of age; meanwhile, output increased by more than 50 percent.[30] After four years of knuckle-down reforms between 1998 and 2001,

---

[30] Interview Q1, Q2, SOE-2, June 2004.

TABLE 2.2. *Sales and market share for China's top-five auto groups, 2012*

Group Name	Sales (10,000 units)	Market Share (%)	Number of Employees[a] (end of 2011)	Ownership	Headquarter Location (city, province)	Foreign Partners
SAIC	446.14	23	150,696	SOE	Shanghai	VW, GM
DFM	307.85	16	162,779	SOE	Wuhan, Hubei	Peugeot S.A. Honda, Kia, Nissan
FAW	264.59	14	125,020	SOE	Changchun, Jilin	VW, Toyota, Mazda
CCAG	195.64	10	55,701	SOE	Chongqing	Peugeot S.A. Ford, Mazda, Suzuki
BAIC	169.11	9	71,509	SOE	Beijing	Daimler AG Hyundai
TOTAL	1383.33	72	594,819			

Note: [a] Number of employees included only formal employees listed on the books of enterprises.

Sources: China Association of Automobile Manufacturers (CAAM), January 2013; CATRC 2012.

FAW reduced its staff by 80 percent, and boosted its profits six fold (Shanghai Information Center 2002). The total number of workers employed in the automobile manufacturing sector dropped by 25 percent, from nearly 2 million in 1997 to 1.5 million in 2001 (CATRC 2002).

Consolidation was further promoted to generate greater efficiencies. Actual market shares in the assembly sector were increasingly concentrated in the five largest auto groups. As of 2012, the top-five Chinese auto groups alone accounted for 72 percent of total vehicle sales in China and directly employed 594,819 workers in automobile manufacture (see Table 2.2).[31]

More dramatic changes came as a result of increased competition. As noted above, the loosening of barriers to entry in the auto sector under China's WTO agreement, combined with the fast-growing domestic auto market, invited a second wave of foreign investment and new domestic entrants in the late 1990s

---

[31] The five auto groups all have JVs with foreign automakers and they sell vehicles under a variety of brand names, most of which belong to their JV partners. One of Beijing's major concerns has been the lack of China's own brand names – especially in the passenger car segment – despite the remarkable development of China's automobile industry over the past decade.

TABLE 2.3. *Changing profitability in the Chinese automotive industry, 2003–2011*

Year	Profitability (%)[a]	Year	Profitability (%)
2003	9.11	2008	5.95
2004	6.85	2009	7.22
2005	4.00	2010	8.62
2006	4.65	2011	8.55
2007	6.31		

Note: [a] Calculations of profitability in 2003–2006 were based on year-end actual sales data; calculations of profitability in 2007–2010 were based on sales data from January through November.

Source: Compiled from China Economic Monitoring Center of National Bureau of Statistics of China (NBS), *Quarter Automotive Industry Index Report*, various issues.

and early 2000s. The ever-growing levels of FDI and the entrance of all the major world auto giants into China not only brought state-of-the-art technology and machinery, new models, and managerial skills, but also global benchmarks and competitive pressures for local producers and early incumbents.

Moreover, spirited local players also sprang up, such as Chery, Geely, Great Wall, and BYD Auto, creating intense competition and driving down sales prices more aggressively. As a result, profit margins, especially for the middle- and low-end automakers, also declined sharply.[32] According to an auto industry researcher at Shanghai Social Science Academy, the price of an average sedan model dropped 30 percent between 2000 and 2005, and the average life cycle of a sedan model was shortened by half compared to the 1980s and 1990s. The average profit margin of a Chinese passenger carmaker was about 12–14 percent as of 2000, yet it stood at a mere 4 percent in 2005.[33] For low-end carmakers such as Chery and Geely, their profit margins were even thinner, at an average of 2.5–4 percent (Wang 2010).

Notably, in the aftermath of the 2008 global economic crisis, the average profitability in the Chinese auto assembly sector rebounded after a short downturn in 2008 (see Table 2.3). Industry analysts generally attributed the rising profitability to the government's stimulus policies in the automobile industry, China's fast-growing domestic auto market, and the optimized production capacity and reduced manufacturing costs (CEIN 2009, 2010).[34]

---

[32] Changing customer markets is another important reason for the steep price declines. As Roberts et al. commented in *Business Week* (2005), "Just a few years ago most auto sales were to state-owned companies that didn't worry much about price. Today most buyers are individuals and they want the best deal for their money."

[33] This estimate excluded luxury car brands, which generally have much higher profit margins. Interview No.31, Shanghai, March 2007.

[34] According to an industry expert whom I interviewed, the profitability of China's auto assembly sector should return to "the normal range" of 6–8 percent in the next two to three years, with

What has often been left out, as we will see in the following pages, is the intensified exploitation of front-line workers through increased work intensity and excessive overtime, as well as the widespread use of low-paid, flexible temporary workers on production lines.

Although automakers in China have so far been able to enjoy higher-than-average profitability compared with their international counterparts, it has become clear that the days of windfall profits in the Chinese auto industry have gone as intensified competition and "ambitious newcomers keep chipping away at the early leaders." The most telling example is SVW, the top passenger car seller in China for nearly two decades: it has continued losing market share, from a peak of 54 percent in 1996 to less than 18 percent in 2005, being overtaken by Shanghai General Motors and FAW-VW. As the head of VW China commented, China had suddenly become "the toughest market in the world" (Dyer 2005).

At the same time, the central government's industrial policy since the mid-1990s has shifted from direct control of the auto sector toward a greater reliance on market mechanisms to decide winners and losers. Although the central government continues to support large, domestic auto groups as they seek to become bigger and stronger and more internationally competitive, it also has promoted "controlled competition" among the dominant auto groups to determine who deserves more support and favorable treatment. At the same time, the remaining companies have been left to "sink-or-swim" at the mercy of market forces. As a spokesman for Ford Motor China Ltd. commented, "It is clear that government subsidies are gone; companies have to stand on their own two feet. Those who can't will be forced into mergers with larger rivals or out of the market" (Young 2001).

The widespread predictions and worries that China's automotive industry would be crushed by floods of imported cars following the WTO accession did not materialize. Between 2001 and 2005, five years after joining the WTO, China's motor vehicle output had nearly tripled, and its export of automotive products had continued growing by 15 percent annually. Export values reached 20 billion *yuan* (about $2.5 billion) in 2005. The auto industry has not only withstood those trials but also has become stronger and more competitive. It is worth noting that the Chinese government did fulfill its commitment to the WTO agreement. On July 1, 2006, China cut tariffs on imported automobiles and auto parts to 25 percent and 10 percent, respectively. In 2005, the government abolished the auto import quotas that had existed for 20 years. China has also opened up its auto financing market since October 2003. As a result, between 2001 and 2005, the annual number of imported vehicles increased

---

the expiration of the government's stimulus policies, the introduction of car-purchase restrictions in a growing number of cities, and the looming production overcapacity concern. But considering the average profitability in the world auto industry has been just 3–5 percent in recent years, 6–8 percent in China is still good news for multinationals. Interview No.41, Shanghai, August 2011.

from more than 70,000 units to over 170,000, and China imported $18 billion worth of vehicles and components in 2005. In spite of the growing absolute number of imported vehicles, the share of imports in the domestic auto market fell from 6 percent in 2001 to less than 3 percent in 2005, and the average price of imported vehicles continued to rise – from $20,000 in 2000 to $33,900 in 2005.[35]

Industry analysts suggested the following reasons for the smooth integration of China's auto industry into the global marketplace. Besides the proactive industrial restructuring prior to China's WTO entry, tariff barriers were dissolved step by step, and only when the domestic market had matured. The last round of tariff cuts, for example, had little impact on the auto market in terms of sales. To minimize the negative effects of increased imports on the domestic auto industry, the government adopted an import control policy for "controlling the total quotas, while promoting orderly competition" (*zongliang kongzhi, youxu jingzheng*). For instance, imported vehicles were mostly luxury cars and high-end models that domestic automakers were still struggling to produce. Perhaps more importantly, auto multinationals chose to expand their investment and production within China, and to sell their Chinese JV-assembled cars locally, rather than importing the same models from abroad. As such, direct competition between domestic automakers and multinationals was largely turned into "bloody battles" between multinationals, waged through their JVs in China.

In sum, leading up to China's WTO accession, the Chinese automobile industry had restructured and transformed itself into a stronger and more competitive sector, and entered a new stage of fast-track development.

Changing workplace and labor regime

The dramatic structural change and intense competition at the industry level had a direct impact on workplace and managerial labor practices at the firm level. To cope with the tougher environment, the major Chinese automakers responded with new strategies to maximize profits and minimize production costs. There were two general trends. In the organization of production, there was a convergence among the major automakers to combine lean production practices and other cost-cutting measures with the existing Fordist/Taylorist mass production techniques, in order to maximize profits (for details, see Chapter 4). In regard to labor and employment policy, as will be discussed in the next section and in Chapter 3, there was a general move toward increased labor flexibility and reduced job security at the major automakers in China.

---

[35] Federation of Automobile Dealers Associations (2006). These figures reflect the rapid expansion of China's domestic auto market, with more and more Chinese people buying cars. They also indicate growing demand for luxury overseas models.

Despite the move toward a leaner and more "flexible" workplace, I found two distinct models of labor practice coexisting in China's auto assembly sector. One resembles the Japanese "lean-and-dual" model, which employs labor force dualism by offering employment security to a core workforce in exchange for cooperation while creating a large buffer of periphery workers without the same rights and benefits (Price 1995: 83; Silver 2003: 67). The other is closer to the "lean-and-mean" model (Harrison 1997), which adopts the cost-cutting measures of lean production but without promising job security. The crucial differences between the two models are whether an employer adopts labor dualism, and to what extent the employer offers its core workforce job security.

My field research found that while some automakers – and especially the newly established ones – adopted the lean-and-mean model, more and more automakers in China had begun to move toward the lean-and-dual model since the early 2000s. As we will see in subsequent chapters, formal workers enjoyed high wages, generous benefits, and relatively secure employment, whereas arbitrary labor control characterized the conditions for temporary workers, who had lower wages, fewer benefits, and little job security. By the early and mid-2000s, the labor regime in the Chinese auto assembly sector had shifted from a "hegemonic" one based on general employment security to a dual labor regime characterized by widespread labor force dualism.

The results of the industrial restructuring were impressive. The total output increased from 1.4 million vehicles in 1994 to 2.3 million in 2001, and rocketed to 18.3 million in 2010 – an increase of 680 percent in a ten-year period. Meanwhile, the total number of manufacturing employees declined, from almost 2 million in 1994 to 1.5 million in 2001. The employment numbers have increased since, albeit to only 2.2 million as of 2010 (see Figure 2.1).[36]

This pattern of rapid expansion and modernization of the automobile industry without a significant increase in employment in China differed from other instances of the rapid expansion of the automobile industry, such as in Brazil, South Africa, and South Korea in the late 1970s and 1980s. In those cases, industrial expansion went hand-in-hand with rapid growth in the number of workers employed in both the automobile industry and in manufacturing more generally (Humphrey 1982; Koo 2001; Seidman 1994; Silver 2003). In the case of China, the take-off of its automobile industry since the late 1990s reflected a simultaneous process of weeding out inefficient

---

[36] CATRC (2002–2011). It should be noted that the CATRC statistics only include formal employees listed on companies' books and payrolls; temporary workers hired through labor agencies are not counted. As such, the actual size of the Chinese auto industry workforce is almost certainly larger (see the next section). The CEIN (2008–2012) data include all employees in the auto industry, likely including temporary workers, but do not provide a breakdown of the categories of employees. Thus, it is hard to gauge the actual size of the temporary workforce from official statistics.

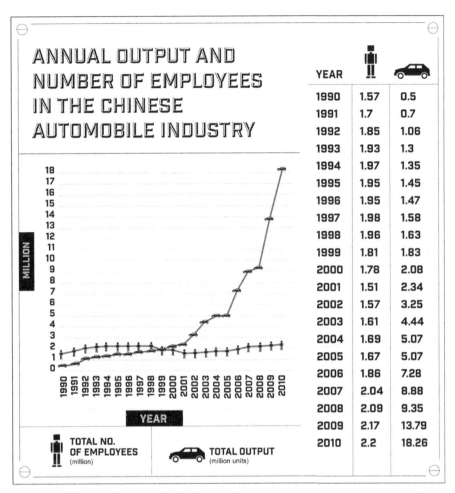

ANNUAL OUTPUT AND NUMBER OF EMPLOYEES IN THE CHINESE AUTOMOBILE INDUSTRY

YEAR	👤	🚗
1990	1.57	0.5
1991	1.7	0.7
1992	1.85	1.06
1993	1.93	1.3
1994	1.97	1.35
1995	1.95	1.45
1996	1.95	1.47
1997	1.98	1.58
1998	1.96	1.63
1999	1.81	1.83
2000	1.78	2.08
2001	1.51	2.34
2002	1.57	3.25
2003	1.61	4.44
2004	1.69	5.07
2005	1.67	5.07
2006	1.86	7.28
2007	2.04	8.88
2008	2.09	9.35
2009	2.17	13.79
2010	2.2	18.26

TOTAL NO. OF EMPLOYEES (million)

TOTAL OUTPUT (million units)

FIGURE 2.1. Annual output and number of employees in the Chinese automobile industry, 1990-2010
Source: Compiled from *China Automotive Industry Yearbook*, various years.

SOEs and the unmaking of the old generation of state workers, along with the expansion of Sino-foreign JVs and the making of a new generation of industrial workers – including a growing number of temporary workers.[37] As a result, although on the surface the numeric change in employment levels

[37] Temporary workers are not counted in China's official statistics. The lack of systematically collected statistics and the frequent fluctuations in the numbers of temporary workers make it difficult to give an accurate estimate of the number of temporary workers. What is clear is that the actual size of the production workforce in the Chinese auto industry is larger than is reflected in the official statistics based on the data gathered from the major auto assembly enterprises included in this study (see Table 2.4).

in the automobile industry seemed not that dramatic, the composition of the workforce had been almost completely transformed.

THE TRANSFORMATION OF THE PRODUCTION WORKFORCE AND THE RISE OF LABOR FORCE DUALISM

The transformation of the production workforce in the Chinese automobile industry involved two processes: the replacement of permanent and long-term workers with contract-based, urban-bred, formal (regular) workers (*zhengshi zhigong*) with relatively short-term labor contracts; and, the introduction of labor force dualism by tapping a large number of rural and urban youths as temporary workers alongside formal workers on production lines. This simultaneous dynamic of flexibilization[38] and dualization, as will be further discussed in Chapter 3, typifies the broader institutional transformation of the Chinese labor system in the reform era.

The replacement of the old generation of permanent state workers was carried out in a relatively smooth way, without provoking overt labor unrest. My fieldwork suggested that three main factors could explain the relatively smooth downsizing during the first round of restructuring in the Chinese automobile industry. First, most state-owned auto assemblers had substantial financial and organizational resources accumulated in the pre-reform era, which allowed them to pay the redundant workers more generous early retirement benefits and severance compensation, or to transfer some of the redundant workers to other less well-paid jobs in service firms spun off from the main enterprise, thus softening the blow of downsizing to workers. Second, at many old SOEs, management relied on the trade union and party Factory Committee, which in turn relied on the accumulated goodwill and political commitment of older workers, to convince those who were to become redundant that the reform was in the collective interests, and that they should therefore step aside without making a major fuss. Third, the central and local governments were more interventionist in monitoring the restructuring process at large automobile SOEs and JVs of "strategic importance."[39] My interviews with managers and local government officials suggested that in the auto assembly sector, enterprise restructuring proposals first needed to be approved by central and local governments. One important consideration was whether redundant workers were properly settled. When restructuring was proposed through the setting up of a new JV, there were often requirements for the new JV to absorb redundant workers from its Chinese partner. Despite the fact that many SOEs were able to use their accumulated resources to soften the blow of

---

[38] By "flexibilization," I refer to Katherine Stone's definition: "the changing work practices by which firms no longer use internal labour markets or implicitly promise employees lifetime job security, but rather seek flexible employment relations that permit them to increase or diminish their workforce, and reassign and redeploy employees with ease" (2006: 77).

[39] Interview Q1, Q2, Q3, SOE-2, June 2004.

downsizing during the first round of reforms, it is not clear whether they will continue to have sufficient resources or motivations to do so in potential future rounds of restructuring.

Another important aspect in the transformation of the production workforce was the introduction of labor force dualism by using temporary workers alongside formal workers on production lines. As seen in Table 2.4, among the seven large automakers in China, four adopted labor force dualism prior to 2006. By May 2011, with the exception of the Sino-Japanese JV JPN-1, all other factories had implemented labor force dualism, with a large number of temporary workers working on assembly lines. The Sino-German JV GER-1 was among the first to use temporary agency workers in the 1990s. The JV had a workforce composed of 11,587 formal employees – 6,950 workers and 4,637 staff – and 3,219 temporary workers as of 2006, with temporary workers accounting for 32 percent of its total production workforce. During peak production months in 2003, the company had over 6,280 temporary workers, making up 60 percent of its total production workforce.[40] As of May 2011, about 48 percent of production workers at GER-1 were temporary workers.[41] Another Sino-German JV, GER-2, also significantly increased the proportion of temporary workers in its production workforce, from 35 percent in 2006 to 60 percent in May 2011.[42] A similar trend can be identified at the state-owned automakers SOE-1 and SOE-2. The Sino-American JVs USA-1 and USA-2 did not introduce labor force dualism in 2006, but they followed suit in 2008 and 2009 respectively. Thus far, JPN-1 has refrained from using temporary workers. It also provides its formal employees with three- to five-year renewable contracts. According to a union official interviewed at JPN-1, this was mainly due to the influence of its Japanese partner in promoting an egalitarian culture and job security in order to maintain a cooperative, committed workforce required for its quality lean production system.[43] It is important to note, however, that such an egalitarian culture and job stability were strategies promoted only within the assembly plants. JPN-1 has one of the highest local sourcing rates and the highest per-car profit margin among the major automakers in China, thanks to its efficient, low-cost auto parts production bases and supply networks (IHLO 2010). As such, although JPN-1 has not adopted labor force dualism in its assembly plants, it has in effect been practicing the lean-and-dual strategy, with a large buffer of

[40] In 2003, GER-1 had a workforce composed of 7,089 formal employees (4,260 workers and 2,829 staff), and 6,280 temporary workers. The number of temporary workers has frequently fluctuated.

[41] Interview S38, GER-1, July 2011.

[42] The dramatic increase in the percentage of temporary workers mainly came from new hires necessitated by the fast expansion of production, rather than from replacing formal workers with temporary workers. This is evident from the steady increase in the number of formal workers since 2006, as seen in Figure 2.1.

[43] Interview H7, JPN-1, May 2007.

TABLE 2.4. *Comparison of labor force dualism at the selected automobile assemblers*

Name	Founding Year	Labor Force Dualism		Formal Employees (2006)[a]			Temporary Workers		
				Number		Contract Terms of Formal Workers[b]	Number (2006) [n]	% in Production Workers [n/(m+n)]	
		2006	2011	Staff	Worker[m]			2006	2011
GER-1	1985	Yes	Yes	4,637	6,950	2-2-3-3—non-fixed[c]	3,219	32%	48%
GER-2	1991	Yes	Yes	3,714	5,570	2-2-3-3—non-fixed	3,000	35%	60%
SOE-1	1997	Yes	Yes	5,900	7,200	1-1-1-3-3—non-fixed	4,800	40%	50%
SOE-2	1993	Yes	Yes	653	2,517	1-1-2-3-3—non-fixed	1,000	28%	40%
USA-1	1997	No	Yes	2,078	3,457	1–2 years renewable	/	/	50%
USA-2	2003	No	Yes	696	2,400	1–2 years renewable	/	/	33%
JPN-1	1998	No	No	1,500	4,120	3–5 years renewable	/	/	/

Notes: [a] Formal employees include both managerial and engineering staff as well as production workers.

[b] Contract terms of formal production workers are different from staff; see Chapter 4.

[c] A non-fixed-term contract (or an open-term contract) is a contract for which an employer and an employee have agreed not to stipulate a definite termination date (equivalent to permanent employment). See Chapter 3 for a detailed discussion on the labor contract system.

Source: The data were collected by the author at the firm level through interviews with managers, union staff, and workers, as well as from company records researched during multiple field trips in 2006, 2007, and 2011.

poorly-paid, insecure parts workers comprising the lower tiers of its subcontracting system and a small number of relatively protected and privileged workers in the upper-tier assembly plants.[44] Clearly, labor force dualism had become a widespread labor practice at China's major auto assembly factories by the early 2010s.

The main reasons for using temporary workers, according to the managers interviewed, were to contain labor costs and to increase labor flexibility. At GER-1 and GER-2, for example, the cost of hiring a formal contract worker (including all the associated social insurance payments and benefits) could be used to hire three or four temporary workers (for a more detailed discussion, see Chapter 3). Management's desire to increase staff flexibility was more prevalent among the longer-established automakers, such as GER-1, GER-2, and SOE-2, which had a relatively large number of permanent and long-term formal employees. During the market downturn in 2004, GER-1 and GER-2 managed to retain their formal workers by letting go of temporary workers. When the market recovered in 2005, they quickly hired back some of the same temporary workers to capitalize on the growing production demand.[45]

This could also explain why those relatively newly-built factories, such as USA-1, USA-2, and JPN-1, initially did not bother to use labor force dualism. Without the burden of a large number of veteran workers, they could simply recruit new workers directly from China's abundant vocational technical schools by offering one- to two-year renewable labor contracts.[46] As they have "matured" and acquired a more veteran workforce, some of these later-built factories – for example, USA-1 and USA-2 – have also adopted labor force dualism.[47]

Certainly, labor force dualism is not unique to the Chinese auto industry. Since the mid- and late-1970s, the rigidity of Fordist mass production has increasingly become an impediment to capital profitability and accumulation. Firms began adopting new and more flexible ways of accumulating capital. One of the key components of this "flexible accumulation" (Harvey 1989) is the rise of flexible labor regimes with the resurgence of labor force dualism and

---

[44] To the extent that auto-assembly workers are generally better off than auto-parts workers, dualism and inequality between assembly workers and parts workers in the subcontracting system is ubiquitous in the Chinese automobile industry. JPN-1 is a good example of this type of dualism, with a well-developed subcontracting system and high in-house and local sourcing ratios compared with other automakers in China.

[45] Interview F15, GER-2, October 2006; S17, GER-1, November 2006.

[46] For instance, the average tenures of production workers at JPN-1 and USA-2 were less than three years as of 2006.

[47] It is worth noting that Chinese HR managers tend to talk to and learn from each other in labor practice. For instance, in 2007, when USA-1 for the first time was faced with having to sign non-fixed labor contracts with some of its formal employees since it was established in 1997, its HR managers consulted with managers at GER-1 about using temporary agency workers. Shortly after, USA-1 introduced temporary agency workers. (Note: GER-1 and USA-1 belong to the same Chinese auto group, which perhaps made it easier for their managers to communicate with and learn from each other.) Interview M26, USA-1, July 2011.

a disparity between "core" and "peripheral" workers (Harrison 1997; Vallas 1999). It has become common for individual firms to adopt a core-periphery staffing strategy to balance the "functional flexibility" provided by core workers and the "numerical flexibility" obtained from peripheral workers (Atkinson 1987; Harvey 1989; Kalleberg 2001, 2003).

In the automobile industry in particular, faced with intense competitive pressures and tight profit margins at the late stage of the automobile product cycle on the one hand, and workers with strong workplace bargaining power and grievances on the other hand, automobile manufacturers worldwide moved toward the lean-and-dual model, even within factories and at firms long characterized by a more regularized internal labor market. Cost-cutting measures associated with "lean production" proliferated. At the same time, labor force dualism became widespread as firms sought to increase flexibility through the hiring of peripheral, temporary workers, while retaining the loyalty of a more permanent, core labor force. For example, in the 1980s, US automakers first emulated some Japanese organizational practices, such as team production, just-in-time (JIT) delivery systems, and quality circles. Throughout the 1990s, they emphasized leanness and downsizing, followed today by the introduction of a two-tier system, with a shrinking group of well-paid, protected, first-tier workers working side by side with a second-tier of new hires whose wages, benefits, and job security have been largely reduced.[48] Although the second-tier workers are not temporary workers, they are still second-class industrial citizens.[49] Similarly, German automakers have also increased their use of temporary workers on assembly lines in recent years. For example, almost 10 percent of the workforce at the Mercedes-Benz factory in Wörth consisted of temporary workers (Palier and Thelen 2010: 127); at another auto plant, they comprised nearly one-third (Mitlacher 2007:591–2).

What seems puzzling, however, is that unlike the conventional core-periphery model, or the flexible firm formula, under which segmentation between core and periphery workers corresponds to functional and numerical flexibilities, automakers in China deploy both formal and temporary workers on assembly lines to perform identical tasks while subjecting them to differential treatment. Why would automakers retain a segment of more expensive and privileged formal workers whose work could be done by temporary workers?[50]

---

[48] The two-tier system was deemed by the rank-and-file workers as "one of the biggest defeats of the UAW (United Auto Workers)," and "detrimental to worker solidarity." Meeting notes of the UAW Meeting at the Labor Note Conference, May 5, 2012, Chicago, IL. I wish to thank Cathy Walker for sharing with me the meeting notes.
[49] I want to thank Nelson Lichtenstein for his insightful comments on the evolution of labor practice in the U.S. auto industry.
[50] In fact, U.S. automakers have already moved toward negotiating buyouts for tenured, first-tier workers, with an eye toward replacing them with second-tier new hires (Welch 2011).

The segmented labor market approach provides us with some clues. This approach sees the workplace as "contested terrain," and labor market segmentation as a "divide and conquer" strategy adopted by management to divide workers, to overcome their resistance, and to gain some workers' consent and cooperation (Edwards 1979, Gordon et al. 1982). In the case of China, as discussed in the previous section, the take-off of its automobile industry in the late 1990s has been *accompanied by* large-scale restructuring and downsizing of many SOEs, as well as waves of labor protests at many other SOEs that experienced mass layoffs. The managers interviewed seemed apprehensive about the possibility of layoff-triggered labor disputes and protests. For instance, when GER-1 dismissed over 2,000 temporary agency workers without laying off its formal workers during the market downturn in 2004 and 2005, it was clearly a conscious management strategy. As the Human Resources manager there explained, "It is rare for our company to lay off our own formal employees because it could harm the harmonious labor relations and the publicity of our company as one of the 'most-respected joint ventures' in China."[51] Similarly, GER-2 let go 1,000 temporary agency workers in late 2004, but protected its formal workers from layoffs. Formal workers responded by actively cooperating with management during the downturn, including agreeing to pay cuts and unpaid overtime.[52] As we will discuss in detail in the following chapters, management concerns with maintaining peaceful labor relations and a cooperative, stable workforce for quality mass production is another important reason behind the spread of labor force dualism, and one that gives protection to a segment of the more expensive, formal workforce.

CONCLUSION

In this chapter, we traced the unique development pattern and the profound structural changes within the Chinese automobile industry during the reform era. Two stages of development can be identified. In the first stage, from the early 1980s to the early 1990s, the automobile industry was highly protected by the central government through high tariff and non-tariff barriers. Foreign direct investment was introduced through JVs but remained limited in scale. The central government took the lead in developing the auto assembly sector by partnering foreign auto multinationals with large, state-owned auto groups through centrally sanctioned JVs. This state-led triple alliance led to a monopolistic sector in which windfall profits accrued to a handful of pre-selected JVs and SOEs. During this time period, most state-owned auto assembly enterprises were operating under government protection and with soft budget constraints. The labor regime in the auto assembly sector was generally characterized as hegemonic based on guaranteed employment and the full coverage of welfare

[51] Interview S17, GER-1, November 2006.
[52] Interviews F11, F12, F13, GER-2, October 2006.

benefits for workers, as was typical in large work units in state-owned and state-controlled sectors.

In the second stage beginning in the mid-1990s, the broader structural change in the Chinese system – including the deepening of SOE and labor reforms, the fast-growing demand for private vehicles, and especially the government industrial policy change in order to prepare the auto industry to meet the challenges of China's WTO accession – led to the large-scale restructuring of inefficient SOEs and layoffs of state workers in the auto assembly sector. Meanwhile, a new wave of foreign investment through JVs and the rapid growth of private domestic automakers led to a dramatic increase in competition and declines in prices and profit margins. Intense competition drove the major Chinese automakers to move toward a leaner and more flexible workplace, including the replacement of permanent and long-term workers with contract-based formal workers, as well as the use of labor force dualism and a large number of temporary workers. By the early 2000s, the labor regime in the auto assembly sector had shifted to a dual labor regime.

Given that labor force dualism has taken hold in the Chinese auto industry, it is necessary to examine the nature and characteristics of this dualism. We begin with the question of the social composition of the automobile industry: Who are the formal workers, and who are the temporary workers? How are the labor markets of formal workers and temporary workers organized, respectively? For instance, how are they recruited, and what are the supply-demand conditions? What criteria do employers use to draw boundaries between the two groups of workers? It is to these questions that we now turn in the next chapter.

3

The labor market and social composition in the automobile industry

Wei was a 25-year-old line operator. When I first met him in 2006, he had worked at the general assembly shop of USA-2 for almost two years. After graduating from a local technical college with a Bachelor's degree in Computer Science, Wei joined the legion of job applicants for the opportunity to work at USA-2, a new assembly plant of a large Sino-US JV that opened in Wei's hometown in 2003. Wei recalled his "proud experience" of being selected as a formal worker at USA-2:

They said there were over 3,000 local people who applied for the 300 vacancies of formal workers, and I was among the 300 lucky dogs. I passed three rounds of physical examination, written exams, and individual and group interviews. I'm very proud of getting this job. You know, USA-2 belongs to a large joint venture with a well-known American automaker. Everyone here tries to get in. You feel good when you tell people you are a formal employee of USA-2.[1]

Although Wei grumbled about his "so-so" paycheck and the repetitive, monotonous, operative work, he was hopeful that he could move up and become a technician or white-collar staff relatively quickly with his Bachelor's degree. Like most other newly hired formal production workers at USA-2, Wei only had a one-year renewable labor contract for his first three years. While Wei hoped to secure a longer-term contract, he was not that worried about his contract terms at the time. The production demand had continued to increase since USA-2 started operation in 2003, and it was rare that formal workers could not renew their contracts annually.

By contrast, Tao, a 26-year-old welder at the Sino-German JV GER-2, had a very different background and labor market experience. Born and raised in a poor family in the countryside of Jilin Province, Tao dropped out of high school and left home to find work to support his family when he was only seventeen. Before starting work in the auto industry, he worked in a private coal mine,

---

[1] Interview D3, USA-2, September 2006.

in a furniture factory, for a construction subcontractor, and in a foundry. Like most rural migrant workers with a rural *hukou* and limited education seeking jobs in cities, Tao found himself stuck in secondary labor markets characterized by jobs that are part-time and temporary, paid low wages without benefits, and that are otherwise undesirable for urban residents. Eventually, Tao was able to land a job as a temporary agency worker (*laowu gong*) at the body shop of GER-2 through a labor agency. When I interviewed him in 2006, Tao had worked at GER-2 for five years and had become a skilled welder. But he was still a *laowu gong*, and could earn only half the wages of a formal worker, with fewer bonuses and benefits. Although Tao was bitter about the unequal treatment he received, working in a large auto assembly factory, even if only as a temporary worker, still was a much better option for him. As he explained:

I used to work at a private coal mine and for a construction subcontractor. I had the miserable experience of not getting paid for three or six months. GER-2 at least always pays us on time, not like those deceitful private employers. So I know how good this job is. Sometimes you feel unfair and bitter for getting paid half for doing the same work. But on second thought, you know, I don't have an urban *hukou*, I don't have much education, and I really don't have many other options. I don't think I can find a better job than this one.[2]

Compared with Wei and Tao, Qiang was much younger – he was only eighteen years old when we met in 2005. At the time, Qiang was working as an assembler at the state-owned carmaker SOE-1. He was among the several thousand student interns drawn from a dozen middle technical vocational schools working at SOE-1 to complete a mandatory one-year internship. Qiang told me that in his three-year vocational school education, he only had the chance to study in school for one and half years. The remaining time was spent completing the internships required by the school in order to graduate. During their internships at SOE-1, Qiang and his classmates worked 10–12 hours a day on the assembly lines, just as did other full-time workers. But they were paid only a meager living stipend of 900 *yuan* ($113) per month, with no benefits. Moreover, they did not have labor contracts because they were student interns, not workers, despite the fact that they were used as full-time laborers. Nevertheless, Qiang still hoped to land a formal job at SOE-1 upon graduation. But he was not very optimistic, "There are hundreds of interns that come in every year, but in the end only a few can stay and become formal employees. It is more convenient for companies to use student interns nowadays."[3]

The three snapshots of Wei, Tao, and Qiang epitomize the different social backgrounds and labor market experiences of the current generation of Chinese autoworkers. In this chapter, we look into the labor market and social composition of the automobile industry workforce. We examine the supply and demand of various types of workers, who they are, how they are recruited,

---

[2] Interview F-19, GER-2, October 2006.   [3] Interview C6, SOE-1, August 2005.

what are their wage and benefit conditions, and what criteria employers use to draw boundaries and to divide them.[4] I begin the chapter by outlining the transformation of the Chinese labor system under market reform and laying out the various institutional arrangements that provide auto manufacturers with different types of workers – namely, the labor contract system, labor dispatch (temporary agency work), and the vocational and technical education system. I found a simultaneous dynamic of flexibilization and dualization of labor markets has taken place in post-socialist China. On the one hand, the market-oriented labor reform has significantly increased labor market flexibility and led to widespread job insecurity. On the other hand, there has been a persistent, albeit evolving, dual labor force structure sponsored by the state. This dualist structure constantly creates boundaries and inequalities between a relatively privileged and secure segment of workers "within the system" (*tizhi nei*), and an insecure and lower-paid segment of workers "outside the system" (*tizhi wai*).[5] The chapter proceeds to examine the social composition and the labor market of formal and temporary workers in the automobile industry, respectively. It highlights the re-composition of the new generation of Chinese autoworkers and the blurring boundaries between formal and temporary workers based on their urban-rural *hukou* status. The final section investigates the wage conditions and demystifies the popular assumption about auto assembly workers as being "affluent workers, contented workers."

CONSTRUCTING FLEXIBLE LABOR MARKETS AND THE EVOLUTION OF LABOR FORCE DUALISM

China's transition from state socialism to a market economy over the past thirty years has profoundly transformed its labor and employment system. One of the fundamental institutional changes was the replacement of the socialist "iron rice bowl" permanent employment system with a market-oriented labor contract system, under which workers can be hired and fired on an open labor market based on legal contracts with their employers. Another important feature has been the persistent but evolving labor force dualism that constantly creates boundaries and inequalities among Chinese workers. Rather than take an economist's view of labor market dualism/ segmentation as an economic trend or "natural" outcome of labor market

---

[4] My main focus in this chapter is on external labor markets; I leave the discussion of internal labor markets – i.e., the HRM policies and the bureaucratic rules that govern appraisal, training, promotion, wage schemes, and job classification – for Chapter 4, when the analysis moves inside the factories.

[5] The terms "tizhi nei" and "tizhi wai" were borrowed from a high-profile article titled, "Tizhi wai yuangong shi erdeng gongmin ma?" ("Are Employees outside the System Second-class Citizens?"), published in the CCP's official magazine, *People's Forum*, which begins with a pointed statement: "We have to admit that the differential treatment between workers within the system and outside the system, the institutional discrimination and unequal treatment of workers, have been a long-lasting and widespread existence in our country" (Zeng 2007).

processes, I will argue that labor force dualism in China has been the result of active state policies and laws that favor some worker groups at the expense of others. The party-state has played a central role in defining boundaries among its working population and in determining who is to be included "within the system," and who will be left out.[6]

Under the socialist planned economy, there were no labor markets because labor was not a commodity and therefore could not be sold and bought in the marketplace. Labor allocation and wage administration were controlled by the state through labor bureaus at various levels, each of which followed set procedures (Hoffmann 1974: 62–92). This state-administered labor system provided full employment, permanent job tenure, and all-inclusive welfare provisions and social services to state-sector workers through their work units. This is known as the "iron rice bowl." Under this system, management could not hire or fire workers freely, nor were workers able to switch jobs easily among work units (Walder 1986).

As many studies have shown, however, even under Maoist socialism, only a minority of the urban working class in the state sector was entitled to the "iron rice bowl" permanent employment.[7] A substantial segment of temporary, contract, and seasonal workers in SOEs, as well as rural workers in rural industries, were systematically excluded from the favorable treatment associated with permanent state employment (Granick 1991; Hoffmann 1977; Howard 1991; Perry 1997: 48; Walder 1986: 40–54; White 1976). The establishment of the household registration (*hukou*) system in the 1950s divided Chinese citizens according to their urban and rural residencies, and relegated rural residents to second-class citizens, with limited access to urban areas and to employment and welfare provisions in cities. Temporary and contract workers in the socialist era were overwhelmingly peasants hired by urban state-owned and collective enterprises to work dirty and dangerous jobs, or to account for seasonal fluctuations in production demand (Blecher 1983).[8] The boundaries under state socialism were drawn by the Communist state according to one's *hukou* status, as well as the type of *danwei* with which workers were associated. From a comparative perspective, when faced with growing population pressure and concern for social stability and its political legitimacy, the Chinese state – like some East Asian developmental states – has a tendency to

---

[6] In a similar vein, Andrew Walder described a dualist employment structure under state socialism, and "a status order that is conceived and enforced by the state itself" (1986: 40). Recent studies of labor markets in developed capitalist economies have found that a salient current trend is the widening and deepening of dualization between insiders and outsiders with explicit state policy support (Emmenegger et al. 2012; Palier and Thelen 2010; Song 2012).

[7] For example, in 1981, only 42 percent of the industrial labor force were state workers with lifetime employment, superior wages, and generous benefits as defined under the State budget (Walder 1986: 40).

[8] There were certain periods, however – such as the 1950s and late 1970s – during which contract workers consisted mainly of the urban unemployed awaiting permanent positions in state enterprises (Howard 1991: 96).

only "incorporate key groups and bind them to the regime" (Holliday and Wilding 2003: 163).

Since China's market transition began in 1978, labor reform has been gradual but central to urban economic reform given its ideological sensitivity and connections with many other urban reforms (Knight and Song 2005). The general aim of reformers has been to put an end to the "iron rice bowl" labor system, to increase enterprises' autonomy, efficiency, and labor flexibility, and to create a flexible and functioning labor market that can effectively allocate labor resources (White 1987). Whereas a labor contract system was first introduced for all new hires at SOEs in 1986, it was still rare for SOEs to lay off urban workers until the mid-1990s. This was largely due to workers' resistance to the "smashing of the iron rice bowl," and reformers' concerns over political and social stability, as well as political sensitivity surrounding commodification of labor at a time when socialist ideology was still relatively strong (Gallagher 2005a: Chapter 5; Lee 2007: Chapter 2; White 1987). One of the results was that a dual labor force structure was reproduced in the form of permanent versus contract system workers, which ran parallel to the two-tier union contracts in the West that allowed for reduced wages and less job security for new workers (Howard 1991: 111). But in general, urban workers were still protected from the vagaries of labor markets during this period, while state firms continued to use peasant temporaries as cheap and flexible hands to adjust to changes in production demand.[9] The boundaries were still largely drawn along the line of urban-rural *hukou* status, plus seniority, which prioritized protection to veteran state workers.

As China's market reform deepened since the mid-1990s, urban labor reform accelerated to prioritize efficiency and flexibility, in conjunction with the large-scale restructuring and downsizing of SOEs. The 1994 Labor Law, which took effect in 1995, codified a universal labor contract system and formally allowed employers to terminate labor contracts with formal employees (Gallagher 2005a). A labor contract can be fixed-term or non-fixed (open-ended) – that is, without a definite termination date. Because an employment relationship ends when a fixed-term contract expires, employers can dismiss formal employees without paying severance compensation by simply not renewing a contract. Until the 2007 Labor Contract Law was passed to limit short-term contracts, most employers chose to sign one-year renewable contracts with their ordinary employees, only offering longer-term or open-term contracts to their core employees (Gallagher and Dong 2011: 40). There was growing job insecurity under the labor contract system. During the same period, over 30 million workers at SOEs and almost 50 million urban workers of all kinds were laid off. Many ended up in the informal sector (Naughton 2007: 184–191), or in non-regular employment in the formal

---

[9] By 1986, the hiring of peasant workers had been legitimized, as the *hukou* system was loosened and a large number of migrant peasant workers entered the cities to work in both the state and non-state sectors (Solinger 1995).

sector. On the other hand, more than two hundred million rural migrant workers left the countryside for factory jobs in cities, most working in non-state or informal sectors. Many of these workers did not even have a written contract with their employers.[10] They consisted of a large and fast-expanding informal and non-regular labor force that existed outside the formal contract employment system.[11]

It is clear that commodification and flexibilization of labor intensified in China between 1995 and 2007, as Beijing's priorities skewed heavily toward supporting rapid economic growth and those interests that most directly helped achieve this goal – namely, capitalists and managers.[12] However, to simply conclude that China's labor system has moved to generalized "informalization" or "casualization" – as some scholars have argued,[13] would be to miss its distinctive, persistent dualist feature. For one thing, the 1994 Labor Law (Article 20) provided that an employee can request to sign an open-term contract without a definite termination date with his/her employer after working for the same employer for 10 consecutive years, and upon agreement of both parties. Despite the ambiguity and difficulty in enforcing this clause, some employers do sign open-term contracts and give tenure to their long-serving formal employees. This is especially the case in large SOEs and state-controlled enterprises where total payrolls and authorized staffing practices (that is, the hiring and firing of formal employees) are subject to state supervision. Moreover, the attack on workers' job security and livelihood has provoked widespread resistance and waves of labor unrest since the mid-1990s, which have pushed the central government to pass new labor laws in order to re-regulate and stabilize labor relations and to provide more protections for workers for the sake of maintaining social stability. The 2007 Labor Contract Law (LCL), for instance, makes the signing of an open-term contract mandatory if a formal employee has worked for his/her employer for 10 consecutive years *or* after two fixed-term labor contracts (Article 14). It also

---

[10] According to a national labor law enforcement inspection conducted by the NPC Standing Committee in 2005, the percentage of workers with labor contracts was less than 20 percent in small and medium enterprises and in non-state enterprises. The inspection also found that more than 60 percent of existing contracts were short-term contracts, mostly for a period of one-year or less (*China Economic Weekly* 2007).

[11] In the Chinese context, non-regular workers include workers employed in the formal sector on a long-term basis but without regular contracts, such as temporary workers in state enterprises and strategic sectors. Many of them are in fact quite "formal." Informal workers comprise a much larger labor force, which ranges from self-employed small business owners to unregistered street vendors and day laborers, many of whom are either working outside the formal sector or are employed on a short-term basis. For informative discussions on China's informal labor force, see Huang (2009); Naughton (2007: 189–191); Park and Cai (2011).

[12] Among the rich literature on the plight of Chinese workers during this period, see, for example, Chan (2001); Chan (2010); Feng (2002); Gallagher (2004, 2005a); Hurst (2009); Lee (1999, 2000, 2002, 2007); Pun (2005); Pun and Chan (2012); Solinger (2002, 2005) ; Zhang (2011).

[13] See, for example, Friedman and Lee (2010); Kuruvilla et al. (2011).

strongly discourages short-term contracts and restricts employers' rights to hire and fire formal workers without cause. But as we shall see in Chapter 7, the compromise in the legislative process allows employers to continue using labor dispatch outside the formal contract system to cut costs and gain flexibility. As a result, a dual labor system is recast as one between formal workers within the contract system and agency workers outside the system. In sum, the Chinese party-state has recreated boundaries and inequalities among its working population, providing some workers with more protection to shore up its legitimacy while excluding others to promote flexibility and profitability.

Thus far, I have highlighted the simultaneous dynamics of flexibilization and dualization in the transformation of the Chinese labor system in the reform era. Below I lay out the institutional arrangements that provide automakers with a large number of temporary agency workers and student workers.

The rise of labor dispatch and the supply of temporary agency workers

Labor dispatch (*laowu paiqian*), also known as temporary agency work (TAW), has been one of the fastest-growing forms of non-regular employment in China since the late 1990s.[14] The core feature of this triangular employment relationship is the separation of hiring from the use of labor: a temporary agency worker is hired by, and signs a labor contract with, a labor agency, and is dispatched to work at (and under the supervision of) the user companies (ILO 2009). Because there is no direct employment relationship between agency workers and user companies, user companies can reduce their responsibility for agency workers to a minimum.

Globally, the fast growth of TAW has been one of the most significant employment trends over the last two decades.[15] Underpinning this trend has been the widespread move toward labor "flexibility," which is a key component of "flexible accumulation," as firms seek new ways of accumulating capital and maximizing profits with explicit state policy support under the "neoliberal turn" since the 1970s (Harvey 1989, 2005; Rubin 1995). Although the proportion of temporary agency workers is relatively small in relation to the total employment in industrialized economies,[16] TAW has remained a controversial subject due to its triangular employment structure, which

---

[14] There are other terms used to refer to labor dispatch, such as labor leasing and triangular employment. The term "temporary agency work" is often used in the West, while the term "labor dispatch" is more commonly used in China, Japan, and Taiwan. I use both terms – as well as the terms "agency workers" and "dispatched workers" – interchangeably in this book.

[15] See, for example, Burgess and Connell (2004); Connelly and Gallagher (2004); Degiuli and Kollmeyer (2007); Knox (2010); Mitlacher (2007); Peck and Theodore (1998, 2002); Peck et al. (2005); Purcell et al. (2004).

[16] For instance, as of 2007, the percentage of agency workers in relation to the total active working population in the US was 2 percent; in Japan, 2.8 percent; in the UK, 4.8 percent; in Germany, 1.6 percent; in France, 2.5 percent and, in the Netherlands, 2.8 percent (ILO 2009: 7, 14–15).

challenges the conventional definition of the employment relationship and complicates the legal and financial obligations employers have to their employees.

Whereas the rapid expansion of labor dispatch in China is a relatively new development since the late 1990s, its significance has been far-reaching. According to a report by the ACFTU, by the end of 2010, the national total of "dispatched employees" had reached 60 million, accounting for 20 percent of the total actively employed population in China (Xiang 2011a).[17] Moreover, instead of confining labor dispatch to "temporary, auxiliary, and substitute" work, many employers in China use agency workers alongside regular employees, in permanent positions on a long-term basis in government agencies, at public institutions, and in SOEs. These include key enterprises in strategic sectors, such as energy, railways, banking, telecommunications, and the automobile industry (Weng 2009; Zhang 2011). There is a growing class of "temporary workers in permanent jobs" in today's China (Zhang 2008: 28). Thus, a significant feature of labor dispatch in China is that, rather than functioning as a supplementary form of employment, it has become a major employment practice that challenges the formal contract system. Large SOEs and public institutions, in particular, have higher demands for temporary agency workers, in part because the wages and benefits of formal employees at those enterprises are generally high, and the hiring and firing of formal employees is more restricted by the state.[18]

Another distinctive feature of labor dispatch in China is that the central and local governments have played a key role in facilitating the development of labor agencies, initially in response to the severe unemployment problems caused by the restructurings and layoffs at SOEs since the late 1990s.[19] In 2002, the central government explicitly promoted labor dispatch as a way to better assist laid-off workers in finding flexible employment. In September 2003, at the National Forum on Re-employment, Party General Secretary Hu Jintao put forward a direct call for "actively developing labor dispatch and other types of employment intermediaries to organize and guide individual laid-off workers to find re-employment" (Li et al. 2009). Local governments responded by establishing labor agencies, including turning their former employment and re-employment service centers into labor agencies affiliated with local labor and social security bureaus. State-owned enterprises with

---

[17] The total number of dispatched workers in China remains in dispute. The Ministry of Human Resources and Social Security estimated the number to be approximately 27 million in 2010.

[18] It was estimated that, as of 2009, there were 25 million-plus agency workers in the public and government sectors, and another 10 million working at SOEs in strategic sectors (Weng 2009).

[19] Labor dispatch agencies first appeared in China in 1979, when the Foreign Enterprises Service Corporation (FESCO) was established by the Chinese government to provide staffing and human resource services for foreign companies' representative offices in China. Foreign companies had to rely on FESCO to hire Chinese employees because they were not allowed to hire Chinese directly at that time, a period when socialist China had just opened its door to foreign investors. Operations of labor dispatch agencies were highly restricted until the 1990s.

a large number of laid-off workers were also encouraged to establish their own labor agencies to absorb their laid-off workers. By the end of 2005, there were 26,158 registered labor agencies in China, of which nearly 70 percent were either directly operated or approved by local labor and social security departments (Pan and Deng 2011).[20] As such, local labor authorities are both players and referees in the labor dispatch industry. Large SOEs and public institutions particularly prefer this type of government-affiliated labor agencies because their official background is considered as a "trouble-free" warranty against potential labor disputes.[21]

Prior to the enactment of the Labor Contract Law in 2007, there had been no nationwide legislation or regulations pertaining to labor dispatch. Labor dispatch expanded rapidly to almost every sector and to enterprises of all ownership types. Accordingly, more and more urbanites joined the ranks of agency workers, including many college graduates.[22] As a result, the boundaries that had existed between formal/regular and informal/non-regular workers based on their urban or rural *hukou* status have become blurred. To be sure, rural migrant workers are still disproportionately concentrated in informal and non-regular employment in cities (Huang 2009: 410; Park and Cai 2011: 28). This indicates that the *hukou* system continues to create boundaries and discriminate against rural residents in urban labor market. Meanwhile, criteria such as education qualifications and social connections (*guanxi*) have become more and more important in determining an urbanite's chance at securing formal employment. The changing social composition of the temporary workforce in the auto assembly sector illustrates this recent trend in China's urban labor market (see discussion below).

In sum, the rise of the labor dispatch industry in China has been embedded in the broad political economy of China's market transition. It is the result of intensified flexibilization of labor with explicit state policy support.

The marketization of vocational education and the supply of student workers

The growing trend of using student interns as full-time laborers remains a gray area in China today. Since its inception in the early twentieth century, China's modern vocational and technical education (VTE) system has followed a

---

[20] There are various types of labor agencies in China. In addition to the government-affiliated type, there are also high-end comprehensive HRM services companies specializing in dispatching white-collar professionals and office workers, and low-end labor brokers dispatching manufacturing workers – most were rural migrant workers – in labor-intensive sectors. There are also unregistered, so-called "black" labor agencies.

[21] Many of these labor agencies are in fact privately-owned, often by families and friends of local labor officials. Interview 37, Shanghai, January 2008.

[22] According to a report by China Talent Group (CTG) (2010), for example, 70 percent of agency workers in the Information and Communication Technology sector had at least a junior college degree.

"work-study" (*gongxue jiehe*) model that combines school-based education with on-the-job training in factories through apprenticeships (Ye and Meng 2008). During the Mao years, VTE was emphasized and the "work-study" model was further promoted to train skilled workers for China's rapid industrialization. Not only were students sent to work in factories as apprentices to learn practical skills as part of their vocational education, factory workers also went to study in technical vocational schools or colleges to advance their skills and knowledge (Hoffmann 1977). Many SOEs established their own technical schools to train their prospective and existing workforce. This system was effective in training technicians and skilled workers from the 1950s to the mid-1990s, a period during which most vocational schools were fully funded by the government. The government was also responsible for assigning jobs to the graduates of technical and vocational schools at SOEs and public institutions during that time period.

Since the late 1990s, with the deepening of market reform, the central government has stopped assigning jobs to graduates, cut funding, and begun promoting marketization and self-sustaining vocational education (Meng 2004). Since then, many vocational schools have suffered from deteriorating educational quality due to funding shortages, the loss of teachers, poor school conditions, and outdated textbooks and training equipment. In order to survive and operate at a profit, many schools collaborate with enterprises and send their teenage students to work full time at enterprises under internships, in exchange for equipment and funding. Some schools also charge students internship fees on top of tuition fees (Zhou 2010). In theory, internships should provide student interns with the training and skills in demand at the enterprises at which they may obtain formal employment upon graduation. In reality, many enterprises conspire with vocational schools to use student interns as cheap, temporary manual laborers with little training provided. It is not uncommon to find illegal internship practices, such as compulsory overtime forced upon student interns, and the organizing of internships through labor agencies.[23] In many cases, local governments are directly involved in facilitating or requiring vocational schools to arrange for "internships" at the factories of new investors, so that they may meet investors' demand for large numbers of cheap and flexible workers.[24] Because vocational students are required to complete at minimum a six-month internship before they can graduate,[25]

---

[23] According to the "Regulations on Secondary Vocational School Student Internship," issued by the Ministry of Education and the Ministry of Finance (2007), student interns should not work more than eight hours a day, and internships should not be organized, arranged, and/or managed through intermediary agencies.

[24] For example, see Pun and Chan's (2012) discussion on the recruitment of labor at Foxconn's new factories in inland China.

[25] According to the State Council (2005), students of secondary technical schools are required to complete a 1-year internship, while students of vocational technical colleges are required to complete a six-month internship.

they are often forced to accept whatever "internship" their school assigns to them – no matter whether the internship has anything to do with their training or specialty. To make the situation more problematic, student interns by definition are students/trainees, not full-time workers, despite the fact that they are used as full-time laborers. Because they lack *de jure* worker status, however, they are neither protected by labor laws nor do they have labor contracts. They are also ineligible to receive social insurance benefits and to join labor unions. This situation makes student workers particularly vulnerable to exploitation and workplace abuse. As one ACFTU official in the Policy Research Department acknowledged, "The use of student workers is currently a gray area that requires new regulations and clearly defined responsibilities and coordinated efforts among several departments of Education, Labor, and ACFTU."[26] In sum, the marketization of vocational education, coupled with the lack of corresponding state legislation and monitoring, have led to the abusive use of student workers in many sectors, including the automobile industry, as we shall see below and in Chapter 6.

Having outlined the transformation of the Chinese labor system and the institutional arrangements to which various types of workers are subject, we now will examine the labor market and the social composition of the automobile industry, which typifies these broader changes.

THE STRUCTURE OF THE LABOR MARKET IN THE AUTOMOBILE INDUSTRY

As a dynamic industry undergoing rapid expansion, employment in the Chinese automobile industry has grown steadily, albeit not dramatically in recent years.[27] In 2011, about 3.62 million people worked in the auto industry (CEIN, 2012: 29), of which 2.42 million were formally employed in vehicle manufacture. This included 994,437 (41.1 percent) working in the auto assembly sector and 1,054,000 (43.6 percent) in the auto parts sector, with the remainder working in the manufacture of modified vehicles (7.5 percent), motorcycles (4 percent), and engines (3.8 percent) (CATRC 2012: 492). Although the automobile industry as a whole is designated as a pillar industry in the Chinese economy, it is the assembly sector that has received the most attention and support from the central government.[28] The overall structure of the industry is highly stratified, with a concentrated, capital-intensive assembly sector at its core and a fragmented parts sector consisting of multiple tiers of suppliers at the periphery, including hundreds of

---

[26] Interview 39, Beijing, July 1, 2011
[27] See Chapter 2 for a discussion on the lack of significant increases in employment in the automobile industry.
[28] In recent years, the central government has also begun to give more attention and support to the auto parts sector.

TABLE 3.1. *Distribution of workers by segment and size of enterprises in the Chinese automobile industry, 2011*

Size of Enterprise[a] Segments	Large		Medium		Small		Total
	Number	%	Number	%	Number	%	Number
Auto Assembly							
Enterprise	87	75.7	23	20.0	5	4.3	115
Employee	651,690	65.5	342,567	34.4	180	0.1	994,437
Auto Parts[b]							
Enterprise	113	4.4	897	35.4	1,526	60.2	2,536
Employee	362,366	34.4	411,544	39.0	280,564	26.6	1,054,484

Notes: [a] According to the NBS, a large enterprise must meet all of the following conditions: 1) employing more than 2,000 persons; 2) having primary business revenues exceeding 300 million *yuan*; and, 3) having total asset values in excess of 400 million *yuan*. A medium enterprise must meet all of the lower limits of the following conditions: 1) employing more than 300 and fewer than 2,000 persons; 2) having primary business revenues in excess of 30 million *yuan* and not exceeding 300 million *yuan*; and, 3) having total asset values in excess of 40 million *yuan* and not exceeding 400 million *yuan*. A small enterprise is defined as one that meets either one of the following conditions: having fewer than 300 employees; or having primary business revenues of less than 30 million *yuan*; or having total asset values less than 40 million *yuan*.
    [b] The auto parts segment does not include engine manufacturers, which are listed separately.
Source: Compiled by the author from CATRC (2012): 461, 465.

small parts suppliers.[29] Correspondingly, the labor market in the automobile industry is segmented into jobs in the core assembly sector and the peripheral parts sector. As seen in Table 3.1, about two-thirds of assembly workers were concentrated at 87 large assemblers, each employing 2,000-plus people, whereas the majority (65.6 percent) of parts workers were employed at small- and medium-sized plants. Assembly workers on average also earn significantly higher wages than parts workers (see discussion, below). Thus the practice of labor force dualism and the protection of a "core" segment of formal workers at large assemblers are conditioned on labor market dualism that exists between assembly and parts workers in the first place.

Within the assembly sector, blue-collar production workers accounted for 60 to 80 percent of the total workforce after restructuring; the remainder consisted of white-collar managerial and engineering staff. The ratio of manufacturing workers is similar to that of Ford Motor Company and GM, where approximately 70 percent of workers were involved in manufacturing and

---

[29] In 2009, there were over 10,000 registered auto parts manufacturers, with the top 10 companies claiming an 18 percent market share (Haley 2012: 5). By contrast, in 2012, there were 115 auto assemblers with the top five groups holding 72 percent of the market (CAAM 2013).

30 percent were corporate personnel.[30] With respect to gender ratios, the overwhelming majority of workers in the auto assembly sector were male; female workers accounted for only 10 to 20 percent of the workforce as of 2006.[31] Female workers employed at factories were concentrated mainly in the off-line divisions such as quality inspection, production scheduling, and statistics, and in auxiliary positions in final assembly shops. Management often cited the high physical demands and challenging work schedules as the main reasons for the low ratio of female factory workers in assembly plants. The female share of the workforce, however, tended to be higher in parts plants, where wages are significantly lower than at assembly plants.[32] In her study of the gender-based division of labor in the prewar and postwar US automobile industry, Ruth Milkman has argued that "the logic of Fordism" – that is, capital-intensive mass assembly production with a workforce earning relatively high wages –held auto assembly work as a gendered stereotype of "men's work" (1989: 131). I observe similar gender dynamics in the Chinese auto industry. Table 3.2 presents some basic information about the composition of the workforce at the selected auto assemblers.

Given that labor force dualism has taken hold in the Chinese auto assembly sector (see Chapter 2), in the sections that follow we will examine the social composition and the labor markets of formal workers and temporary workers, respectively.

SOCIAL COMPOSITION AND THE LABOR MARKET OF FORMAL WORKERS

Under the labor contract system, all formal employees sign fixed or non-fixed term contracts with their employers, but their job security and labor market conditions vary widely. At each of the studied enterprises, about 10–15 percent of workers were "core talents" (*hexin rencai*) who were deemed essential to the company's long-term development. This core group consisted largely of managers and engineers with strategic knowledge, skills, and functions. A very small number of senior technicians and craftsmen with rare skills were also

---

[30] According to Rogozhin et al. (2009), Ford Motor Company reported 64,000 hourly workers (73 percent) and 23,700 salaried workers (27 percent) (Ford 2007: 12). General Motors reported expenditures for manufacturing labor of $27.9 billion (66 percent) and selling, general, administrative, and other personnel expenses of $14.4 billion (34 percent).

[31] While no industry-wide statistics on the gender ratio in China's auto industry are available, my field data collected from seven large auto assemblers as well as my discussions with managers and industry experts inform this estimate. Among my cases, SOE-2 had the highest percent female in its labor force (19.4 percent), while USA-1 had the lowest (10.6 percent), with the remaining five companies falling between the two (Table 3.2).

[32] According to *China Labor Statistics Yearbook* (2005–2012), the overall female share of employment in the manufacturing of transport equipment – including both motor vehicles and parts – remained around 30 percent from 2004 to 2008. It declined to 27 percent in 2011, but that figure was still higher than the ratio for the auto assembly sector alone.

TABLE 3.2. *Workforce composition at selected auto assemblers in China, 2006*

	USA-1		GER-1		GER-2		SOE-1	
	Number	%	Number	%	Number	%	Number	%
Staff[a]	2,078	37.5	4,637	31.3	3,714	30.2	5,900	33.0
Production Workers	3,457	62.5	10,169	68.7	8,570	69.8	12,000	67.0
Formal Workers	3,457	(62.5)	6,950	(47.0)	5,570	(45.4)	7,200	(40.2)
Temporary Workers	0	0	3,219	(21.7)	3,000	(24.4)	4,800	(26.8)
Total Formal Employees[b]	5,535	100	11,587	78.3	9,284	75.6	13,100	73.2
Female	587	10.6	2,132	14.4	1,375	11.2	3,240	18.1
Male	4,948	89.4	12,674	85.6	10,909	88.8	14,660	81.9
TOTAL WORKFORCE	5,535	100	14,806	100	12,284	100	17,900	100

Notes: [a] "Staff" includes white-collar workers and management.
[b] "Total Formal Employees" includes staff and formal (production) workers

Sources: Data were collected by the author from the respective HR departments at the company level: USA-1, November 2006; GER-1, December 2006; GER-2, October 2006; and SOE-1, March 2007. See also Table 2.4 for worker/staff ratios at other studied enterprises.

included in this core group. However, there were institutionalized status distinctions between white-collar staff and blue-collar workers (see Chapter 4). The core employees enjoyed job security, high wages, generous benefits, and good prospects for advancement – in short, the characteristics of a primary labor market (Doeringer and Piore 1971).

A tier just below the core group consisted of white-collar specialists and technical professionals, who accounted for 15–20 percent of the workforce. This group included office workers with relatively narrowly specialized skills. Most held university degrees, and their contract terms ranged from two-year renewable to open-term, depending on one's position and seniority (see Chapter 4). Some members of this group were management trainees and "reserved talents," who were expected to enter the core talent group in the future. My interviews suggested that employees belonging to this group generally considered their jobs to be secure, given that their specialized knowledge and skills were necessary to the smooth operation of the company and were in demand on the labor market.

Further down the hierarchy were the blue-collar production workers. I found that, except for a small segment of skilled, veteran workers with permanent or long-term contracts, the majority of the post-restructuring formal production workers were young, semi-skilled, urban-born workers with short-term contracts. Many were directly recruited from technical and vocational schools with little industrial experience. According to a 2005 survey conducted among twelve large auto assemblers in China, 32 percent of their production workforce were under the age of 25, and 51 percent were between the ages of 25 and 35. The average seniority was between 2–5 years, and more than two-thirds of workers had one- to two-year renewable contracts. About 45 percent of formal workers had been recruited directly from the secondary vocational and technical schools (equivalent to a total of 12-year education). An additional 40 percent held a degree from a technical junior college or higher vocational school (equivalent to a 14-year education) (CAAM 2005). My interviewees and the general composition of the workforce at the seven large assemblers conformed to these general features,[33] but there were notable variations between the studied factories – for instance, between the early-established and the newly-built plants – as I will discuss in greater detail in Chapters 4–6.

Notably, leading auto assemblers tended to require higher education and skills qualifications for their formal production workers. New recruits were required to have at minimum a 12-year education. Some automakers, such as USA-1 and GER-2, required a degree from a technical junior college or higher vocational school. Nearly two-thirds of the formal workers I interviewed had a junior college or higher vocational school degree. About 90 percent had at least "intermediate" vocational qualification certificates (VQCs) – equivalent

[33] See Methodology Appendix for detailed sample information and sample selection methods.

to semi-skilled status – in certain skilled trades related to the automobile industry.[34] More than half had completed a 6–12-month apprenticeship at the factory where they later became formal workers.

Despite their relatively advanced qualifications, the majority of formal production workers were semi-skilled line operators performing repetitive and routine manual tasks. Only 20–30 percent of formal workers were classified by management as core skilled production workers. For instance, USA-1 had the highest percentage of skilled workers among the automakers I studied. According to the company's own classifications, 59 percent of its formal production workers were semi-skilled, 11 percent were unskilled, and only 30 percent were classified as skilled. At the state-owned truck-maker SOE-2, roughly 20 percent of production workers were classified as skilled workers. The percentages of skilled workers at the other five automakers fell between 20–30 percent. The basic training for line operators could be carried out in a matter of a week or less. Formal workers belonging to this group might be termed as "the periphery of the core," in that they were formal employees on the authorized payroll, but they were relatively easy to replace, requiring short training time and working under renewable, short-term contracts. It was alongside this group of formal workers that temporary workers were deployed on the assembly lines.

There were generally two types of skilled workers: skilled workers in off-line divisions, such as technicians, maintenance and repair workers, quality control inspectors, and tool-and-die makers; and skilled line workers, such as painters, welders, and metal finishers (including team leaders). Most skilled workers I interviewed had worked for their current employers for at least three years, with contract terms ranging from two-year to open-term. Some had worked for their current employers for more than ten years; some had earned tenure at a SOE before being transferred to a newly-built JV between a foreign partner and the same parent auto group. It should be noted that since the late 1990s, China has established a system of occupation classifications and certifications to regulate and accredit occupation-based skills. However, due to the lack of standardized and unified certification administration, as well as the low quality of vocational education in the eyes of employers, large auto groups such as SAIC and FAW have developed their own systems of skills appraisal and certification to train and assess skilled workers for their subsidiary companies. Thus standardization of skills has been limited within the same auto group, and the supply of skilled workers mainly relies on company-specific, on-the-job training. As such, it comes as no surprise that there is an overlap between workers' skill

---

[34] According to the latest *PRC Occupation Classifications Dictionary* (2012 edition; http://www.ostami.org.cn/show.asp?id=436), there are 7 occupations and 59 skilled trades classifications (*gong zhong*) related to the automobile industry, not including engineering personnel. For each skilled trade, there are five skill levels: "elementary," "intermediate," "advanced," "technician," and "senior technician." Skilled trades classifications are occupation-based, and thus are related to, but different from, job classifications at the factory level (see Chapter 4).

TABLE 3.3. *Skill level of production workers in China's auto assembly sector, 2005*

Skill Rank	Current %	Desired %	Expected Recruitment % Change
Semi-skilled line worker	25.27	38.42	+ 52%
Technician & Maintenance worker	2.17	23.10	+ 965%
Skilled line worker	55.60	21.81	– 60%

Source: CAAM (2005).

levels and seniority, given that obtaining skilled worker status in China's large automobile factories is achieved mainly through accruing seniority (see Chapter 4).

It is important to note that with the continued mechanization of the auto assembly sector, not only have the skill levels required for the majority of line operators been reduced, but also the types of skills in demand have changed. For instance, mechanization and automation have created a high demand for technicians and maintenance workers who can keep the machines running properly. Such a change in demand for skill types can be seen clearly in the CAAM report (2005). Management would prefer to reduce the number of skilled assembly line workers – based on their VQCs – by 60 percent, while looking to increase the number of semi-skilled line workers by 50 percent. Management also expressed a need for many more technicians and maintenance workers to keep the machines running properly (Table 3.3). In the words of a production manager of GER-2, "We have an oversupply of 'low-level' skilled workers. But what we really need are experienced technicians who can identify and fix specific machine problems on the spot."[35] The changing demand for the levels and types of skilled workers in China is in line with the general trend in the global automobile industry, as the increasingly mechanized and automated production process has reduced workers' tasks to "baby-sitting" machines and responding to machine problems (Ishida 1997: 51).

As such, the impact of technological change on autoworkers' skills and labor market conditions is uneven and less straightforward than is widely thought. On the one hand, mechanization reduces the required skills for many assembly line workers, weakening their skills-based marketplace bargaining power. On the other hand, it has also created a high demand for technicians and maintenance workers who can keep machines running properly, thereby substantially increasing their marketplace bargaining power. As we will see, even semi-skilled operators have certain marketplace bargaining power under the

[35] Interview F20, GER-2, October 2006.

capital-intensive, quality mass production system, derived from the fact that performance improves with experience, such that management has an interest in keeping labor turnover rates low.[36] This brings us to the discussion of management recruitment strategies and hiring standards for formal production workers.

Recruitment strategies and hiring standards

Traditionally, under the *danwei* work unit system, large state-owned auto enterprises had their own technical schools and an apprenticeship system to ensure a supply of skilled workers. Admitted students usually spent the first two years studying related theoretical and technical knowledge. They then spent their last year as apprentices in the factories at which qualified students were expected to become formal workers upon graduation. Many early-built automobile factories – such as the Sino-German JVs GER-1 and GER-2 – continue to use this system to recruit their formal production workers. For instance, about two-thirds of new hires at GER-2 in the past five years were graduates from AutoStar (pseudonym), an automotive technical junior college founded by FAW in 1979. AutoStar offers specially-tailored training programs to supply "graduates by order" for dozens of FAW's subsidiary companies, including GER-2 and SOE-2. The automakers often select their formal workers from AutoStar's tailored pool of quality graduates through apprenticeships and careful screening. Similarly, at GER-1, about half of the formal workforce was recruited from the automaker's own technical vocational school upon completion of an apprenticeship.[37] Although to become a truly skilled worker requires further on-the-job training and 3–5 years of work experience, management believed that workers trained under this system were better suited, more technically proficient, and committed to their work. They were also considered easier to fit into the company's culture and more likely to stay with the company for a long time.[38]

Newly-built automobile factories, by contrast, tend to rely more on open recruitment from external labor markets, through job fairs, online and newspaper advertisements, and employment service agencies. For skilled positions, they often directly recruit experienced workers from other companies – as in the case of USA-2 and SOE-1 – or incorporate skilled veteran workers from their Chinese partners, as in the case of USA-1 and JPN-1. As to semi-skilled workers, the most common strategy is to openly recruit recent graduates from technical and vocational schools and provide them with a

[36] Thelen and Kume (1999: 499) made a similar argument, stating that semi-skilled workers are central to the continued smooth operations of quality mass production in Germany and Japan. For a discussion on different types of workers' bargaining power, see Chapter 1.

[37] Both schools attracted a large number of applicants and required high entry-exam scores given the promising prospects of their graduates to become formal employees at either of the two leading auto assemblers.

[38] Interviews S2, GER-1, June 2004; F2, GER-2, August 2004; Q2, SOE-2, June 2004.

brief period of on-the-job training. In recent years, faced with rapid production expansions and a growing shortage of skilled workers, many newly-
established automakers have become more proactive in the training and
recruitment of skilled workers. Some have also established long-term collaborations with selected colleges and technical and vocational schools to design
tailored training programs and internships, in order to ensure a regular supply
of graduates with the required skills. At the same time, it has also become
common practice in the industry to use student interns as temporary laborers
with little training and no intention to offer them formal employment upon
completing the internship.

Despite these differences, large automakers tend to share similar hiring
standards and screening procedures when recruiting formal workers. They
all emphasize the need for job candidates to exhibit disciplined behavior and
a cooperative attitude, as reflected, for instance, in low absenteeism, good
discipline, an ability to work in teams, and a willingness to adjust to change
and to obey orders at work. They also take great efforts to screen candidates in
order to select qualified and suitable formal workers. As the HR manager of the
Sino-Japanese JV JPN-1 explained:

We want disciplined and committed workers who can work cooperatively under the
integrated just-in-time production system. Our employees have all gone through several
rounds of rigorous selection of written, skill, and physical tests, personal interviews, and
team play. For operators, we prefer fresh graduates from vocational and technical
schools and junior colleges, because they tend to be more willing and capable to learn
new skills and adjust to changes on the job quickly. They also have a down-to-earth
work attitude desirable for daily operative tasks and team work. We also pay close
attention to job applicants' educational attainment because it reflects one's comprehensive quality and disciplinary attribute.[39]

In other words, the "integrated just-in-time production system" requires
"behaviorally highly skilled" workers who may be technically semi-skilled
or unskilled (Sayer and Walker 1992: 187). Especially when skills are largely
acquired on the job and through company-specific training, "general and gen-
eric" qualifications such as work attitude and educational attainment become
the primary criteria employers rely on to select workers (Kirpal 2011: 25). It also
shows that management has an interest in recruiting and retaining quality and
committed production workers, including ordinary operators. This is one of the
main incentives to the operating of internal labor markets for formal production
workers, as we will discuss in Chapter 4.

In sum, formal workers are a diverse lot, and there are important intra-group
distinctions along the lines of staff-worker status, skill and education levels, and
age and seniority. Accordingly, their labor market conditions and job security
vary widely. Notably, there is a generational divide between a minority of
skilled veteran workers with permanent or long-term contracts and the

---

[39] Interview H1, JPN-1, September 2006.

majority of young, semi-skilled, urban-bred workers with one- to two-year renewable contracts. Whereas the job security of the majority of young formal workers has been reduced, they still have relatively secure employment as the core segment of workers in China's booming auto industry – especially given the buffer provided by the flexible segment of temporary workers.

SOCIAL COMPOSITION AND THE LABOR MARKET OF TEMPORARY WORKERS

The practice of using temporary workers in Chinese automobile factories evolved in two stages. In the first stage, in the early and mid-1990s, most temporary workers were peasant workers hired by automobile factories in relatively small numbers to cope with seasonal changes in production demand. Peasant workers were either directly hired by the automobile factories or were recruited through local labor bureaus from nearby suburbs and the surrounding countryside, as a type of "rural redundant labor export" (*nongcun fuyu laodongli shuchu*). Peasant workers usually signed six-month to one-year renewable contracts with the automobile factories, and were paid about 70 percent of the wages formal workers received for doing the same work. Notably, peasant workers hired by large SOEs through local labor bureaus received better treatment than temporary agency workers hired through labor agencies at a later stage. For instance, at the state-owned truck maker SOE-2, peasant workers were paid close to the same wage, and received two-thirds of the bonus formal workers received – perhaps a sign of the residual strength of egalitarian mores within the SOEs. They also received work-related injury insurance and were enrolled in a pension plan. This concurs with Solinger's (1995) findings that the treatment of peasant workers in the 1980s and early 1990s was generally better in state enterprises. But because of their rural *hukou* status, peasant workers were ineligible for the social insurance and benefits to which urban workers were exclusively entitled, such as medical, maternity, and unemployment insurance, and access to a public housing fund. Most peasant workers were drawn from the surrounding countryside, or from townships close to the automobile factories. They lived in their own rural homes, and commuted daily to the factories. Some peasant workers from more distant rural areas lived in rented housing near the factories. In general, peasant workers dispersed into their local (rural) communities after work, and remained invisible as a distinct worker group.

At this stage, the boundary between formal workers and temporary workers was easy to draw and to maintain based on the state-enforced rural-urban *hukou* system. As noted in the previous section, peasant workers often are channeled into secondary labor markets characterized by jobs that are part-time and temporary, pay low wages, and are otherwise undesirable to urban residents. Working at auto assembly factories is considered one of the very few good jobs available to peasant workers because wages in the auto assembly sector are generally higher than those paid at other temporary jobs, and sometimes are even higher than the local average of urban workers.[40] As such, competition for temporary jobs at large automobile factories is high, and the recruitment and selection process is strict and more tightly regulated. Local labor bureaus during this stage were often closely involved with the recruitment and training of peasant workers, to ensure that the quality of the selected peasant workers would meet the needs of the automobile factories. For instance, the Q district, a suburb of Shanghai, was one of the main suburban districts from which GER-1 sourced peasant workers. It supplied the Sino-German JV with over 2,200 peasant workers between 1995 and 2004. The district labor bureau directly recruited and trained local peasants, and competed with labor bureaus in other districts to provide peasant workers to GER-1. A labor bureau official from the Q district commented:

We have very strict selection criteria and training programs to guarantee the quality of our selected peasant workers. That's why GER-1 has come back to us every year, in spite of the factory's recent cut in hiring temps from other districts. It is a win-win situation for the factory (GER-1), the local economy, and individual peasants in our district. The annual income of a peasant worker at GER-1 is about 35,000 *yuan*, which is almost three times as high as the average annual income of a rural family. It has also brought in over 80 million *yuan* annual revenue to our district government. People in the Q district regard working at GER-1 as a decent job, no matter whether it is temporary or formal work.[41]

A handful of peasant workers I interviewed at SOE-2 and GER-2 in the summer of 2004 also expressed satisfaction with their wages, even though in most cases they could earn only between one-half to two-thirds the wages of formal workers for doing the same or heavier work. The following quote from a peasant worker at GER-2 is representative:

Although we [peasant workers] can only earn 1,500 *yuan* per month – about half of the wages of those formal workers – it is much better than staying in my home village, and it is even better than many urban workers in other factories in the city, especially given that many urban workers can't even find jobs nowadays.[42]

When I revisited the factories in 2006, however, most peasant workers had since left.[43] In their place on the assembly lines, I found a large number of temporary

---

[40] Interview Q5, SOE-2, June 2004. See Table 3.8 for a comparison of formal and temporary autoworkers' wages to local average wages.

[41] Interview No.5, Shanghai, July 2004.   [42] Interview F6, GER-2, August 2004.

[43] According to the managers I interviewed, the main reason for letting peasant workers go was because the ongoing *hukou* system reform since the 2000s had made the use of peasant workers "inappropriate." Instead, labor dispatch had become the "new trend," and the more convenient option for using temporary workers. The workers interviewed believed that management kicked out most peasant workers who had worked at the factory for long tenures in order to avoid potential labor disputes over signing open-term contracts – for which those peasant workers would have been eligible after a period of 10 years, according to the Labor Law. Interviews Q15, Q16, SOE-2, September 2006; F15, F17, GER-2, October 2006.

agency workers who were hired through labor agencies.[44] As noted in the previous section, because there is no direct employment relationship between agency workers and user companies, the auto factories can simply "return" (dismiss) agency workers to the labor agencies without having to pay any severance compensation. Furthermore, agency workers are ineligible for tenure (open-term contracts) no matter how long they work for the auto factories. Thus the automakers can reduce their responsibility for agency workers to a minimum.

I also found a fast-growing number of student interns from vocational and technical schools working full time on assembly lines. For instance, at the Sino-German JV GER-2, it was estimated that student workers accounted for 30 percent of the total workforce on the line as of July 2011. At the state-owned carmaker SOE-1, the number of student workers on the assembly lines increased from 20 percent in 2005 to an estimated 30 percent in early 2007. Most student workers I interviewed received only basic wages and overtime pay, plus work-related injury insurance, making them even cheaper to employ than temporary agency workers. More appallingly, I found some schools operated like labor agencies, sending their students to factories as agency workers and charging commission fees deducted from the students' monthly pay. For example, LY Technique School had been providing student workers to the state-owned truck maker SOE-2 on a yearly basis since 2001. The students received only 70 percent of their monthly pay from the truck maker, while the school kept 30 percent as service fees.[45] As noted in the previous section, the lack of *de jure* worker status and labor law protection leaves student workers particularly vulnerable to abusive labor practices during their internships. Moreover, student workers were often perceived by management to be more docile and easier to control because they would have to stay at the factory for 6–12 months to complete the required internship before they could graduate. Thus student workers were subject to control and discipline from both the school and the factory. As a student worker at SOE-1 tellingly described their vulnerable situation in the factory:

When other workers cannot bear the hard work anymore, they can simply quit. But we have to stay to complete the internship in order to get our diplomas. We are the most exploited here. We are at the bottom here.[46]

It should be noted that student workers differ from apprentices in that the former are hired as temporary workers and automakers often have no intention to recruit them as formal workers beyond the completion of their "internship." By contrast, apprentices were the "real" trainees, and they were often recruited from the vocational school affiliated with the particular automaker. They have a good chance of becoming formal employees of the factory following their apprenticeship.

---

[44] GER-1 still retained some of its "old temp" peasant workers, hired through the labor bureaus of the surrounding suburban districts, but it also introduced "new temp" agency workers in 2005. The agency workers received reduced pay and benefits compared to peasant workers (see Chapter 6).
[45] Interviews Q6,Q7,Q8,Q9, SOE-2, June 2004.   [46] Interview C6, SOE-1, August 2005.

In sum, by the mid-2000s, the social composition of temporary workers in the auto assembly industry had changed from the "old temp" of peasant workers to the "new temp" of agency workers (70 percent) and student workers (30 percent). Most were between 18 and 24 years old and had an average of 9–12 years of education, which tended to be higher than the average education level of temporary workers.[47] Around two-thirds of agency workers were rural residents from the suburbs and countryside surrounding the automobile factories; the remaining third were predominantly local urban youths who were unable to find formal employment. Student workers included both rural and urban youths drawn from all across China (Figure 3.1).

As a result of the change in social composition, the boundary between temporary and formal workers as based on their rural-urban *hukou* status became blurred. Management intended to emphasize education and skill qualifications as the new yardstick in drawing boundaries between formal and temporary workers. In many cases, however, temporary workers had similar education and skill levels as compared to formal assembly line workers – for instance, having completed 12 years of education and obtained the semi-skilled VQCs. In other words, there was growing homogeneity between formal and temporary workers on the line. As we will see in Chapter 6, the re-composition of temporary workers has delegitimized labor force dualism and contributed to the rising labor activism among the new temporary workers, against the unequal treatment they experience in the workplace.

WAGE CONDITIONS IN THE CHINESE AUTOMOBILE INDUSTRY

Since Henry Ford introduced the "five-dollar day" wage policy, high wages have been part of the control and organization of labor that accompanies automobile mass production. Chinese autoworkers, especially those working at large automobile assembly factories, are known for their high wages and generous benefits compared to auto parts workers and workers in other manufacturing sectors in China. It is commonly assumed that high wages is one of the main reasons for the relative quiescence of auto assembly workers. However, a closer look at the wage conditions of blue-collar workers in the Chinese auto assembly industry suggests a varied and complicated picture that does not support this popular assumption.[48]

---

[47] According to a survey conducted by the Shanghai Federal Trade Union in 2004, the average level of education of temporary agency workers in Shanghai in all industries was less than 9 years (Tu 2007).

[48] China is known for the lack of reliable official statistics on employment and labor compensation that are comparable to international standards (Banister 2005). Companies in China also tend to keep secret of their labor compensation information. Given these obstacles, I mainly rely on my field research data and on survey reports by reliable news media and business consulting firms, and checked those sources against one another to get a relatively accurate picture of Chinese autoworkers' wage conditions.

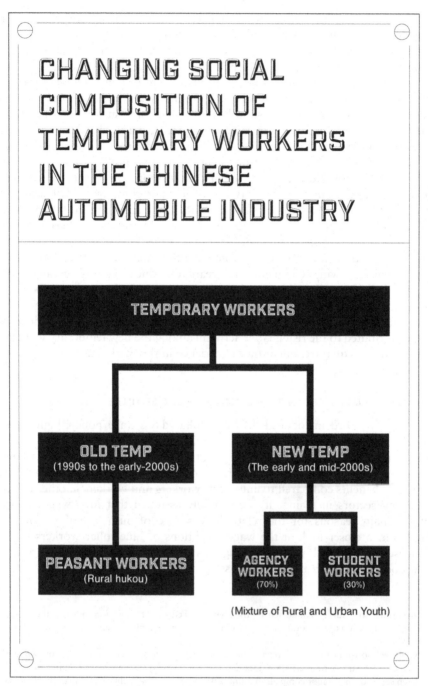

FIGURE 3.1. Changing social composition of temporary workers in the Chinese automobile industry

Note: The diagram is based on the author's field data and company records of four large auto assemblers using temporary workers in late 2006.

TABLE 3.4. *Average annual earnings in the manufacturing and transport equipment manufacturing sectors in China, 2004–2011*

	2004	2005	2006	2007	2008	2009	2010	2011
								Chinese RMB (*yuan*)
Manufacturing [x]	14,251	15,934	18,225	21,144	24,404	26,810	30,916	36,665
Transport Equipment [y]	18,485	20,204	22,990	26,922	31,658	34,730	40,493	45,635
National Average	15,920	18,200	20,856	24,721	28,898	32,244	36,539	41,799
Ratio [y]/[x]	1.30	1.27	1.26	1.27	1.30	1.30	1.31	1.24

Source: Compiled from *China Labor Statistics Yearbook*, various years. Beijing: National Bureau of Statistics.

TABLE 3.5. *Motor vehicles and other transport equipment hourly compensation costs in selected countries, 2008–2011[a] (US dollars)*

Country	2008	2009	2010	2011
Germany	59.59	57.70	54.80	60.53
United States	41.97	45.19	45.34	46.11
Japan	32.82	35.66	37.21	42.37
South Korea	21.99	19.01	23.42	24.26
Brazil	14.62	13.88	17.22	19.88
Mexico	8.69	8.01	7.95	8.15
China (manufacturing, urban)[b]	2.58	2.85	n/a	n/a
China (Transport Equipment)[c]	3.35	3.71	n/a	n/a

Notes: [a] Compensation costs include direct pay, social insurance expenditures, and labor-related taxes. For complete definitions, see the technical notes at www.bls.gov/ilc/ichcctn.pdf

[b] BLS, "Manufacturing in China," "Table 2: Average hourly compensation costs of manufacturing employees in China, 2002–2009," www.bls.gov/fls/china.htm.

[c] The hourly compensation cost in China was estimated by multiplying hourly compensation in the manufacturing sector (b) by the ratio of average annual earnings in Table 3.4. Given the long working hours typical in the Chinese automobile industry, we can expect annual working hours to be close to the manufacturing average.

Sources: US Bureau of Labor Statistics (BLS) (2013a); US BLS (2013b); NBS and MOHRSS (2009–2012).

First of all, although Chinese autoworkers' hourly compensation costs are very low by international standards, they are about 30 percent higher than the average of all urban manufacturing workers in China (see Table 3.4 and Table 3.5). When the auto assembly sector is separated from the general

TABLE 3.6. *Average annual growth rates in vehicle output, labor productivity, and remuneration in the Chinese automobile industry, 2006–2010*

Year	2006	2007	2008	2009	2010 (%)
Vehicle output growth rate[a]	27.3	22.0	5.2	48.3	32.4
Productivity growth rate (output per capita)[b]	29.2	16.5	0	22.3	23.8
Remuneration growth rate in the auto industry[c]	9.0	9.0	8.6	6.4	10.6
National pay growth rate[d]	8.7	9.7	11.7	7.8	12.3
GDP growth rate[e]	11.6	13.0	8.9	9.1	10.3

Notes: [a, b] Compiled from CATRC, various years.

[c] The remuneration growth rates for 2006–2009 are drawn from figures published in *First Financial Daily* (2010); the growth rate for 2010 is drawn from a report on an HRM Auto Industry Survey conducted by one of China's largest recruitment services websites, 51job. com (2011). It should be noted that both sources had a bias toward representing autoworkers whose earnings tended to be higher than the industry average. The former is based on a survey conducted among Sino-foreign JVs, where workers' annual earnings are typically higher than those of workers at SOEs and at domestic private automakers; the latter is based on information from nine large automakers recognized for their HRM practices in the "100 Best HRM Companies in China," with remuneration at those companies being higher than the industry average.

[d, e] National Bureau of Statistics.

category of "Manufacture of Transport Equipment," the wage level can be even higher (see discussion below).

However, wage increases for front-line workers have not kept pace with the remarkable growth of China's auto industry in the past decade. As shown in Table 3.6, total output and labor productivity in the auto industry grew at a double-digit rate annually between 2002 and 2010, excepting 2008, yet the average wage growth rate of production workers remained in the single digits. In 2009, for example, the total vehicle output in China increased by 48.3 percent, yet the average wages of autoworkers increased only by 6.4 percent. Even this moderate wage increase was achieved primarily through extensive overtime and a significant increase in work intensity, as I will detail in later chapters.

Second, there were significant variations in autoworkers' earnings across segments, enterprise ownership types, regions, and workers' skill levels. One such notable disparity is that assembly workers receive much higher pay than do parts workers. According to a 2007 survey report by China's leading recruitment website, ChinaHR.com, the average annual pay of production workers in the auto assembly sector was 29,842 *yuan* ($4,265), 55 percent higher than that of other manufacturing workers in China (19,258 *yuan*, about $2,752) (ChinaHR.com 2007). By contrast, an automotive industry income survey conducted by *China Business News* (CBN) found that, in 2009, most auto parts workers' annual earnings were a mere

TABLE 3.7. *USA-2 monthly monetary compensation for production workers, April 2007*

		Chinese RMB (*yuan*)	
Category	Base Pay	Total with Bonus, Regular Time	Total with Bonus, Overtime
Non-skilled/Semi-skilled Worker	940–1,060	1,500–1,800	2,000–2,500
Skilled Worker/Technician	1,400	2,100	2,800–3,000
Team Leader	1,500	2,100–2,200	3,000–3,200

Notes: Annual income is based on 14 months – 12 months base pay, plus two months' salary in bonus.
Management classifies team leaders as workers (see Chapter 4).
Overtime pay: Mon–Fri: 7 yuan/hour
Sat, Sun: 1.5–2 times the normal hourly rate
Holidays: 3 times the normal hourly rate
Source: The authors' interviews with workers and shop-floor managers at USA-2, April 2007.

10,000–20,000 *yuan* ($1,477–$2,954). Only those workers at a handful of large, first-tier parts suppliers earned an annual income of 30,000 *yuan*, comparable to the earnings of assembly workers (Liu 2010). Such a steep wage gradient between assembly and parts workers – and the fact that a larger proportion of workers are employed in the parts sector – is reminiscent of the structure of the Japanese automobile industry, in which large assemblers like Toyota "exploit a steep wage gradient into the supplier network" to achieve competitive cost structures (Williams et al. 1995: 23). But this wage disparity has been increasingly challenged by parts workers, as seen in the case of Honda strike.[49]

Within the auto assembly sector, monthly earnings of production workers could range from 1,800 *yuan* to 4,000 *yuan*. Skilled workers such as mechanics and technicians were in high demand and they could easily earn an average of 3,000–5,000 *yuan* per month. But in general, workers' base pay was low and high earnings were mainly a product of overtime and bonuses, which were directly tied to the performance of their employers (see Table 3.7).

There are also large wage differences by enterprise ownership type and by region. The CBN survey reported that the average annual pay of front-line

---

[49] A major grievance of the striking auto parts workers was their substandard wages compared with Honda assembly workers' in the same area. Whereas the average annual pay of Honda parts workers in Foshan was a mere 15,000 *yuan* ($2,216) in 2009, the average annual pay of workers at Honda's assembly plants in Guangzhou, just 15 miles from Foshan, was 57,000 *yuan* ($8,420) – almost four times that of the parts workers (*National Business Daily*, 2010). Clearly, striking parts workers were aware of the large wage disparity when they put forward their demand for pay increase.

workers at JVs was about 10,000 *yuan* ($1,464) higher than that of workers at Chinese state-owned and private-owned automakers. Similarly, *Southern Metropolis Daily*'s (2010) income survey among blue-collar autoworkers found in 2009 that the average annual earnings of front-line workers at Sino-foreign JVs were 35,000–45,000 *yuan* ($5,124-$5,857), while workers at domestic Chinese automakers only earned an average of 25,000–32,500 *yuan* ($3,660-$4,758). Another survey conducted by a management consulting firm found that JVs with European and American companies generally paid their workers higher salaries than did JVs established between Chinese companies and Japanese and Korean companies. For example, the median annual total cash income of auto assembly workers in 2011 was 62,354 *yuan* ($9,652) at JVs with European and American companies, 42,732 *yuan* ($6,615) at Sino-Japanese and Sino-Korean JVs, and only 31,433 *yuan* ($4,866) at Chinese state-owned and private automakers (Puxin Management Consulting Co., Ltd., 2012). This wage gradient tends to be consistently correlated with automakers' profitability levels, with European and American JVs dominating the most profitable, high-end brands, Chinese domestic automakers concentrating on low-cost models, and Japanese and Korean JVs occupying the middle tier of the car market. The survey also found that remuneration levels in the auto industry varied widely by region. Among the six major vehicle production regions, the Yangtze River Delta ranked the highest (assuming pay coefficient P=1), followed by the Pearl River Delta (P=0.94), the Bohai Sea region (P=0.92), the Central region (P=0.88), the Southwest region (P=0.85), and the Northeast region (P=0.74).[50]

Finally, I found that in the automobile factories that had adopted the policy of labor force dualism, temporary agency workers earned only one-half to two-thirds the pay of formal workers,[51] even though their earnings were comparable with – and in some cases, higher than – local average earnings (see Table 3.8). Temporary workers also received less generous social insurance contributions through their labor agencies, usually at levels 25–50 percent of the standard for formal workers. Temporary workers were also ineligible to receive the fringe benefits auto companies provided to their formal employees. Given that social insurance premiums and fringe benefits constituted as much as half of the wage bills, for the total cost of hiring a formal worker, automakers could afford to hire 3–4 temporary workers.

Formal workers, by contrast, not only earned significantly higher wages in comparison to the local average, they also enjoyed generous benefits. In addition to the government-required social insurance contributions and

---

[50] Puxin Management Consulting Co., Ltd. (2012). See also Chapter 1 for a discussion about the six major vehicle production regions in China.

[51] Student interns in most cases only received basic living stipends of 800–1,200 *yuan*, with some also able to secure overtime pay.

TABLE 3.8. *Monthly monetary earnings[a] of formal and temporary workers at the selected auto assemblers in comparison with local average wages[b]*

Chinese RMB (yuan)

GER-1

Firm/Year	Formal worker	Temp worker	Local average
2004	4,000	2,500	2,272
2005	3,500	2,200	2,479
2006	4,000	2,500	2,588
2009	5,000	3,200	3,004

GER-2

Firm/Year	Formal worker	Temp worker	Local average
2004	3,000	1,500	1,310
2005	2,500	1,500	1,479
2006	3,500	1,800	1,663
2009	5,800	3,000	2,537

SOE-2

Firm/Year	Formal worker	Temp worker	Local average
2004	2,917	2,200	1,161
2005	2,583	1,800	1,335
2006	2,667	2,000	1,548
2009	3,000	2,500	2,116

SOE-1

Firm/Year	Formal Worker	Temp worker	Local average
2004	1,200	1,000	800
2005	1,500	1,200	1,188
2006	1,800	1,500	1,434
2009	2,800	2,500	2,470

USA-1

Firm/Year	Formal Worker	Local Average
2004	4,500	2,272
2005	4,000	2,479
2006	4,500	2,588
2009	5,500	3,004

USA-2

Firm/Year	Formal Worker	Local average
2004	1,500	1,197
2005	1,800	1,400
2006	2,100	1,772
2009	3,000	2,548

JPN-1

Firm/Year	Formal Worker	Local average
2004	3,000	1,809
2005	3,200	2,006
2006	3,300	2,094
2009	4,750	3,075

Notes: [a] Workers' monetary earnings include base pay, merit bonus (monthly), overtime and other allowances. Annual bonuses, which were usually distributed at the end of the year or early the following year, were not included. On the wage system and its components, see Chapter 4.
[b] The "average wages in the manufacturing sector" are used for Shanghai, Guangzhou, and Wuhu, where such wage statistics are available; "average wages of working staff and workers" are used for Changchun, Qingdao, and Yantai, where no sectoral wage information is available.

Sources: Formal and temporary workers' earnings data are drawn from interviews with production workers conducted in June–August 2004, June–August 2005, September 2006–July 2007, and August 2010; Data on local average wages were compiled from the respective local statistical yearbooks (various years) for Shanghai, Guangzhou, Changchun, Qingdao, Shandong Province (Yantai), and Anhui Province (Wuhu).

TABLE 3.9. *Social insurance contributions and benefits for formal employees at GER-1, 2010*

Social Insurance and Housing Fund (Shanghai City Standard)

| No. | Item | Rate of Base | Contribution Breakdown | | Explanation |
			Employer	Employee	
1	Pension Insurance	30%	22%	8%	The base is an
2	Unemployment Insurance	3%	2%	1%	individual's average monthly salary of
3	Statutory Medical Insurance	14%	12%	2%	the previous year. The maximum is
4	Occupational Injury Insurance	0.5%	0.5%	0%	triple the average monthly social salary of the
5	Maternity Insurance	0.5%	0.5%	0%	previous year; the minimum is 60% of
6	Housing Public Accumulation Fund	14%	7%	7%	the average monthly social salary of the
	SUB-TOTAL	62%	44%	18%	previous year.

Selected Supplementary Benefits (Voluntary employee contribution with employer subsidy)

No.	Item	RMB *yuan*/Month	No.	Item	RMB *yuan*/Month
1	Life Insurance	40	6	Single-child Insurance	42
2	Medical Insurance	91	7	Healthcare	50
3	Additional Medical Insurance	30	8	Risk Fund	10
4	Serious Illness	30	9	Training & Recreation	30
5	Hospitalization Subsidy	30	10	Property Insurance	Complimentary with items (1) & (2)

Source: The Human Resources Department, GER-1, July 2010.

public housing funds contributed by their employers,[52] they also received company-subsidized supplementary benefits (see Table 3.9), car purchase discounts, monthly gas subsidies, free meals at work, shuttle service between their workplace and home, and free annual physical examinations.

[52] In many cities, local governments require employers to provide a public housing fund for their local, urban-based employees.

Despite their higher-than-average wages and good benefits, more than three-quarters of the formal production workers interviewed felt they were underpaid considering the rapid growth in output, the profits of their employers, and the long work hours and grueling nature of their daily work.[53] There was a strong sentiment among the workers that their employers could afford to pay them higher wages. Workers felt they were squeezed and did not receive fair reward and recognition for their work. As one formal worker at the state-owned carmaker SOE-1 commented:

It is not just about money, it is how you feel about how the company treats you! You feel they really do not care about you as a worker. The managers always promise to increase our wages when the company becomes more profitable. But after all these years of rapid growth, the paychecks and bonuses of managers and salesmen have gotten bigger and bigger. We workers still earn that little! But it is we front-line workers who make the cars, do the heavy and dirty work, and generate the profits for the company! But we are the least paid and cared for here! This is not the right way to treat employees![54]

Workers were especially indignant about the large and growing wage gap between themselves and management. For example, the wage grades at the Sino-German JV GER-1 were divided into 7 levels and 59 grades, with the highest management earning on average 20 times the lowest workers. Since bonuses and overtime were calculated based on the pay grade of one's position, the total income difference between managers and workers could be even larger. During interviews, workers expressed their dissatisfaction with such a large wage gap. Thus there is no reason to assume a high wage in and of itself can guarantee workers' consent and commitment.

However, higher-than-average wages and good benefits for semi-skilled formal assembly line workers do attract a large pool of job applicants, which in turn allows employers to conduct strict screening to select disciplined and quality formal production workers. It also enables management to impose stringent labor discipline based on the assumption that line workers can be replaced relatively easily given an oversupplied labor market. As one 26-year-old team leader at USA-2 recounted while discussing his job-hunting experience:

After graduating from a local college, I was unable to find a satisfying job since there were so many college graduates but very few white-collar office jobs. When USA-2 held a big job fair in 2004, I thought it was a great opportunity. But almost all the office positions required degrees from top universities or work experiences, except for team leaders and assembly line operators. The HR people said that there were piles of

---

[53] Workers' opinions on their wages, however, varied across factories. At SOE-1, every worker I interviewed complained about their low wages compared to the wages at other leading automakers in China. At the Sino-German JV GER-2, by contrast, more than half of the interviewed workers considered their wages "good" based on the local standard of living.

[54] Interview C16, SOE-1, March 2007.

applications on their desk. After all, it is a well-known, large joint venture and the pay is not bad compared to the local standard.[55]

Although high wages and relatively low skill requirements make for an especially competitive labor market for line workers, management does not want constant turnover, since performance and productivity improve with experience. As a production manager explained:

Most assembly line operators don't need advanced skills. All they need is to follow the job descriptions strictly and do their work carefully and proficiently, which can be improved with experience over time. Thus for line operators, we prefer disciplined and committed young workers who can stay with the company for a long time. That's why we are willing to pay our line workers higher wages than the local average. But to be honest, if we simply look at the value of line workers' labor based on their skills, I think they are overpaid.[56]

This resonates with previous discussions, which suggest that management has an interest in maintaining a relatively skilled and stable formal workforce. It also indicates that even semi-skilled operators have some marketplace bargaining power.

The evidence presented in this section is sufficient to reject the popular notion that auto-assembly workers were relatively quiescent because they were satisfied with their high wages. Rather, the auto industry has not formed a long-term, normalized wage-increasing mechanism consistent with the rapid growth of the industry and in labor productivity – a situation faced by Chinese workers at large.[57] Despite China's meteoric rise to become the world's top vehicle-manufacturing nation and largest auto market, Chinese autoworkers have not received a fair share of the fruits of the auto industry boom.

CONCLUSION

This chapter has examined the labor markets and the social composition of the workforce in the Chinese auto assembly industry. What we found in the auto industry exemplifies the broader labor market dynamics of flexibilization and dualization in post-socialist China. On the one hand, my evidence shows a clear move toward flexibilization of labor and reduced job security for ordinary workers. The fact that one-third to two-thirds of production workers at the leading auto assembly enterprises – key enterprises in a pillar industry – were temporary workers reflects the scale and depth of flexibilization of labor in China as marketization has deepened since the mid-1990s. On the other hand, despite the notable intra-group distinctions, formal workers still enjoy more job security as the core segment of workers under labor force dualism.

---

[55] Interview D2, USA-2, September 2006.   [56] Interview F20, GER-2, October 2006.

[57] According to Lu (2006), between 1995 and 2004, the growth rate of average annual wages in the manufacturing sector was estimated 5 percent lower than the average annual growth rate in labor productivity.

As we will see in subsequent chapters, rather than produce a generalized "race to the bottom," the movement toward flexibilization has encountered resistance from both formal and temporary workers. Having examined "ways of life" as seen from the organization of labor markets at the first of the "-experience-near" levels, in the next chapter we will go inside the hidden abode of production – that is, the organization of production and factory settings in the automobile plants.

4

Organization of production and factory social order

> We expect the men to do what they are told. The organization is so highly specialized and one part is so dependent upon another that we could not for a moment consider allowing the men to have their own way. Without the most rigid discipline we would have the utmost confusion... The men are there to get the greatest possible amount of work done and to receive the highest possible pay. If each man were permitted to act in his own way, production would suffer and therefore pay would suffer. Anyone who does not like to work in our way may always leave.
>
> ——Ford and Crowther (1926), *Today and Tomorrow*, 111

In this chapter, we go inside China's gigantic auto assembly factories to examine the organization of production, working conditions, and factory social order – that is, the factory settings under which managers, different groups of workers, and factory Party and union cadres make their decisions, act, and interact with one another in the factory on a daily basis.

The first section of this chapter takes a close look at the organization of production and the work regime at the seven studied auto assembly factories. I find that the current production system in the Chinese auto assembly sector is essentially a Taylorist/Fordist mass production model in a leaner and more efficient formula.[1] The work regime under this production model is inherently exhausting and authoritarian, which is one of the main sources of workers' grievances. The second section examines the cadre-managerial personnel system, the role of enterprise unions, HRM practices, and issues of status and hierarchy in China's large automobile enterprises. I find that although management generally seeks to obscure the status distinctions between white-collar managerial staff and blue-collar workers, the overall factory social order in China's large automobile enterprises is very hierarchical. The institutionalized

---

[1] Many scholars have argued that Taylorism is integral to the success of lean production. See, among others, Babson (1995), Moody (1997) and Price (1997).

inferior status of blue-collar workers is another main source of production workers' complaints and discontent. The last section investigates the operation of internal labor markets and the structure of opportunities for a blue-collar, formal worker to move up in today's large and hierarchical automobile factories in China.

THE ORGANIZATION OF PRODUCTION: A LEANER VERSION OF THE MASS PRODUCTION PARADIGM

The automobile industry, which Peter Drucker once called "the industry of industries" (1946: 149), is essentially a mass assembly industry *par excellence* (Dicken 2011: 332–9). Despite some variations, I found the core elements of the production system at China's major automakers converge with global industrial practices, which can be characterized as a leaner version of mass production paradigm – that is, a Taylorist/Fordist mass assembly production system combined with lean production techniques pioneered by Japanese automakers.[2] What seems unique in the Chinese model, however, is that along with incremental mechanization and automation, automakers in China also adopt "human wave tactics" (*renhai zhanshu*),[3] in which they mobilize a large number of young, relatively low-cost, semi-skilled, male workers to work in two or three shifts to ensure nonstop production and thereby maximizing output.

Just-in-Time (JIT) mass production

The basic organization of production at the major auto assembly plants I visited conformed to the typical automobile assembly plant found anywhere in the world. It consisted of four main production workshops, corresponding to the four major manufacturing processes of an automobile, and connected by a network of conveyors carrying sub-assemblies from one shop to another. The main assembly line originates in the press shop, where a series of gigantic, automated stamping machines press and mold raw steel sheets into the various metal pieces to be used to make a car body. Workers in the press shop are mainly responsible for machine operating, monitoring and maintenance, as well as for conducting quality inspections of the finished metal pieces. Next is the body shop, where the metal pieces from the press shop are welded into a

---

[2] Lean production (*jingyi shengchan*) is also known as the Toyota Production System (TPS) in China.

[3] This term was first mentioned to me by a manager I interviewed at SOE-1. It came up several times in my subsequent interviews with managers and workers at other factories. I use this term instead of "labor intensive" because, despite the large number of workers employed in production, the capital-to-labor ratio in China's auto assembly sector is still high compared with traditional, labor-intensive manufacturing sectors. See discussion below.

bare car body. The main body frame is welded by robots, using articulating arms and laser welding equipment. The remaining body welding work is done by workers with welding torches and other tools. After inspection, the line continues to the paint shop, where the bare body of the car is painted. The painted shell is then carried to the final assembly shop. Traditionally, the body shell proceeds along the interior assembly line, to have all of the internal components assembled and integrated into the body. Meanwhile, the chassis is built on the chassis assembly line, and the body and chassis are then mated to complete a car. This method was widely utilized during the plant visits I made between 2004 and 2006.[4] However, when I revisited those plants in 2011, almost all of them – with the exception of SOE-2 – had adopted the modular assembly method, which breaks down the traditional long assembly lines into several modules: powertrain, doors, instruments, and front end assembly. The different modules then are assembled on separate sub-assemblies – or in many cases are provided, pre-assembled, by first-tier parts suppliers – and then sent by conveyers to the main assembly line. The guiding principle behind the modular production method is the use of the same key components, such as engines, gearboxes, and steering systems, across several different car models, but with designs that are flexible enough to allow for individual models with a variety of external dimensions. This way, auto assemblers can boost production efficiency and cut costs and the number of parts and workers needed. The completely assembled vehicle is then driven to the test and inspection area for four-wheel positioning, spray testing, and test driving before rolling off the line to either the defect repair section if a problem was detected, or to the parking lot for additional polish, after which it would be considered a complete product and ready to be delivered to dealers.

It should be noted that today's assembly plants represent only the final stage of automobile manufacturing, where workers and robotic systems put together tens of thousands of parts drawn from hundreds of outsourced suppliers in multiple locations to manufacture a vehicle.[5] In fact, all seven studied assemblers had subcontracted part of their assembly work – including seat systems, cabin modules, front-end modules, and front and rear axles – to their first-tier suppliers, to reduce their own labor input requirements and manufacturing time. They also outsourced their logistics functions to third-party logistics companies to ensure that they meet their JIT inventory delivery requirements.[6] Under this JIT system, a combination of computerized

---

[4] The one exception being the Sino-American JV USA-1, which used a modular assembly method at that time.

[5] In most cases, key components such as engines were manufactured by the automakers' own engine plants or shops. For example, five of the seven assembly plants, excepting JPN-1 and SOE-2, had at least one engine plant next to their assembly plants, to provide the "heart" of the vehicles they build.

[6] The lead time for imported auto parts can be as long as three months, making advanced ordering essential to smooth production.

production scheduling and the *kanban* method was utilized.[7] Each month, the assemblers send their estimated orders to their major domestic parts suppliers and logistics companies through computerized production scheduling systems. Actual orders were placed on a weekly or daily basis. Most major suppliers are located near the assembly plants. The logistics companies are in charge of coordinating shipments from more distant suppliers. They deliver the exact types and amounts of parts to the assigned gates of the workshops based on the actual orders and the *kanban* signals, or to the exact work stations at the precise time according to the synchronous JIT online systems. Five of the studied assemblers explicitly required their major suppliers to set up factories located within a 3-mile radius – or a maximum driving distance of 30 minutes – of the assembly plants, so that the suppliers could respond to the *kanban* signals sent by the assembly plants within 1–2 hours.[8]

On the shop floor, electronic display boards hanging over both ends of assembly lines display real-time production progress with daily production targets, actual output, down time, and remaining quotas to be met. An *andon* system is implemented to monitor and signal quality or process problems on the line with different color signal lights: green (normal), red (abnormal), and yellow (assistance needed). An error-proofing method (*poka-yoke*) is adopted with specified parts packaging, equipment designs, and tool setups to prevent and correct inadvertent errors. All of the studied assemblers had introduced flexible production lines, with different models sitting side by side and assembled on the same line. Synchronized flows of different parts and sub-assemblies must reach their designated body shells on the main assembly line at a precise time. The finely-tuned JIT mass-production system runs seamlessly under the control of a computerized system, which sets the speed and rhythm of the overall production system.

Organization on the shop floor

On the shop floor, the organization of production has remained largely the same as in the pre-reform era (cf. Walder, 1986: 95–102). At each workshop (*chejian*) I visited, there was a workshop office headed by a shop manager, a Party branch secretary, and a shop union chairman – the latter position often being held by the Party branch secretary as well. The shop manager was in full charge of production and of various administrative matters within the shop. He/she usually reported directly to the factory production and engineering department. Each workshop was divided by assembly lines, with each led by a line chief. Each line was divided into a number of work sections (*gong duan*),

---

[7] *Kanban* is a type of visual control method used in the JIT system that signals whether inventory pallets or dollies need to be replaced, ensuring that the right type and amount of material inputs are in the right place at the right time, thereby preventing the unnecessary buildup of inventory.

[8] The author's field notes, June 2007.

TABLE 4.1. *Organization of the shop floor in Chinese automobile factories*

Organizational Level	Work Position
Work Shop (*chejian*)	Shop Director (*chejian zhuren*)
Shift (*ban*)	Shift Chief (*zhiban zhang*)
Line (*xian*)	Line Chief (*xian zhang*)
Work Section (*gong duan*)	Foreman/Section Chief (*gong duan zhang*)
Work Group (*ban zu*)/Work Block (*gong qu*)	Team (Group) Leader (*banzu zhang*)
Work Station (*gong wei*)	Operator (*caozuo gong*)

with each led by a foreman or section chief. Since production was usually organized into two or three shifts, there were two to three shift chiefs overseeing several lines during a given shift. Within each work section, production lines were further divided into dozens of work blocks (*gong qu*) organized according to the specific technical operations on assembly lines. Each work block was assigned to a work group (*ban zu*), and led by a team (group) leader. Within each group, an individual production worker was assigned to a specific work station (*gong wei*) by his team leader.

The work group is the basic unit in carrying out daily production tasks on the shop floor. It was an innovation introduced during the Mao years, and has remained one of the most effective means of organizing production and reaching out to ordinary workers in Chinese factories.[9] Each group assumes direct responsibility for product quality, safety, and cost control for its work block, and is expected to be the first to respond to any problems in daily production. In the factories I visited, a group usually consisted of 10–20 workers, led by a team leader who himself was a worker appointed by his shop manager, and who represented the lowest level of the management hierarchy in the factory. Team leaders played a pivotal role in organizing and carrying out daily production, reaching out to individual workers to ensure the timely and reliable completion of production tasks allocated to the group, mediating shop-floor conflicts, and promoting participation and cooperation from their fellow workers. While not officially recognized as managerial personnel, team leaders fulfilled a wide range of managerial functions and were granted some power, such as making decisions on job assignments, conducting performance appraisals, and determining bonus distributions within their work group. On the other hand, team leaders still engaged in direct production, including filling in for absent workers and assisting group members who encountered difficulty in completing

---

[9] For a detailed discussion on the extensive functions and the pivotal role of work group and group (team) leaders in pre-reform Chinese factories, see Walder (1986: 102–113).

their tasks.[10] Given their worker status but with substantial managerial responsibilities, the position of Chinese team leaders may be understood as standing
halfway between the "straw bosses" and foremen of the interwar years in the
U.S. automobile industry.[11] In a broad sense, the Chinese work group system
resembles the Japanese "team" concept, in that both are fundamentally a
managerial strategy designed to increase productivity and quality.[12] But the
Chinese work group system tends to place a greater emphasis on the social
and ideological dimensions of labor control and "harmony-building" through
group-building and group-centered worker participation – perhaps a legacy of
the Maoist democratic management experiment (for more detail, see Chapter 5).

Each shop also had a number of off-line sections, such as repair and
maintenance, quality control, inspection, and test driving. Workers considered
those off-line positions to be much more desirable than working on the line,
and they were often staffed by senior or skilled formal workers who were seen
as having higher status than regular line operators. Most other ancillary jobs,
such as logistics and cleaning, were subcontracted. It was common to see
workers from subcontracting companies, in different color uniforms, working
on the shop floors.

Rotation and skill training

The rotating of workers among tasks within a work group was common. It aimed
to train workers to perform multiple tasks and to reduce the incidence of repetitive
motion injuries. But positions like quality control and relief were reserved for
team leaders and acting team leaders – the worker activists able to assist team
leaders. Also, rotation outside of one's work group was rare. With respect to
on-the-job skill training, all of the studied factories had "multi-skill training"
programs for their production workers. My interviews with workers, however,
indicated that such skills training opportunities for line operators were limited
and selective. Among the interviewed line workers, more than two-thirds said
that they only received on-the-job skill training when they were newly recruited.
Opportunities for off-line training in technical skills were offered only to
selected workers with at least two years of seniority and good work attitudes
and performance. A worker who wanted to attend an off-line training session
needed first to be nominated by his team leader, and then approved by his foreman

---

[10] There were some variations in the amount of time team leaders spent working on the production
line. At USA-1, USA-2, and SOE-1, team leaders spent approximately two-thirds of their time
working on the line; at other factories, team leaders spent about 50–70 percent of their work
time fulfilling managerial functions off the line. Generally, team leaders did not work at fixed
work stations, nor did they work full time on assembly lines.

[11] Labor historian Nelson Lichtenstein describes the "straw boss" of the interwar years as a
"combination pusher, relief man, spy, and all around foreman substitute," who himself was a
worker, as well (1989: 157). See Chapter 5 for a more detailed discussion on the role of team
leaders in Chinese automobile factories.

[12] For a succinct explanation of the Japanese team concept, see Rinehart et al. (1995).

FIGURE 4.1. The Welding Shop at a Sino-Japanese JV, 2013
Source: Reference News (cancaoxiaoxi.com)

and shop manager. Alternatively, regular work group meetings proved to be the main channel through which ordinary workers could learn useful techniques and tips applicable to their daily work from their fellow group members.

Mechanization, standardization, and "human wave tactics"

As mentioned in Chapter 2, the massive foreign investment into the Chinese automobile industry through Sino-foreign JVs since the late 1990s has driven Chinese automakers to rapidly adopt global industrial standards in machinery and technology, organization of production, and managerial practices. The government policy of promoting technology upgrading has further facilitated the introduction of the most advanced technology and machinery at China's leading JVs. Among the seven studied auto assemblers, all five of the JVs had reached a fairly high level of mechanization and automation,[13] with state-of-the-art production machinery and robotic systems imported from their foreign partners. For example, the Sino-Japanese JV JPN-1 boasts a world-class plant

---

[13] It is important to note that both processes of mechanization (the introduction of machines operated by workers) and automation (the use of robots to replace workers entirely) have been progressing in China's automobile assembly factories since the late 1990s.

in terms of mechanization and automation levels. Its body shop has 267 advanced welding robots that are used to conduct difficult welding tasks to make a perfect car body. At the Sino-German JVs GER-1 and GER-2, advanced laser welding equipment and robots imported from Germany are used in the body shop; paint spraying and glass installation are completely automated. The state-owned carmaker SOE-1 used to be known as a low-end carmaker in China.[14] In recent years, it has aggressively upgraded its technology and imported advanced machinery from Germany and other industrialized countries. Today, in its highly automated press shop, most work is done by huge, complex, and expensive press machines and robotic systems. Only a dozen on-the-scene control and tooling engineers and technicians are needed to oversee the operations, along with 5–6 skilled workers positioned at the end of each press machine line to inspect the quality of the finished pieces. By contrast, the state-owned truck maker SOE-2 still relies on relatively old production equipment and a lower automation level; production workers there have to put up with more physical work, with manually operated machine tools (see Figure 4.2).[15]

Along with the continuous push for increased mechanization and automation, there has been a greater emphasis on standardized operations. Each position on the line is analyzed and broken down to its basic constituent gestures, and its sequence of movements is refined and optimized for best performance. Each line operator is expected to perform his task in the prescribed manner and time. A spot welder in the body shop at GER-2 described the standard operating procedures of his job:

I have been working on *gong wei* (work station) OP185-MA7 for about one-and-a-half years. I need to follow 11 operating procedures in order to weld 25 points within 88 seconds. It used to be 96 seconds when I first came. I need to use No. 14 and No.15 soldering turrets. I need to move back and forth four times and a total three meters distance to complete one unit. It does not look that difficult, but you have to do it several hundred times a day in exactly the same manner. We have job rotations within the group. But they are all similar, just need to use different soldering turrets and follow somewhat different orders of operation.[16]

The above quote reflects the sophisticated application of Taylor's time and motion studies and technique control over line operators through standardization and deskilling. Yet, as noted in Chapter 3, the weakening of workers' marketplace bargaining power is less straightforward than widely thought. While the skill-based marketplace bargaining power of most line operators has been weakened, mechanization and automation has also created a high

---

[14] As a fast-growing, state-owned automaker, SOE-1 was known for its low-price small cars when it first entered China's domestic auto market. The interviewed managers at JVs generally considered the levels of technology and management at SOE-1 low compared with their companies.

[15] The author's field notes, June 2004.   [16] Interview F8, GER-2, August 2004.

FIGURE 4.2. Workers of the state-owned truck maker SOE-2 assembling a truck chassis, 2004
Source: Photograph by the author.

demand for skilled workers, such as repairmen and maintenance workers, who thus have gained substantial marketplace bargaining. Even regular line operators have some marketplace bargaining power, derived from the fact that performance improves with experience, and so management has an interest in keeping labor turnover rates low. Moreover, capital-intensive, JIT production requires continuous and smooth operation of machines to keep down-time to an absolute minimum if profitability is to be achieved. That suggests localized stoppages or disruptions by a small group of workers, whether skilled or semi-skilled, can lead to large losses for capital, which potentially boosts workers' workplace bargaining power.

It is worth noting that the scope of automation in the Chinese auto industry has thus far been limited to certain labor processes and production areas. The major drivers behind automation, according to the interviewed managers, are to enhance productivity and product quality, to perform tasks that are impossible or difficult for human beings to accomplish, and to improve the work environment and reduce work-related physical strains and injuries. Few managers considered labor savings as a major motivator for automation. In fact, the interviewed managers and industry experts have generally recognized that the Chinese auto assembly sector occupies an intermediate position between the capital-intensive industries, in which labor costs are relatively insignificant, and the labor-intensive industries that rely on low-cost labor. Chinese automakers therefore seek to take advantage of both intensive capital/technology inputs and China's competitive advantage in low-cost, quality labor. This point was made clear by a production manager at SOE-1, "To achieve large scales and high volumes in a short time, we rely not only on highly advanced machinery, but also on our hard-working workers – our comparative advantage."[17]

As such, it is common to find automakers in China using the "human wave tactics," by which they mobilize a large number of young, relatively low-cost workers to work long hours at an intense pace on assembly lines, along with incremental mechanization to maximize output. This leads us to a discussion of the working conditions in China's automobile factories.

Working conditions

Working conditions at the major Chinese automobile factories are characterized by heavy workloads, an intense work pace, long working hours, and excessive overtime, although the physical working environments are generally good. To have a sense of how fast assembly lines move in Chinese auto assembly factories compared to the international standard, I take JPN-1 as an example. As of 2006, it took 51 seconds for workers at the Sino-Japanese JV to assemble a compact car. That was only 1.3 seconds slower than at the JV's Japanese partner's flagship plant in Japan (49.7 seconds per car), which is among the fastest assembly plants for compact sedans in the world. During my fieldwork at JPN-1, I observed that workers in the assembly shop had to run to the toilet.[18] About 89 percent of the interviewed workers considered the current production pace to be "very intense." More than 85 percent of the interviewed workers in their 20s did not think they would be able to sustain the current work intensity by the time they had reached their 40s. Similar complaints about the high work intensity were reported by the interviewed workers across all of the studied auto assembly factories.

Working hours in China's auto assembly factories were notoriously long, and compulsory overtime was common. Production lines usually operated in two shifts of 10–12 hours each.[19] Most workers felt exhausted after their shifts. When operating in two shifts of 10 hours each, a regular day shift would often start at 7 a.m., but most automobile factories required workers to arrive at the factory 20–30 minutes ahead of the normal shift starting time to attend pre-shift meetings led by their team leaders and set up their group work areas. At JPN-1 and SOE-1, for example, employees were "encouraged" to participate

---

[17] Interview C3, SOE-1, August 2005.   [18] The author's field notes, JPN-1, May 2007.
[19] Repair and maintenance workers had a different work schedule, usually working three shifts of 8 hours each.

TABLE 4.2. *Regular work schedules at USA-1, June 2007*

Day Shift		Night Shift	
6:30 a.m.	Arrival at factory (required)	5:00 p.m.	Arrival at factory (required)
7:00 a.m.	Shift begins	5:30 p.m.	Shift begins
9:30 a.m.	First break (10 minutes)	7:30 p.m.–8:00 p.m.	Dinner break
11:30 a.m.–12:00 p.m.	Lunch break	11:00 p.m.	First break (10 minutes)
3:00 p.m.	Second break (10 minutes)	1:30 a.m.–2:00 a.m.	Meal Break
5:30 p.m.	End of shift	4:30 a.m.	End of shift
6:00 p.m.	Company bus departure	5:00 a.m.	Company bus departure

in the 10-minute morning calisthenics sessions with martial music, to build "a cohesive enterprise culture."[20] By 6:55 a.m., all workers were expected to report to their work stations and get ready for production. Sharply at 7:00 a.m., the multiple assembly lines started moving. During the day shift, usually there was a 30-minute lunch break and two 10-minute breaks in the morning and afternoon, respectively. Table 4.2 shows regular working hours during the normal production season at USA-1 in June 2007.

Workers often spoke bitterly about the mandatory overtime that management imposed on them without advance notice. As one young line operator at SOE-1 recalled:

During the peak production season, I often go to work without knowing what time I would be off. The line runs until the daily production quota is made. If the manager tells you: today's off time is 7 p.m., then it is. Simple as that.[21]

Moreover, lean production methods have created a more demanding and stressful workplace that requires workers to work longer, harder, and faster, with more pressure and responsibility but little real empowerment and autonomy over their own work. For instance, after the implementation of *kaizen* activities at the body shop of GER-2 in 2006, line speed increased from 85 seconds per sedan to 75 seconds. Together with overtime, production output more than doubled while the number of workers was reduced from 121 to 105.[22] A team leader at the body shop complained:

---

[20] Interview H1, JPN-1, September 2006.   [21] Interview C4, SOE-1, August 2005.

[22] It should be noted that technological change and management's push for increased productivity has not, thus far, cost the jobs of redundant workers, who are often transferred to newly built factories as automobile production in China has continued to expand rapidly. The author's field notes, October 2006.

We have operated three shifts for about a year and production capacity has almost doubled. We have cut 12 workers over the past six months, but the production engineering department keeps on asking us to reduce an extra five people. We all work as hard as we can. You cannot just talk about productivity without considering workers' physical limits! Plus, with the old equipment under the extended service, we have reached the real limit![23]

Indeed, what Parker and Slaughter had observed within the Japanese lean production system can also be seen at China's leading auto assemblers today:

[W]ork standards are constantly *kaizened* upward so that team members work fifty-seven out of sixty seconds; buffers are eliminated so that workers cannot pace themselves and create a break; relief personnel are reduced or eliminated and absent workers are not replaced; responsibility for handling these disruptions is forced downward; the supervisor is therefore pressured to fill out more papers and takes on more tasks; he protects himself by holding out the team leader for production breakdowns, which means team members cannot get bathroom relief when they need it. The result that management desires is for workers to pressure each other to reduce absenteeism and bathroom breaks. (1995: 45–6)

To be sure, physical working environments were generally good at China's leading automakers, especially at the large JVs. Workshops were clean, bright, and air-conditioned. Flexible production devices were installed to help workers identify comfortable postures. Both the workers and managers interviewed took pride in the relatively good working environments, advanced technology and high level of automation of their factories.[24] Nevertheless, there are still particular parts of automobile production that remain dirty, strenuous, and damaging to workers' physical health. For example, workers in the body shop – where a bare car body is assembled – frequently complained about the poor air quality, unbearable heat from welding activities, and the noise.[25]

In sum, the evidence presented above suggests that the current production system in the Chinese automobile industry is in essence a Taylorist/Fordist mass production paradigm in a leaner and more efficient formula. On the one hand, this production model prioritizes large economies of scale and high volumes through intensive capital investment, reckless expansion of production capacity, incremental mechanization and automation, and the intensive use of a relatively inexpensive, young workforce on assembly lines. On the other hand, it adopts lean production techniques and cost-cutting measures to reduce overall production costs and maximize profit. To a large extent, this model resembles the cost-leadership mass production paradigm employed by large South Korean automakers in the 1980s and early 1990s (cf. Rodgers 1996: 87–135).

---

[23] Interview F17, GER-2, October 2006.
[24] It was widely held among the interviewed workers that JVs offered better working environments, higher wages, and were more "modern and advanced" than SOEs.
[25] Interviews F6, F7, GER-2, August 2004.

The dramatic growth of China's automobile production speaks to the effectiveness of this production model: between 2001 and 2010, total investment in production increased by 557.9 percent, output increased by 680 percent, total profits increased by 1,169.3 percent, and average labor productivity increased by 357 percent (CATRC 2011: 8, 11, 466). Yet as discussed in Chapter 3, wage increases of front-line workers have not kept pace with the rapid growth in productivity and profitability during the auto industry boom, suggesting the intensified exploitation of labor. However, this model also has notable limits. On one hand, the labor regime under this production system remains largely the same as the traditional Fordist production system, which is inherently exhausting and authoritarian. Such a work regime has been known to constantly engender strong workplace grievances and antagonism. On the other hand, the JIT system is extremely vulnerable to any disruptions caused by workers' individual and collective actions. Management must find ways to better elicit workers' consent and cooperation. As we will see in Chapters 5 and 6, some leading automakers in China have encountered major problems in labor control due to their adoption of lean production techniques without implementing related employment policies to gain workers' consent and cooperation.

It is important to remember, however, that a factory is not merely a production site; it is also a social institution of certain organizational structures and social relations. In order to understand workers' grievances, bargaining power, and collective actions, we also need to consider the fabric of the personnel system, the factory social order, and the structure of opportunity under which different groups of workers, managers, and factory Party and union cadres make their decisions and interact with each other on a day-to-day basis.

PERSONNEL SYSTEM, HRM PRACTICE, AND FACTORY SOCIAL ORDER

Since China launched the SOE and labor system reforms in the mid- to late 1980s, the ways in which Chinese enterprises manage their employees have undergone profound change. A new terminology – Human Resource Management – came to China, along with a normative, bureaucratic approach to management. At each factory I visited, there was a large HRM department in charge of recruitment, training, job classifications, performance appraisals, compensation, career development, grievances and firing processes. Concurring with previous findings, the HRM practices I observed at China's large automobile enterprises, including both SOEs and JVs, were influenced by both Western and Japanese management systems (cf. Warner 1995, 2000). However, both Western and Japanese approaches to management were only selectively adopted, and "blended" with certain Chinese SOE management practices and socialist legacies.

Four mechanisms are constitutive to the fabric of personnel systems, HRM practices, and factory social order in state-owned and state-controlled large automobile enterprises: (1) the cadre-manager personnel system, which establishes the rationale behind the daily decisions and practices of Chinese cadre managers (including Party and union cadres); (2) the job classification system, which allocates formal employees for different work positions and determines their statuses within the factory hierarchy; (3) the performance appraisal and position wage systems, which constitute the centerpiece of a meritocratic system; and, (4) the operation of internal labor markets and career advancement paths, which form the basis of opportunity structure for formal workers in factory settings. Whereas temporary workers are subject to the same factory rules and regulations, they are largely excluded from the operation of internal labor markets and from the career advancement opportunities available to formal workers.

The cadre-manager personnel system

Under state socialism, Chinese managers were cadres representing the Party-state in the factory (Walder 1986). Studies have suggested that managers running large SOEs and state-controlled JVs in the reform era are still cadre-managers controlled through the Party's *nomenklatura* system (Taylor, Chang & Li 2003). I found this was largely the case at the state-owned and state-controlled large automobile enterprises, including JVs. At each automobile enterprise I visited, there was an enterprise Party committee (EPC) in charge of mobilizing Party members, from top managers to ordinary workers, through various party branches and affiliated organizations such as trade unions and youth leagues. In fact, China's 1994 Company Law mandates that companies in China establish Party organizations, which are considered "an essential feature of the modern enterprise system with Chinese characteristics."

Although the Communist party has withdrawn from direct enterprise administration and management since the factory director (manager) responsibility system was established in 1984, it still maintains its political leadership and makes key personnel appointments in the state sector (Naughton 2007: 317). For example, the Chinese managers of middle rank and above at GER-2 and SOE-2 were appointed by the head office of their Chinese parent company, FAW Group, a centrally-controlled key SOE. Each year, the Organizational and Personnel Department (*zuzhi renshi bu*), under the leadership of the FAW Party Committee, sends evaluation teams to its dozens of subsidiary enterprises to review the work of the preceding year. The evaluation teams conduct interviews with a range of enterprise employees, review the enterprises' finances, and evaluate the work of each manager. The evaluation teams not only examine "hard" criteria, such as production and financial performance, but also look at "soft" criteria, including "cadre-mass relations" and "opinions of masses". The goal is to guarantee that enterprise managers fulfill their economic, political, and social responsibilities in accordance with government priorities – including, among others, improving enterprise efficiency and profitability, generating more employment, building harmonious labor relations, and maintaining social stability. The evaluation results serve as important references when personnel decisions are made concerning who should be promoted or demoted, and who should be transferred to other subsidiaries.[26] Similarly, key personnel appointments and evaluations of Chinese managers at GER-1 and USA-1 were controlled by their Chinese parent company, SAIC, a large public SOE under the supervision of the Shanghai State-owned Assets Supervision and Administration Commission (SASAC).[27]

Moreover, in SOEs, managers traditionally had, for the most part, moved up into the ranks of management from positions as workers on the shop floor. This was the case at SOE-2, a state-owned auto factory built in the late 1960s, for those who had made it into management positions before the 1990s.[28] This also was the case at some JVs, since many Chinese managers were assigned and evaluated by their Chinese parent companies. They were thus influenced by their own shop-floor experiences and tended to be more empathetic toward workers. Although the younger generation of managers has been increasingly recruited directly from China's top-ranking universities as managerial trainees, as opposed to being promoted from shop floors, it was common practice to have the new managerial trainees work on the shop floor for 3–6 months to "accumulate shop-floor experiences."[29] It was believed that such experiences could contribute to their management skills and provide them with crucial experience, including how to effectively deal with workers' grievances and demands.[30]

To be sure, after more than two decades of market and SOE reforms, Chinese SOEs have embraced the logic of a market economy. The intensified competition combined with the share-holding system of ownership has driven major Chinese automakers to prioritize efficiency and profitability. Yet my fieldwork found the resilience of some socialist legacies that have survived in the Chinese management practices on factory shop floors, such as enterprise paternalism, "heart-to-heart talks" and "thought work" with ordinary workers, regular group study meetings among Party members and activists, and campaign-style production mobilization efforts. As we will discuss in detail

---

[26] Interviews Q1, SOE-2, June 2004; F2, GER-2, August 2004. It was rare that a manager could be fired based on the evaluation results, but according to my interviewees, there were cases in which certain managers were transferred to other less important departments due to poor evaluations. Eric Thun's (2006: 120–1) earlier study found similar situations with respect to the personnel system at China's large auto groups.

[27] Interviews S16, GER-1, November 2006; M18, USA-1, December 2006.

[28] Some workers were even sent by the factory to study at the university, after which they returned to the factory to take up positions in management. Interview Q1, SOE-2, June 2004.

[29] The shop-floor training was usually followed by another 3–6 months of comprehensive training in the office, to familiarize managerial trainees with the company's structure and work procedures, as well as the functioning of related departments before they were assigned to a specific department.

[30] Interview S1, GER-1, June 2004.

in Chapter 5, such practices have tended to be effective in mitigating direct labor-management conflicts and eliciting workers' cooperation.

It might be tempting to draw a dichotomy between management practice before and after China's economic reforms, and to consider paternalism, fairness, and concern and sympathy for workers as "socialist residuals," in contrast to the rational, profit-maximizing principles of the market economy in reform-era China. This viewpoint, however, misses the essence of institutional continuity in China's SOEs, and the fact that the incentives for SOE managers in the reform era are continually shaped by the Party-state.[31] As Barry Naughton put it:

Although the Communist Party has...become more meritocratic and development oriented, it obviously does not, and will not, appoint directors to companies solely on the basis of their ability to maximize profit and the value of the government's ownership stake... The Communist Party holds on to its appointment power and thereby continues to shape the career paths and incentives of enterprise managers. (2007: 317)

The following "pragmatic philosophy" of one HR manager at GER-1 makes clear the rationale of cadre-managers at China's large auto enterprises:

Our great leader Deng Xiaoping has a famous saying, "It doesn't matter whether the cat is white or black, as long as it can catch the mouse." We apply the same philosophy to manage our company. That is to say, it doesn't matter what management methods we use, as long as they work for our goal – to make our customers happy, our partner and shareholders happy, our workers happy, and more important, the government happy.[32]

In other words, rather than merely maximizing profit, cadre-managers need to strike a balance between pursuing profitability (to make shareholders happy) and maintaining legitimacy with workers (to make workers happy), which are both essential to making "the government happy." This rationale can help us better understand the resilience of certain socialist legacies, including enterprise paternalism – a common practice under the socialist *danwei* system, and one that has been widely practiced at China's large auto enterprises. As the Vice Chairman of the union at GER-2 indicated:

We always try to provide our workers with higher wages and better benefits based on our company's profitability. Our workers all understand that only if the enterprise, the "big family" (*dajia*) is doing well, can their individual small families (*xiaojia*) do well. That's why both workers and managers work together towards the same goal to make our enterprise more profitable and competitive.[33]

The above quote indicates that management recognizes that certain socialist legacies, such as enterprise paternalism and empathy for workers, do not conflict with the principle of profit-making at all. Instead, if properly combined with modern HRM methods, they can be more effective in eliciting workers' cooperation and extracting labor power that can contribute to a company's

---

[31] For a nuanced analysis of the institutional change and continuity in Chinese firms and management practices under market transition, see Guthrie (1999).

[32] Interview S17, GER-1, November 2006   [33] Interview F11, GER-2, October 2006.

profit making. One might ask how we can be certain that practices such as enterprise paternalism are the results of socialist legacies rather than a reflection of a general capitalist interest in maintaining labor peace and extracting more labor power for profit making. As I will show in subsequent chapters, there continue to be tensions between the goal of increasing profitability and the need to maintain legitimacy with workers. While it is true that all managers have to strike a balance between these two contradictory imperatives, in factories where socialist legacies and norms remain strong, managers have to place greater weight on accommodating workers' legitimate demands based on the same ideology and rhetoric they officially uphold.

The enterprise union

In China, all unions belong to the ACFTU, the sole official union under the leadership of the Chinese Communist Party. Traditionally, trade unions in socialist countries are known for their dualist functions: delivering the State's instructions from the top to workers, and mobilizing workers for production while submitting the demands of workers to the top, in an effort to protect workers' welfare and interests (Pravda and Ruble 1986). This "classical dualism," however, is self-contradictory (Feng 2002). Tensions between the dualist functions of Chinese trade unions have become more apparent under market reform, as the state has retreated from its socialist social contract and from its commitment to protecting workers' interests. Meanwhile, the divisions and conflicts between workers and managers have significantly increased with the rapid development of a capitalist economy and rampant violations of workers' rights and interests (Chan 2001). Critics view the ACFTU as merely a state apparatus whose priority is to service the state's goals of maintaining social stability and upholding political authority, rather than protecting workers' rights (CLB 2009a: 3). A more nuanced view recognizes the "double institutional identity" of the ACFTU and its regional branches as both the state apparatus and the labor organization, whose power in "representing, mediating and pre-empting" labor conflicts derives from their formal government status (Chen 2003: 1006–7; 2009).

Yet at the enterprise level, branches of the ACFTU are generally viewed by workers as incapable of representing their interests and negotiating with employers because they are both financially and organizationally dependent on, and are part of, management.[34] In fact, union officials in state enterprises are often appointed by the Communist Party. They are expected to cooperate with management to promote production rather than to bargain with management over wages and workers' welfare. The enterprise union officials I interviewed all held that trade unions under the leadership of the Communist

---

[34] The majority of funding for the union's operational expenses comes from a 2 percent payroll tax on employers and from the state (Chen 2009).

Party should first assist management to mobilize workers to increase the productivity and profits of the enterprise, and they should at the same time work to represent and protect workers' interests. They emphasized the shared common interests between managers and workers in promoting production and increasing the profits of their enterprises. When asked how the union would react if the interests of managers and workers came into conflict, the union officials simply responded that this was rarely the case. But if conflicts did arise, unions would help to mediate and defuse the conflicts as quickly as possible. When asked about the union's response to the use of temporary agency workers and student intern workers, the union officials either responded that, "This is necessary for our enterprise to stay competitive," or, "This is the trend in the industry."[35] Apparently, there was no resistance from unions to the spread of labor force dualism. This inability or reluctance to recognize the existence of conflicts of interest between workers and managers indicated that the enterprise unions were not effective in representing workers' interests and protecting their rights. As we will discuss in more detail in Chapters 5 and 6, the enterprise unions' primary functions are to organize social and recreational activities among employees and to assist management in promoting production and mediating labor-management conflicts.

Job classifications, status, and factory hierarchy

Unlike the detailed job classifications and descriptions that existed at the "Big Three" U.S. automakers in Detroit decades ago, I found job classifications at China's major automobile enterprises were more loosely defined categories based on authority, level of responsibility and the nature of each position.[36] It was probably closer to the Japanese job classification system, as team-oriented production required multi-skilled workers and broader job classifications so that each team member could be allocated to different posts within his work team. For example, as seen below, the Sino-American JV USA-1 classified job posts into ten categories and 18 classifications, of which only four categories and six classifications (A, B1, C1, C2, D1, and D2) were designated for production workers. By contrast, Kochan and colleagues (1994) reported that the unionized plants in a multidivisional U.S. automobile firm had an average of 96 job classifications for production workers. In recent years, under pressure from U.S.-based auto companies to reduce

---

[35] Interviews S16, GER-1, June 2004; F5, GER-2, August 2004; C3, SOE-1, August 2005; Q18, SOE-2, October 2006; M16, M17, USA-1, December 2006; D11, USA-2, April 2007.

[36] Job classifications at the plant level are based on job positions (*gang wei*), which are related to, but differ from, occupation-based skilled trades classifications (see Chapter 3). The general trend in the Chinese automobile industry is to simplify job classifications at the enterprise level to improve work flexibility, while developing more specific and standardized skilled trades classifications at the industry level, for the purposes of better training and assessment of skilled workers. In other words, workers are required to master multiple skills so that they will be able to perform more than one job.

the number of job classifications and improve work flexibility, the United Auto Workers (UAW) agreed to fewer job classifications at unionized U.S. auto plants. For instance, under the terms of a 2011 contract, the number of skilled trades classifications was reduced from 27 to a mere five (Jones 2013).[37]

Job classifications at USA-1

Classification A: Manufacturing On-line Operator
Classification B1: Off-line Operator
Classification B2: Clerk
Classification C1: Manufacturing Repair Team Member
Classification C2: Manufacturing Maintenance
Classification D1: Production Team Leader
Classification D2: Maintenance Team Leader
Classification E1: Secretary to Section/Shop Manger
Classification E2: Engineer
Classification E3: Chief Engineer
Classification G1: Administrative Supervisor
Classification G2: Supervisor of Specialized Functions
Classification G3: Senior Supervisor of Specialized Functions
Classification H1: Executive Committee Secretary
Classification H2: Shift Leader
Classification I: Shop Manager, Chief Designer, Chief Engineer
Classification J: Executive Director, Director
Classification S: Expert

However, unlike Japan, where status differences between staff and workers within companies were diminished as a result of the postwar labor movement (Gordon 1996; Kume 1998), the job classification system in China has tended to group workers and managerial staff into different ranks and statuses based on their work positions and to institutionalize these distinctions in the factory hierarchy. The job classifications are based on performance appraisals and directly linked to the position wage system. Each formal contract employee is appraised and allocated to a specific work position within a certain job classification based on education and skill qualifications, experience, competency and performance. Each job classification corresponds to a position wage grade (*gangwei gongzi dengji*), a certain labor contract term (job security), specified functions, duties, and rights, and channels for advancement – in short, a classification signals a worker's status within the factory. For example, at USA-1, the HRM department

---

[37] See also the "2011 UAW-Ford Contract Settlement Agreement," Appendix F: Classifications: 049B–050B. This move has caused wide concerns and criticism among rank-and-file UAW members. See, for example, Eisenstein (2011), and Kaminski (2007).

TABLE 4.3. *Labor contract terms for formal employees by job classification at USA-1*

Job Classification		Number	%	Contract Term (renewable)
Operator (A,B1)	Unskilled	375	6.8	1 year
	Semi-skilled/ Skilled	2,030	36.7	1 year
Clerk (B2)		44	0.8	1 year
Maintenance, Technician (C1–C2)		508	9.2	2 year
Team Leader (D1–D2)		500	9.0	2 year
Specialist, Technical Professional (E1–E3)		1,226	22.1	2 year
Supervisor, Lead Engineer (G1–G3)		511	9.2	3 year
Shift Leader (H1–H2)		131	2.4	3 year
Senior Manager, Chief Designer, Chief Engineer (I)		156	2.8	Open-term
Executive Director, Director, Expert (J,S)		54	1.0	Open-term
TOTAL		5,535	100.0	

Source: The HRM Department of USA-1, November 2006.

classified those with job classifications A to D2 as blue-collar production workers, and those with job classifications E1 and above as white-collar managerial employees and technical staff (Table 4.3). Temporary workers were listed separately on the companies' official employee rosters; most were classified as unskilled/semi-skilled line operators, except for a very few skilled temporary workers. Temporary workers were at the bottom of the factory hierarchy.

Staff and workers were drawn from different labor markets through different recruitment channels, and upon being hired entered into separate career tracks and training programs. They also had different work hours and separate work environments. The crucial yardstick management used in determining a formal employee's status as staff or worker was his/her educational attainment. Most newly recruited managerial and engineering staff had at least a Bachelor's degree from one of China's top-ranking universities. As seen in Table 4.4 and Table 4.5, at GER-1 and GER-2, a formal employee's education directly determined his work position, wage grade, labor contract term – in short, his status as a white-collar staff member or a blue-collar worker. Moreover, as in Japan, not only was a 4-year university degree "the ticket-of-entry into managerial ranks" (Dore 1973: 48), but also the prestige of universities largely decided a graduate's chance of being selected into the managerial ranks. Until recently, the leading automakers in China would only consider applicants from top universities when

TABLE 4.4. *Work position and wage grade by education level at GER-1ᵃ*

Work Position	Required Education Degree	Wage Gradeᵇ in Probation	Wage Grade after Probation
Direct and Subsidiary Production Workers	Technical secondary school	A2/Z2	A3/Z3
	Junior college & above	A3/Z3	A4/Z4
Technician	Technical secondary school	B1	B2
	Junior college & above	B2	B3
	Junior college with work experience	B3	C1
Engineering & Management Staff	Bachelor's	C1	C2
	Master's without work experience	C2	C3
	Master's with >=3 years work experience	C2	C4
	Ph.D. without work experience	C4	C5
	Ph.D. with >=3 years work experience	C4	C6

Notes: ᵃ This table only applies to formal employees; temporary workers have pre-set wage rates.
ᵇ The position wage grades of formal employees are divided into 7 categories and 49 grades, starting from A1 for direct production workers and Z1 for subsidiary production workers. F4 is the highest grade, applicable to special experts and senior managers.

TABLE 4.5. *Labor contract terms by education and work position at GER-2*

Education Degree	Work Position	Terms of Labor Contract
Bachelor's & above	Management staff	5-5 – non-fixed
	Non-management	2-2-3-3 – non-fixed
Below Bachelor's	Non-management	2-2-2-2-2 – non-fixed

recruiting managerial and engineering staff.[38] It has also become more and more common to recruit professional managers and engineers with substantial work experience from outside.

[38] With the rapid expansion of the automobile industry in recent years there has come a severe shortage of managerial and engineering talents. According to a 2006 report by the China Automotive Talents Society, the supply-demand ratio of university graduates with an automotive engineering specialty to open positions requiring such talents was 1:20. The intense competition for university manpower has driven many large automakers to establish long-term collaborations with universities, including some second-tier universities, to build "talent reservoirs" through college internship programs and pre-selected recruitment.

To be sure, overt status distinctions between white-collar staff and blue-collar workers varied among the automobile factories studied. At GER-1, for example, the factory organization was very hierarchical. Managers had reserved parking lots, and a separate dining hall was designated for foreign managers and senior Chinese managers. Management also adopted a "visual control method," and workers of different "statuses" wore different colored work uniforms – technicians and team leaders wore gray uniforms, formal workers dark blue, and temporary workers wore two different sky-blue uniforms, with the different shades being used to identify the "old" and the "new" temps. At JPN-1, by contrast, in order to embody the company's egalitarian culture promoted by its Japanese partner, workers and managerial staff wore the same uniform, ate in the same cafeteria, shared the same parking lots, and performed morning exercises together. Managerial staff worked in a large office with open cubicles adjacent to the production shop floor. Even the general manager's office had only a glass wall to separate it from the other offices. The difference might be explained by the organizational legacies of the Chinese partners, as well as the different roles played by the foreign partners. For example, GER-1 is one of China's earliest and most successful auto JVs. Its Chinese partner had more confidence and a stronger voice in the operation of the enterprise. Its German partner opted to take control over the technology in the JV while leaving HRM and labor control to its Chinese partner. Accordingly, GER-1 inherited more of the SOE "traditions" from its Chinese parent company. At JPN-1, on the other hand, a past failure at operating a JV with another foreign automaker led the Chinese partner to rely more on its current Japanese partner. The Japanese automaker thus took a leading role in management at JPN-1, from production to HRM, including the implementation of an egalitarian culture as the JV's core value.

In general, excepting GER-1, management has sought to conceal or obscure the outward status distinctions between managerial staff and production workers. However, the overall factory structure in China's large automobile enterprises remains very hierarchical, and distinctions between blue-collar workers and white-collar staff are institutionalized through the job classification and position-status systems that link work position to status.

Discrimination against blue-collar workers in wage and social status is not unique to China, and it has been documented in both Western and Eastern factories. Using education credentials to divide workers is also a common strategy of employers. It often leads to antagonistic employment relations and labor-management conflicts.[39] This issue tended to incite more resentment among the

---

[39] For instance, Hagen Koo (2001) documented the sharp division between manual and non-manual workers in South Korea, a main factor contributing to the labor-management conflicts and labor militancy in South Korea in the 1970s and 1980s. David Collinson's (1992) case study of a truck factory in England also found that manual workers' deep discontent was a direct consequence of their status as "second-class citizens" compared to white-collar employees at the factory.

interviewed Chinese workers. That might have to do with the socialist egalitarian legacy, especially the Maoist "democratic management" experiments in the factories, as they raised workers' awareness of workplace democracy and of the inequality between factory cadres and workers (Zhang 2005). China's market and SOE reforms, however, changed labor relations profoundly, making the divisions between managerial staff and production workers sharper and more apparent. In interviews, I often heard veteran workers at the early-built factories expressing nostalgia for the "good old days," when workers had a higher status and managers tended to be more "democratic" and accessible within the factory. As a veteran team leader at GER-2 recounted:

Workers nowadays don't have any power. I used to work at a tool factory in the "big yard" (*da yuan*, referring to FAW's headquarters) in the early 1980s. Back then, it was much more democratic. Workers could say what they thought directly to factory cadres (*ganbu*). Everyone, cadres and workers alike, was expected to work together to contribute to our factory. When sacrifices were needed, cadres took the lead. Now, it is one-man rule. No one dares say anything negative about managers. You don't need someone to tell you to shut up if you don't want to make things hard for yourself in the factory. You know, back to the early 1980s, a skilled worker could earn as much as a shop manager. Now, managers can earn as much as 10–15 times of what workers make.[40]

The hierarchal factory structure and institutionalized inferior status of blue-collar workers was one of the main sources of formal workers' complaints and discontent. The difference in status between white-collar staff and production workers was further entrenched by educational credentialism, which made it even harder for a blue-collar worker to advance from the shop floor. Nevertheless, there were some opportunities for ordinary workers to move up within the factory hierarchy as the major Chinese automobile factories moved to adopt a meritocratic system.

The rise of meritocracy: Performance appraisals and the position-merit wage system

Another notable feature of the factory social order at China's large automobile factories is the rise of a meritocratic system based on performance appraisals and a "position-merit wage system" (*gangwei jixiao gongzi zhi*), which takes into account both one's work position and daily performance. It is similar to the Japanese *satei* system (meritocratic system) that prevailed from the post-WWII period until the crisis of the early 1990s. The performance appraisals include not only the objective results of one's work, but also an evaluation of one's behavior and attitude, in particular, the employee's level of conformity with the expected standards of the employer – that is, "the subjective dimension of the evaluation" (Durand et al. 1999: 28). The results of the performance appraisals are directly linked to employees' wages and bonuses. More

[40] Interview F10, GER-2, October 2006.

important, they are a key factor used in determining raises and promotions. In practice, shop-floor managers often placed some limitations on the competition between workers based on certain percentage quotas for the distribution of appraisal results. For example, at a body shop of GER-2, a team leader would mark 10 percent of workers in his group as "excellent," with an extra 10 percent in bonus over the average; 10 percent of workers as "unsatisfactory," with a bonus 10 percent less than the average; and, the remaining 80 percent of workers as average or "satisfactory." If the difference in bonuses paid to two workers in the same work group exceeded 200 *yuan*, a team leader would have to get approval from his foreman. This was considered necessary to avoid causing conflicts within work groups, a residual of the SOEs' egalitarian culture that is still evident on the Chinese shop floor.[41]

Job classifications and performance appraisals are the centerpieces of the position-merit wage system, which is in essence a merit wage system that emphasizes an employee's capabilities and performance. It consists of four components:

1) **Base Pay** – Position Wage* + Seniority Pay
2) **Bonus** – Individual Merit Bonus (monthly)** + Company Profitability Bonus (annually)
3) **The Comprehensive Premium (allowance)** – Mid-night and night shift premium, whole attendance bonus, the nationally-stipulated subsidy of non-staple food, housing, and transportation, etc.
4) **Overtime Pay**
* *Position Wage= Basic wage rate* based on *position wage grade* + (maximum-minimum) * *range percentage*.
** *Individual Merit Bonus = Basic wage rate * range percentage * Appraisal coefficient*

From the four components above, we can see that, unlike in a piece-rate system, a worker's performance appraisals are at the center of the position-merit wage system. After being classified into a certain work position, a formal employee will be appraised for competency and performance by his/her department director, to receive a "range percentage" – sometimes referred to as a "position coefficient."[42] The range percentage is modified each year to reflect changes to

---

[41] Notably, the Japanese performance-appraisal system also sets certain threshold percentages for evaluators, to limit competition and bonus differences between employees. The interviewed team leaders and foremen regarded such practices in Chinese factories as the residue of SOE's egalitarian culture.

[42] The Range Percentage, which fell between 0 percent~100 percent, was determined by comparing the experience of the relevant employee with other employees with the same job classification in the same department. An employee classified from A to H2 was appraised by his department director, and that appraisal was confirmed or adjusted by the HRM Department. The Executive Committee was responsible for conducting appraisals of employees classified as I, J, and S. Interview M1, USA-1, January 2005.

an employee's "merit" rank, which has a direct influence on the employee's wages. Besides the annual performance appraisals, production workers are appraised once per quarter or per month, depending on the individual company's policy. The performance appraisal results, or the appraisal coefficients, are also linked to employees' monthly and annual merit bonuses. Under this position-merit wage system, bonuses are the major component of the total wage, usually accounting for 1/2–2/3 of a production worker's total wages. For instance, the monthly base pay of a formal maintenance worker who had worked at USA-1 for eight years was only 2,200 *yuan* ($340) in 2010; but, he could earn as much as 8,000 *yuan* ($1,240) per month through overtime, "double-pay" (*shuang xin*), and an annual bonus.[43] In fact, using regularized double-pay – remunerating workers with two-months' pay for certain months – has become common practice among China's leading automakers.[44] One might wonder why management would use regular double-pay to increase workers' income, rather than achieving the same end through normalized wage increase mechanisms. The reason, according to the HR manager of USA-1, is revealing:

Although our company has been doing pretty well, there is a great deal of uncertainty in China's competitive auto market. Once you raise workers' base pay, it would be very difficult to bring it down. By using double-pay and other bonuses to motivate workers in good times, we can also cut back easily the bonuses in bad times."[45]

To put it in the workers' words, "such a wage system is designed for management to have all the control and say over workers' pay."[46]

Notably, I found some early-built automobile factories, such as GER-1 and GER-2, used a "position-grade wage system" (*gangwei dengji gongzi zhi*) that combined both seniority-based and merit wage systems.[47] As its name indicates, the basis of this wage system is the "position grade," based on one's work position and seniority. Each grade has three steps, each with an associated position coefficient. One can expect to get a one-step wage increase every year, unless they are promoted to a managerial position or become a mechanic or technician. Thus, seniority still plays an important role in the position-grade wage system. For example, during my fieldwork at GER-1, a new hire working at the same line-operating position with the same skill level could earn only 2/3 or less the wages of a senior operator. The position-grade wage system consists of the same three components as the position-merit wage system discussed above, but the former differs in that base pay accounts for a larger percentage of a formal employee's total monthly income – 50–70 percent – which is a

---

[43] Interview M32, USA-1, July 2011.
[44] For example, management at USA-1 and USA-2 designated the months of April and September as double-pay months, thereby regularizing a 14-month annual pay schedule. At JPN-1, workers expected double-pay every other month, meaning they were able to receive up to 18 months of salary annually. The author's field notes, July 2011.
[45] Interview M31, USA-1, July 2011.   [46] Interview M32, USA-1, July 2011.
[47] In late 2006, GER-2 carried through a wage and reward system reform in which it adopted the position-merit wage system.

relatively fixed item in determining an employee's work position and seniority. While the bonus is also based on performance appraisals, it has become a relatively small component in the total wage package, particularly when compared to the position-merit wage system. The position-grade wage system is said to provide employees with a more stable monthly income and to better recognize seniority, while still rewarding employees' with bonuses based on merit. It reflects a compromise between the status quo, seniority-status-driven wage system and the market-oriented, merit-based wage system. In general, China's major automakers have continued their move toward meritocracy and the position-merit wage system by placing greater emphasis on workers' merit and performance and downplaying seniority, and by linking individual workers' economic rewards to their employers' performance and profitability.

The rise of a meritocratic system based on performance appraisals and the position-merit wage system directly affects workers' opportunities for advancement and economic well-being in the factory. First, it encourages workers to view themselves as sharing common interests with their employers in a highly competitive market environment. It also resonates with the Chinese state's strategy in the reform era to develop a new set of market values and foster individualism by emphasizing competition, individual merit, and market-based solutions. Second, given the centrality of performance appraisals in a meritocratic system, it is very important for workers to receive good performance appraisal scores if they are to advance in the factory. That means workers have to conform to management expectations, especially those of their direct supervisors who conduct performance appraisals – their team leaders and foremen. As Richard Edwards (1979: 151) put it, "bureaucratic control establishes not only a real hierarchy of persons but also an ideal hierarchy of traits characterizing the good worker." At the same time, a meritocratic system promises, at least rhetorically, equal opportunities for workers to advance based on their own efforts. It gives young workers the hope that they will be able to move up relatively quickly if they work hard. Veteran workers in their forties, by contrast, are more likely to feel ill-treated as their seniority-based privileges are further reduced and their chances for promotion become slim. This has a direct impact on workers' coping strategies in the workplace, as we will discuss in Chapter 5.

What, then, are the paths available for a blue-collar worker to advance from the shop floor at a large automobile factory today? This brings us to another important aspect of the factory social order – the operation of internal labor markets and the structure of opportunity for a blue-collar worker to move up in a hierarchical factory setting.

THE OPERATION OF INTERNAL LABOR MARKETS AND THE STRUCTURE OF OPPORTUNITY

Studies utilizing the notion of internal labor markets (ILMs) can be sorted into two broad groups. One views ILMs as a set of administrative rules governing the hiring, firing, promotion, and pricing of labor (Doeringer and Piore 1971:4–5). This approach argues that the existence of an ILM is due to the employers' need for firm-specific skills that can only be obtained through on-the-job training and the maintenance of a highly skilled and stable workforce. The other emphasizes ILMs as part of management "bureaucratic control" (Edwards 1979), with the operations of job classifications, graded career ladders and seniority-based wage systems being designed to win employees' loyalty and to encourage workers to identify their own interests and goals as being concordant with those of the company and management (Burawoy 1979; Edwards 1979).

I found both views were relevant in the operation of the ILMs at the large automobile factories in China. First, concordant with the functionalist view, large automakers use ILMs to stabilize a skilled and committed core segment of workforce. As detailed in Chapter 3, starting from the pre-employment vocational training and apprenticeship system and followed by strict screenings, the large automobile enterprises recruit new workers from a pool of quality candidates in the external labor markets at the bottom of the job hierarchy, and then fill more advanced posts through a process of internal training and promotion (cf. Doeringer and Piore 1971: 165–7). The view of ILMs as a means of management bureaucratic control is more relevant when it comes to promotions and opportunities for advancement. The HRM departments of the major automobile factories fulfill an important function in the "career development" of their formal employees. A "dual career path" model is widely used to direct new recruits toward either a managerial path or a technical path, and then to guide them as they climb the career ladder in accordance with the specific rules and requirements of each path (Figure 4.3).

As seen from Figure 4.3, in theory, a blue-collar formal worker can either take the managerial path by trying to become a team leader and then look to climb the ladders of management; or, choose the less prestigious technical path and become a skilled technician or craftsman,[48] and then, hopefully, an engineer.

In reality, the technical positions require seniority, and are often reserved for workers from certain departments, such as maintenance/repair and quality control. New hires with a 12-year education – the minimum requirement – but without any related previous work experience are classified as unskilled workers, and they can expect to attain semi-skilled worker status within one to two years by working on the line. For semi-skilled workers to become skilled workers, they must remain at their current post for at least two years and obtain an advanced-level vocational qualification certificate. For skilled workers to become mechanics or technicians would require that they work at

---

[48] Technicians start with a higher level of school education, usually having attended at least a technical junior college or a higher vocational school, whereas craftsmen are required only to have completed secondary vocational and technical education.

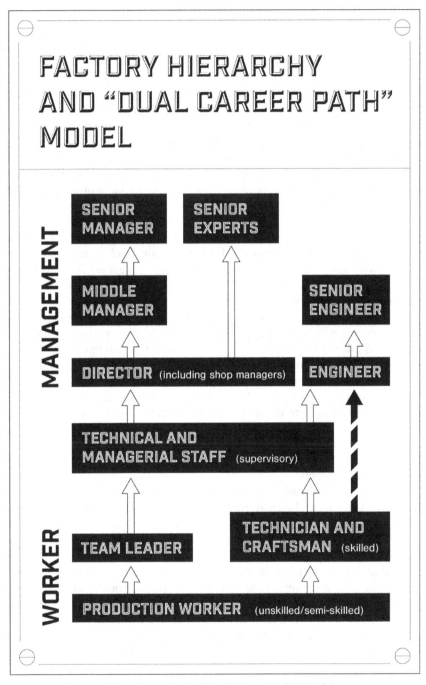

FIGURE 4.3. Factory Hierarchy and the "Dual Career Path" Model

the factory for at least three years and pass the factory-organized examinations before they are qualified to apply for a technician position in the factory.

Therefore, for a young line worker, becoming a team leader is perhaps a more feasible path to move up through individual efforts. Then how is a team leader selected? My interviewees indicated that there were generally two channels: a blue-collar worker with a junior college degree or equivalent could be selected from the ranks through open competition; and, a managerial trainee with a Bachelor's degree, directly assigned to the team from above, could be promoted after obtaining some shop-floor work experience. Among the 15 team leaders I interviewed, 11 had worked their way up from the bench. My interviews with firm-level managers also suggested that the "worker turned team leader" was preferred because they tended to be more capable and popular among workers than the "top-down" managerial trainees. Certainly the specific selection criteria and processes varied by factory. For example, at GER-1, GER-2, and USA-1, team leaders were selected from a "team leader candidate pool," which consisted of reserve team leaders and "advanced workers" with good performance appraisal scores. Whenever there were new openings, workers already in the candidate pool had priority in applying for the positions by virtue of having completed the relevant training and passing the required examinations. The shop manager then could choose a new team leader based on the examination results. At SOE-1 and SOE-2, all employees could submit an application to their foreman in response to a job opening; however, they would need recommendations from their current team leader. There was often an upper limit of two to three candidates that each team leader could recommend from his group. The foreman then selected and submitted a short-list for his work section to the shop manager, and the shop manager made the final decisions. At JPN-1, team leaders were selected exclusively from a pool of workers who had graduated from the "Team Leader Training Program" at a local technology junior college, with the training program tailored to meet JPN-1's specific requirements.

The next question is, what are some criteria for a blue-collar worker to be selected as a team leader? According to the interviewed workers and managers, educational credentials and personal merit and ability mattered most. All the studied factories required a minimum of a junior college degree for a team leader position. Criteria such as good performance appraisal records, demonstrated skill and proficiency in conducting quality work, good work ethic, faithful adherence to company rules, and other qualifications were often listed as selection criteria for a team leader position. But educational credentials and demonstrations of merit were not in themselves enough. The interviewed workers all mentioned the importance of having good connections (*guanxi*) with their team leaders and foremen in order to secure recommendations and have a better chance of being promoted.

Workers differed widely, however, in their opinions about how important merit and ability – that is, workers' individual efforts – were considered as prerequisites for becoming team leaders. On the one hand, there were success stories of capable, blue-collar line workers becoming team leaders through open competition on the strength of their merit and ability. For instance, a team leader whose nickname was "Versatile Hand" described his successful experience in moving up from the ranks (Table 4.6):

I graduated from Changchun Automobile Industry Institute in 2001 with a middle-level qualification as a repair electronic mechanic. I worked one-year as a student apprentice at the factory before becoming a formal contract worker. All new workers here start from the bottom as line operators. So I worked as a line operator on the Jetta line for 3 years. I was ranked at the 4th grade and the 3rd step – the highest among operators. I also became the multi-functional man in my work group and entered the "team leader reservoir" during this time period. My team leader and workmates trusted me. When they posted five openings for mechanics in my shop on the factory billboard, I submitted an application and took the training and exam. I felt I had a good chance. And I did. A year later, when my team leader was promoted to an assistant foreman, he recommended me and I became a team leader. I think the system is good and everyone has a fair chance to move up through hard work and persistent efforts.[49]

On the other hand, criticisms about opaque selection processes and management favoritism and corruption in the selection process were often heard from the interviewed workers. For example, a 31-year-old skilled machine operator who was frustrated by his "failed experience" of competing for a maintenance electrician position was sharply critical:

I have been working as a skilled machine operator for 5 years, and I am ranked the highest among operators. When they had five openings for maintenance electrician in my shop two years ago, I submitted an application and took the examination. My score was the fourth highest among the 39 applicants. But in the end, I was not selected because I did not have close *guanxi* (connections) with my team leader and the foremen. Nor did I give them bribes – I was too naïve and believed it was a fair merit system. Now I have no faith in this system any more. You know, here, just like all the other SOEs, the most important thing is to have good *guanxi* with your *lingdao* (supervisors), no matter whether it is to get promotions, to get a good job assignment, or to attend off-line training classes. How can you build good relations with your *lingdao*? Well, it's simple – flattery and bribery.[50]

Young workers in their 20s tended to be more optimistic about their advancement prospects within the factory than veteran workers in their 30s and 40s. As one ambitious and hopeful 25-year-old assembler at SOE-1 commented:

I would say it's probably half merit and half *guanxi*. They cannot just pick someone they like but who is incompetent [as a team leader] because that would hurt production. And production is the most important thing here. So I think there are chances out there and you just have to work very hard to seize any opportunities.[51]

---

[49] Interview F17, GER-2, October 2006.   [50] Interview F12, GER-2, October 2006.
[51] Interview C8, SOE-1, August 2005.

TABLE 4.6. *Career path of a team leader at GER-2*

(RMB *yuan*)

Year	Work Position	Position Grade	Scale Rank	Contract Term	Position Pay	Bonus	Allowance	Total Monthly Income
2000	Student Apprentice		1st		600	0	0	600
2001	Semi-skilled Operator	(3rd)	1st	1 year	600	1,000	400	2,000
2002	Semi-skilled Operator		2nd	1 year	700	1,000	600	2,200
2003	Skilled Operator (Multi-function)	(4th)	3rd	3 year	800	1,000	600	2,400
2004	Electrical Mechanic	(5th)	4th		900	1,000	800	2,700
2005	Team Leader	(5th)	5th		1,100	1,200	800	3,100
2006	Team Leader	(5th)	5th	3 year	1,800	1,400	1,000	4,200 (Wage Reform)

In general, my interview data suggested that, although there was skepticism and criticism concerning the fairness and efficiency of the meritocratic system and the operation of ILMs, young workers tended to see more opportunities to move up based on their own efforts and merits. Especially given the rapid expansion of automobile production in China, young workers feel optimistic that they might have more opportunities to become team leaders or skilled technicians and mechanics as new plants continue to be built and new lines and shifts continue to be added. But the important question is: how many blue-collar workers have actually been able to move up from the ranks in China's large and hierarchical automobile factories thus far? We will return to this question in Chapter 5.

In summary, the factory social order at China's major automobile enterprises can be characterized by three main features. First, the organizational structure is very hierarchical, and there is a marked distinction between staff and workers, with blue-collar workers' inferior status being institutionalized. Second, China's major automakers have established a formalized, comprehensive, and meritocratic HRM system based on job classifications, performance appraisals, and a position-merit wage system. Third, ILMs operate in a way that creates "dual career paths." Together, they tend to create some institutional opportunities for blue-collar formal workers, especially for younger workers, to move up from the ranks. By contrast, temporary workers were largely excluded from the operations of ILMs. As we will see in Chapter 6, most temporary workers have little chance for advancement at work, no matter how long and how hard they have worked for the automobile factories.

Having examined the factory setting, we now proceed to the third and fourth levels of Katznelson's (1986) framework of working-class formation, to explore workers' lived shop-floor experiences, their aspirations, grievances, bargaining power, and collective actions in Chapters 5 and 6.

5

Hegemonic consent? Formal workers' compliance and resistance

> The working class is neither pure combativity, nor pure passive dispersal, nor pure institutionalized apparatus. It is a complex, moving relation between different practical forms.[1]
>
> ——Connell (1983), "Class, Gender and Sartre's Theory of Practice," 69

> Social agents are not passive bearers of ideology, but active appropriators who reproduce existing structures only through struggle, contestation, and a partial penetration of those structures.
>
> ——Willis (1977), *Learning to Labour*, 175

One of the central arguments of this book is that the dynamics of labor politics in the Chinese automobile industry largely depend on the directions and outcomes of labor force dualism. More specifically, they depend on the inter-relationships between management, the core segment of formal workers, and the flexible segment of temporary workers. This chapter focuses on the formal workers, their contradictory dispositions and their changing relations with management. On the one hand, I found that, far from the assumption of "affluent workers, contented workers," the current generation of formal auto-workers had major grievances, derived from a grueling workplace as well as their inferior status as blue-collar manual workers in a hierarchical factory. On the other hand, formal workers still enjoyed higher-than-average wages and relatively secure employment as core workers in China's booming auto industry. In particular, the buffer created by the presence of a large number of temporary workers under labor force dualism has provided formal workers with some sense of protection. Moreover, management labor control strategies over formal workers at China's large automobile factories were sophisticated and hegemonic in nature. As a result, most formal workers tended to resort to

[1] Quoted in Fantasia 1988: 17.

individual coping strategies when faced with a more demanding workplace and management prerogatives. However, intense competition in the automobile industry has driven management to gradually reduce the protections and privileges afforded to formal workers. As a result, there has been declining consent and emerging resistance among formal workers on the shop floor, ranging from hidden "everyday forms of resistance" (Scott 1985) to open protest, and in extreme cases, sit-down strikes. The seeming quiescence of formal workers can best be understood as a process of negotiated compliance, not consent.

COLLECTIVE CHARACTERISTICS OF FORMAL WORKERS: YOUNGSTERS AND VETERANS

As noted in Chapter 3, the new generation of formal production workers consists of a vast majority of semi-skilled, urban-bred youngsters with relatively short-term, renewable labor contracts, and a small segment of skilled, veteran workers with permanent or long-term employment.

Hopeful youngsters: Aspirations to "Exit" from the line

The younger generation of formal production workers has relatively high educational qualifications, and they tend to have high expectations for wages, working conditions, and advancement opportunities at the "well-known, modern and advanced" large automobile enterprises. But the reality of the monotonous and grueling work on the assembly line often causes feelings of frustration and dissatisfaction among them. At the same time, the operation of ILMs (see Chapter 4) and their relatively high qualifications, have given many young workers the hope that they will be able to "exit" the line and move up in the factory hierarchy. The following quote from a 24-year-old welder is representative:

I graduated from an automotive technical junior college three years ago. I was trained as a maintenance electrician, but now I am here wasting my life doing these nasty, boring, spot-welding tasks every day! I've got the senior-level skilled trades certificate. I am waiting for a new opening for an electrician position at the maintenance and repair division so that I can apply and get out of here.[2]

The meritocratic rhetoric based on educational credentials also motivates young formal workers to pursue further education and training in their spare time, hoping to get out of the shop and find a "9 a.m.–5 p.m. office job." As a 23-year-old assembler recounted:

I have been attending night schools preparing for the National Computer Rank Examination and Public English Test for two years. My goal is to pass the examinations

---

[2] Interview F18, GER-2, October, 2006.

and get intermediate level certificates in both Computer and English. I wish I could eventually find a 9 a.m.–5 p.m. office job. You know, there is no future as a factory worker nowadays.[3]

Such aspirations among the young workers to "exit" from the line, and from manual work, are reminiscent of Ely Chinoy's 1950s study of American autoworkers. Chinoy found that American autoworkers tried to "maintain the illusion of persisting ambition by defining their jobs in the factory as 'temporary' and by incessantly talking of their out-of-the-shop goals and expectations" (Chinoy 1992: 123). Similarly, young autoworkers in early twenty-first century China express the same aspirations and hopes as their U.S. predecessors half a century ago – to get an off-line position, to move up from the ranks, to get out of the factory, and to achieve the "rich and full sense of self" that they rarely find on the automobile assembly line (Chinoy 1992: 86). Among the 45 formal line workers under the age of 30 that I interviewed, 38 expressed their aspirations to "exit" from the assembly line. Among them, 26 hoped to move up within the factory as they followed one of the dual career paths. The remaining 12 planned to get out of the factory altogether – to get a "9 a.m.–5 p.m. office job," to become an auto salesman, or to open their own small business. They were all youngsters in their 20s, with one- to two-year renewable labor contracts and relatively short tenures. The details of their plans varied, but what was important to them was to do something "more interesting, not tying you to the conveyors and pressing you to catch up with the line all the time"; something that offered "the freedom to move around and do things at your own pace"; or something that "makes you feel like a human being, not a machine." A 26-year-old assembler who had worked on the line for five years revealingly remarked:

I am only here for the money. This job would leave me without any other knowledge, skill, or mind even if I continue doing it for another ten years. And I would definitely be worn out by then. Who knows what is going to happen in the next five years? For now, the market is booming, the company is doing well, and the pay is good. I am trying to save as much as possible so that I can open my own business one day. I don't have a clear business plan yet. Maybe an auto parts and repair/maintenance shop. I know it is not easy, but I want to be my own boss, doing something I like and building up things for myself.[4]

Cynical veterans: "Voice" with no faith in change

About one quarter of the formal workers interviewed had worked for their current employers for more than five years.[5] Most held skilled positions or worked as shop-floor managers, in roles such as foreman and team leader.

---

[3] Interview D19, USA-2, April 2007.   [4] Interview M6, USA-1, January 2005.
[5] See Methodological Appendix for detailed information on the age and seniority of the interviewed formal workers.

Compared to young workers, veteran workers generally had more job security, with three- to five-year renewable contracts or open-ended contracts with no set termination date (until they reached retirement age).

As discussed in Chapter 4, a merit-based system has been established in the Chinese automobile factories. On the shop floor, however, seniority still plays a big role in wages and job assignments, especially at those early-built factories. At the Sino-German JV GER-1, for example, the annual income (including benefits and bonus) of a senior production worker could reach 100,000 *yuan* ($14,700) in 2004, almost twice the income of a new hire in the same position. The young workers interviewed often complained about the unequal treatment of veteran and young workers:

It is unfair that we have to do most of the heavy work, and those *laoren* (old workers) can just walk around and do some light tasks, but they can still earn twice as much as we do.[6]

Veteran workers, by contrast, tended to see themselves as founding members and the backbone of the factory where they had worked for many years. They expected to receive favorable treatment and rewards from their employers in return for their long-term service and loyalty. However, with the general move toward a more meritocratic system that does not pay special respect to seniority in the way that it used to, many veteran workers felt they were being ill-treated and harbored resentment over their lost privileges. For example, a maintenance worker who had worked at the Sino-US JV USA-1 since the factory was founded grumbled:

I have worked here since the factory began production eight years ago. I have contributed my youth and the best of my working life to this place. But we, the first generation of [USA-1] workers, earn almost the same as those young workers who entered the factory one or two years ago. I think many other companies treat their loyal senior employees much better.[7]

Veteran workers, especially those in their late 30s and 40s, tended to be more cynical about overall company policies and management. They were often disillusioned about the meritocratic rhetoric and saw slim prospects for further advancement in the factory. A veteran electronic mechanic who had worked at the assembly shop of GER-1 for twelve years remarked:

Every manager here, no matter his rank, so long as he has some sort of power, he is trying to use his power to grab personal gains. It looks like a modern joint venture, but only the machines and technologies are from the German partner. Management is still the same SOE in nature – corrupt and bureaucratic. If you want to get a promotion, good *guanxi* (connection) with your superiors is still the king. I won't put my hope in them [managers] for any meaningful change.[8]

---

[6] Interview S24, GER-1, November 2006.   [7] Interview M5, USA-1, January 2005.
[8] Interview S5, GER-1, July 2004.

At the same time, veteran workers were well aware of their bargaining power based on their skills and experience, which allowed them to voice their discontent without worrying too much about being sacked. As an experienced technician at USA-1 commented:

I know they [managers] dislike me because I always speak out about the problems. But I tell the truth. They should feel lucky that there is still someone who can tell the truth nowadays. Unfortunately, they just want workers to listen and obey their orders. They want hierarchy and authority. But they cannot easily get rid of me because there aren't many people who know those machines better than I do.[9]

In sum, there was a significant generational divide between young and veteran workers. The majority of young formal workers were hopeful that they would eventually exit the line and move up through further education and skill training. In contrast, a minority of veteran workers with more job security were dissatisfied over their reduced privileges and slim chances of advancement in the factory. They voiced their complaints but were cynical about the potential that management would be willing to undertake any meaningful changes. These collective dispositions, as we shall see later in this chapter, directly affected workers' coping strategies and actions when they were faced with a more demanding workplace and management prerogatives.

WORKPLACE GRIEVANCES AND BARGAINING POWER OF FORMAL WORKERS

I found formal workers generally had two types of grievances. The first type was derived from their daily experiences of working on the line under a leaner and meaner mass production system; the second was incited by the arbitrary exercise of managerial authority and workers' inferior status as blue-collar, manual laborers in a hierarchical factory.

The majority of the workers I interviewed described the line as a dreadful place where they had to confront both intense and demanding physical challenges and monotonous and grueling work. The first major complaint among the interviewed workers focused on the physical rigors and tedium of auto assembly line work. I frequently heard stories about how new workers would lose 10 pounds in their first months working on assembly lines. As one 23-year old assembler at the Sino-US JV USA-1 described:

When I tell people that I work at USA-1, people always say, 'Gee, lucky you!' But they don't know how much it costs to get that high wage and benefits! If you have to work 10 hours a day, sometimes even 12 hours a day continuously except for half an hour lunch break and two 10-minute breaks, dealing with two-ton steel sheets, knocking 3,000 screws, wrenching 600 screw bolts, connecting 600 wiring harnesses, turning around 600 times, and bending down 300 times, every day, do you still think I'm lucky? It's the same exhausting work over and over again! You just want to get out of here![10]

---

[9] Interview M10, USA-1, November 2006.   [10] Interview M7, USA-1, January 2005.

Similarly, a 22-year old welder at the body shop of GER-2 recalled his first-month "nightmare" of working on the line:

It took me a month to get used to this tough job. It felt like a nightmare. I lost 10 pounds during the first months, even though I ate much more than what I normally eat, even though the food at the factory cafeteria was not tasty at all. I drank like a horse during work but I didn't even need to go to the toilet – the water in my body all went with sweats. My hands shook even after work from holding the air gun. At night I was even unable to find a proper position for my body to lie down, because it felt like every bone was painful after 12-hour's work. It's a damn tough job, and you know that you hate it and there is no future if [you're] just working on the line![11]

Workers also complained about management arbitrary decisions to speed up the production pace without giving enough time for them to adjust and catch up with the new line speed. Production quotas and line speed were usually set by the production engineering department in consultation with shop managers. Once a decision had been reached, shop managers implemented the decision through line or shift chiefs, down to foremen, to team leaders, and finally to production workers. Workers simply had no control over how fast and how long they had to work. They were often forced to adjust to the new line speed within a day or two. For instance, a newly-hired line worker at SOE-1 described his difficulty in catching up with the line:

I am still having a hard time catching up with the line. They constantly increase the speed and I am always worried about being unable to finish my tasks within the given time – I could get [a] 50 *yuan* fine for one quality defect. I only earn 1,200 *yuan* per month as a new hand. One of my workmates who entered the factory together with me even owed the company money last month because he had so many quality defects.[12]

A related common complaint was work-related injuries caused by having to perform repetitive motions at an intense pace over long working hours. My interviewees reported various degrees of muscle strains in their hands, wrists, and arms, as well as chronic pain in their necks, shoulders and backs. The following testimony from an assembly worker at the Sino-US JV USA-2 is telling:

Folks here have all kinds of work-related injuries. My back hurts every time I bend down, and I am only 24! The lines just keep moving faster and faster. We are making an overdraft of our body and youth. But what else can you do? Unless you switch to do something else, manufacturing jobs are basically all the same. Workers in other factories may be even worse off.[13]

Another major grievance arose from the excessive compulsory overtime that management imposed on workers without advance notice. Because workers on auto assembly lines are paid an hourly wage rather than by piece rate, work time was thus a major source of contention between workers and managers.

---

[11] Interview F8, GER-2, August 2004.   [12] Interview C13, SOE-1, March 2007.
[13] Interview D20, USA-2, April 2007.

In theory, under a position-wage system, overtime is one of the very few means available for a line operator to increase his monthly earnings. That explains why some of the interviewed workers wanted more overtime when I first visited GER-1 and SOE-2 in the summer of 2004.[14]

Since the market downturn in late 2004 and 2005, however, the major automakers imposed two adjustment measures on working time that dramatically changed workers' attitudes toward overtime. The first measure was to increase the daily planned production quotas, and to count the work time needed to meet the quota as regular working hours, which made it very difficult for workers to earn overtime pay. As an assembler at SOE-2 explained:

At our factory, everyone knows it is almost impossible to meet the daily production quota within the regular working hours. So we end up by routinely working "overtime" but without overtime pay, because they [managers] say we are just "finishing up the quotas that should have been done within regular working hours. Isn't it a blatant capitalist exploitation?!"[15]

The second measure was to use a comprehensive work-time calculation system that considers a year-long period when accounting for overtime, in order to evade the regulations on overtime stipulated by China's Labor Law. The Labor Law stipulates that if an employee's actual working time is more than the statutory standard working time of forty hours per week and 2,008 hours per year, the excess will be regarded as extended working time, and the employee would be owed overtime pay at 150 percent of his/her normal wage (Item 1, Article 44); if overtime occurs on a statutory holiday, the overtime should be paid at 300 percent of one's regular salary (Item 3, Article 44). The statutory limitation on total working time, including overtime, is forty-eight hours per week.

In my fieldwork, a common practice used by Chinese automakers was the installation of a comprehensive work-time calculation system, which took one year as the calculated period for overtime. That means that if an employee's total actual work time was less than 2,008 hours for the year, they would receive no overtime pay – no matter how many hours they actually worked in a given day, week, or month.[16] Management explained that the purpose of the system was to balance workers' working hours between peak and low seasons, so that workers' monthly income would not be affected dramatically due to market fluctuations. But workers resented this system. First off, workers found it harder to get paid for overtime because the company could always find ways to balance a worker's actual working time between peak seasons and low seasons within the one-year period, such that the worker's total working hours would not exceed the limit of 2,008 hours per year. Moreover, as a team leader

---

[14] Interviews S3, S4, GER-1, July 2004; Q3, Q4, SOE-2, June 2004.
[15] Interview Q21, SOE-2, October 2006.
[16] This calculation of overtime is common in many labor-intensive industries in China, and is not in violation of the 1994 Labor Law because many local governments have specific regulations that allow this type of practice.

at USA-1 pointed out, the real trick is that overtime pay was 150 or 300 percent the pay for regular working hours, but the system actually left them with a 1:1 pay rate for both regular working hours and overtime by counting extended hours within the 1-year statutory standard working hours.[17] It is no wonder that workers criticized the system as a cost-cutting strategy that allowed management to "steal" their overtime pay, and that workers described it as "naked exploitation."[18] The resentment over unpaid, compulsory overtime provoked overt resistance among formal workers, as we will see later in this chapter.

While workers generally disliked the physically demanding and monotonous nature of their jobs, they found it virtually impossible to make any change to the established movements of the assembly lines or to the relentless pressure to produce as rapidly as possible. But what workers resented most was management's arbitrary exercise of authority and the lack of respect for blue-collar workers.

Each of the studied automobile factories had strict and comprehensive codes of conduct. Given that the JIT mass production system requires low absenteeism and disciplined workers, many companies impose strict attendance rules and severe punishments for lateness and absenteeism. Being late for work more than twice or absent for up to one day in a month would incur a verbal warning and a 50 percent deduction to an employee's monthly income. Three verbal warnings would lead to dismissal. Being absent from work more than three days in 12 months would lead to immediate dismissal. Emphasis was also put on workers' proper social behaviors, such as no drinking at work or before work, no smoking on the shop floor, cleaning up the tool and production area every day after work, and wearing the proper uniform and personal protective (safety) equipment at all times during work. Workers generally accepted those rules that were considered reasonable and relevant to production, but resented those seen as "unnecessary" or "inhumane" rules imposed by management. For example, at the assembly shop of GER-1, the line workers were all indignant about a new rule put in place by the new shop manager that did not allow them to talk to each other during work.[19] As a young assembler sharply criticized:

We are human beings, not robots. How can you forbid people to talk while doing such boring and monotonous work? That's inhumane![20]

Formal workers also felt bitter about the hierarchical factory structure that institutionalized their inferior status as blue-collar workers, and the lack

[17] Interview M8, USA-1, January 2005.   [18] Interview M4, USA-1, January 2005.

[19] Such rules were also in place at U.S. auto plants in the pre-union era, and were a source of great discontent. See, for example, Jefferys (1989).

[20] Interview S11, GER-1, July 2004.

of recognition and respect for their work. As a formal worker at USA-2 commented:

A blue-collar worker here is just a piece of tool. If it breaks, they'll simply replace it. They don't care about workers as individuals. They don't care how long you have worked here and how much you have contributed to the company.[21]

At the same time, there is clear evidence that formal workers have gained substantial workplace bargaining power. The Chinese government policy combined with the massive foreign investment has increased the scale and concentration of automobile production in China since the late 1990s. Chinese autoworkers are concentrated in factories of enormous size. For example, the production base of SVW in Shanghai, hosts approximately 22,000 employees. More impressive still is the concentration of around 120,000 autoworkers employed by the centrally-controlled FAW Auto Group in its various subsidiary firms and plants within the "FAW auto city," a 12-square-kilometer district in the city of Changchun, where over 300,000 FAW employees and their families work and live. Moreover, the widespread adoption of the JIT production system and highly mechanized assembly lines have indeed increased the vulnerability of production to any interruptions and to the disruptive effects of slowdowns and stoppages by workers, thus boosting the potential workplace bargaining power of Chinese autoworkers. This point can be seen clearly in the Honda strike: a nineteen-day strike at a transmission and engine plant was able to shut down Honda's four assembly plants throughout China. It is also evident in the instances of worker resistance that I observed during my fieldwork, as will be discussed later in this and subsequent chapters.

The evidence has shown growing grievances among the current generation of formal workers, derived from the dreadful nature of assembly line work, constant speedups, management's arbitrary exercise of authority, and their inferior status as blue-collar workers in the hierarchical factory. These grievances are highly reminiscent of workers' grievances in the U.S. auto industry, in Western Europe, Japan, Brazil, South Korea and other automobile manufacturing countries.[22] At the same time, growing workplace grievances go hand-in-hand with strong workplace bargaining power of autoworkers. Likewise, as we will see in the following sections, in both union and non-union settings, in China as well as the United States, management seeks to use a varied set of organizational, cultural, and ideological techniques to control labor, to not only increase production but also to generate and secure workers' consent to a labor regime that is inherently exhausting and authoritarian.

---

[21] Interview D20, USA-2, April 2007.
[22] Among the rich body of literature on autoworkers' grievances in the U.S. and other countries, see, for example, Asher and Edsforth (1995), Beynon (1973), Durand and Hatzfeld (2003), Gartman (1986), Graham (1995), Humphrey (1982), Jefferys (1986), Kamata (1982), Koo (2001), Meyer (1981), Milkman (1997), Seidman (1994), and Widick (1976).

LABOR FORCE DUALISM AND JOB SECURITY
OF FORMAL WORKERS

A key control mechanism in the Chinese automobile factories, as I have high-lighted, is labor force dualism that divides formal workers from temporary workers. One of the important questions concerning the outcome of this dualism is to what extent formal workers have real job security. As noted in the previous chapters, factories that have adopted labor force dualism tend to provide their formal workforce with some sense of job security by using temporary workers as a buffer to adjust the workforce to fluctuations in production demand. For instance, during the market downturns in 2004 and 2005, GER-1 and GER-2 dismissed several thousand temporary workers but protected their formal workers from layoffs.

By contrast, before USA-1 and USA-2 adopted labor force dualism in 2008, more than three-quarters of the formal workers I interviewed in 2006 felt uncertain about their job security. The anxiety seemed particularly strong among workers in their 30s who had not advanced into either managerial or technician positions. For instance, a skilled painter at USA-1 in his 30s expressed his concerns:

Rumor says they [management] don't want workers over 40. They say the logic is if you are good enough, you should have already moved up rather than working on [the] line by your 40s. We currently don't have workers over 40 yet, but it might be true since they only sign one- to two-year renewable contract with production workers every year. That means if they don't want you any more, they can simply not renew your contract. It is tough for many of us. Folks around my age who are still working on the line are anxious and feel the pressure to climb up.[23]

Notably, the Sino-Japanese JV JPN-1 had not yet adopted labor force dualism. Instead, it provided relatively secure employment to its entire assembly plant workforce. Blue-collar workers were given three-year renewable contracts, and white-collar staff typically had five-year contracts, and both production workers and staff could expect their contracts to be renewed at the end of the contract terms. The HR manager at this JV reported an average annual labor turnover rate of two percent, one of the lowest among the studied auto assem-blers. As noted in previous chapters, JPN-1 places great emphasis on retaining a loyal and committed workforce. It also has been one of the most profitable automakers in China since it began operations in 1998.

Certainly, even among those that have adopted dualism, the job security of formal workers at those plants varies widely. At the Sino-German JV GER-2, formal workers reported a strong sense of job security. The JV has been among China's top-three carmakers since 2001. Most young formal production workers at GER-2 were graduates of the technical vocational school set up by the JV's Chinese parent company, FAW. Many of the formal production

---

[23] Interview M9, USA-1, November 2006.

workers had grown up in the "FAW auto city," and they were multi-generational members of the community. The SOE culture was still strong at FAW, making it less likely that formal workers would be laid off. As a 28-year-old formal worker at GER-2 commented, "It is nice to be a formal employee here. It feels like a big family – once you get in, you become a member of the family, and you will be taken care of."[24] In this case, guaranteed job security created a strong sense of belonging and was effective in eliciting the consent of formal workers.

At the other Sino-German JV GER-1, the SOE culture was still influential and both the Chinese managers and formal workers were habituated to stable employment and generous benefits. Although the market downturn in 2004 and 2005 caused concerns among some formal workers about losing their jobs, the carmaker managed to recover quickly and maintain a competitive market position. In particular, given that almost half of its production workforce was made up of temporary workers, one could imagine that it would take a rather dire financial crisis before the employment security of the formal workers was threatened.

At the state-owned truck maker SOE-2, however, all production workers received only one-year renewable labor contracts. The market logic had been fully implemented at SOE-2 in response to the growing competition and the factory's declining sales. Even the long-term and permanent employees had to "compete for work posts" (*jingzheng shanggang*) each year to determine whether they were qualified to continue working at their current posts. If not qualified, they were relegated to post-waiting (*dai gang*) status and were often advised to take early retirement. As such, most interviewed formal workers at SOE-2 did not feel they had much job security. As a formal worker at SOE-2 with a one-year renewable labor contract commented:

There's no job security nowadays as long as you work for others. They [managers] can just let you go by not renewing your contracts. You cannot rely on your *danwei* [work unit] any more. You have to take care of yourself and plan for yourself in advance.[25]

The prospects for job security among formal workers at SOE-1 were even less promising. As one of the fastest growing state-owned automakers in China, SOE-1 made headway by targeting low-end markets. The "low-price" strategy drove the automaker to cut labor costs more aggressively. Newly hired formal production workers were given only one-year renewable labor contracts for their first three years. In fact, SOE-1 had basically stopped hiring formal workers as line operators since 2004. Instead, most newly hired line operators were temporary agency workers. The carmaker also used a large number of student intern workers from all over the country, rotating cohorts on a yearly basis. As of March 2007, it was estimated that around one-third of the production workers at SOE-1 were student workers. Together, temporary agency

---

[24] Interview F9, GER-2, August 2004.   [25] Interview Q11, SOE-2, June 2004.

workers and student workers accounted for nearly two-thirds of the total production workforce at SOE-1.[26] Clearly, intense competition in the Chinese auto industry has driven some automakers, like SOE-2 and SOE-1, to reduce the protections for their formal production workforce.

To be sure, job security depends first and foremost on whether a given economic sector is in structural ascent or decline. The Chinese automobile industry has continued to expand over the past fifteen years, and there have not been large-scale layoffs since the first round of industrial restructuring in the late 1990s. Most formal workers were able to renew their labor contracts in the past several years. Meanwhile, during the interviews, management of both SOEs and JVs predicted more cost-cutting measures and possibly another round of restructuring down the road, as competition intensified in the auto assembly sector. There was a growing sense of insecurity and lack of commitment among the young formal workers with short-term contracts. For example, during the market downturn in 2004 and 2005, formal workers at GER-1 were able to keep their jobs thanks to the buffer of temporary workers. But their wages were cut by more than one-third, and some formal workers were worried about whether they would be able to renew their contracts. The following quote from a formal worker at GER-1 is illustrative:

No one really knows what would have happened if the company had not been able to come back on track after laying off all the *laowu gong* [temporary agency workers]. Many of us were worried that it would eventually come to our turn to be 'let go' if things did not get better. Fortunately, we came over it. But many of us realized that you could not count on the company, no matter how long you have worked for it. It is a market economy. Profitability always comes first. No *renqingwei* [sentiments and feelings], no security nowadays.[27]

As their job security declined, so did formal workers' commitment and loyalty to their employers. Many young workers I interviewed had taken or were taking night classes and other training programs in their spare time. Their goal, besides moving up in the factory hierarchy, was to stay competitive on the job market and to prepare for the uncertain future. As a 25-year-old operator at USA-1 explained:

For the past three years, I've seen many people around [me] come and go. It is true that almost everyone here can renew his contract if he wants because the company has been doing very well. But you never know. The market can change quickly and there is little security for us ordinary workers. I'm taking night classes for the advanced-skill qualification examination and office automatic management. Hopefully, I can pass the examination and get the certificate this year. I think that will make me more competitive on the job market. Many of my coworkers are doing the same. You know, competition is high nowadays. You have to rely on yourself and prepare for your own future in advance.[28]

[26] The author's field notes, March 2007.   [27] Interview S19, GER-1, November 2006.
[28] Interview M4, USA-1, January 2005.

The interviewed managers complained about the deteriorating worker morale. Especially when economic incentives were cut back, there were immediate withdrawals of worker cooperation. For example, a shop manager mentioned that when USA-1 reduced workers' annual bonuses in 2005, workers complained a lot and there were 20 percent higher repair rates during the first quarter of production in 2006.[29]

The evidence presented in this section shows a positive correlation between formal workers' job security and their consent and cooperation with management. We have seen reduced job security going hand in hand with declining consent among formal workers at some large auto assemblers. Given the prediction of more cost-cutting measures and the likely further reductions in the protection for formal workers, it is hard to say to what extent management can maintain a relatively quiescent formal workforce. Before we draw any conclusions, however, it is important to investigate other labor control strategies employed in China's large automobile factories.

BUILDING "HEGEMONIC" CONSENT: LABOR CONTROL OVER FORMAL WORKERS

The concept of "hegemony," derived from the Italian Marxist Antonio Gramsci, emphasizes the ideological power of the ruling class to establish and maintain its dominance by persuading the subordinate classes to accept its own worldview and values as "common sense," and to elicit "spontaneous consent" (Gramsci 1971: 12). Marc Blecher, for example, uses this concept to argue that Chinese "workers' hegemonic acceptance of the core values of the market and the state under the market reform" was the main reason for the political passivity of the Chinese working class in the face of massive layoffs, economic predicament, and the degradation of its class position since marketization and commodification of labor deepened in the 1990s (2002: 283).

Focusing on shop floor, labor process scholars employ this concept to explain how management controls labor and extracts their effort in production through consent rather than outright coercion (Burawoy 1979, 1985). In his study of a piece-rate machine shop, Michael Burawoy (1979) showed how managers, by deliberately giving workers some sense of autonomy, were able to bring forth workers' self-control and consent that, in effect, minimized the potential for class consciousness and labor-management conflict while maximizing productivity. Richard Edwards argued that, through "bureaucratic control," management was able to incentivize "workers to identify themselves with the enterprise, to be loyal, committed, and thus self-directed or self-controlled" (1979: 150).

Studies of labor control on the Chinese shop floor have highlighted the important role of the Party-state ideology and of cultural mechanisms in

[29] Interview M14, USA-1, November 2006.

hegemonic labor control. For example, Ted Fishman, citing Prasenjit Duara, argued that "the Communists made the workforce docile and organized labor to be a managed entity that could be continuously mobilized" (2005: 52). Michel Chossudovsky (1986) observed that "scientific management" in reform-era China, which combined Confucian authoritarianism with western Taylorism, made labor control more effective in Chinese factories. My fieldwork in China's large automobile enterprises partly concurs with previous studies. I found that, besides relying on technical and bureaucratic control as discussed above, management also placed great emphasis on cultural and ideological control mechanisms to elicit formal workers' cooperation and consent. Labor control over formal workers was "hegemonic" in nature, and in some degree could be effective. However, compliance does not equate with consent. As we shall see, the very effort to legitimize the hegemony of managerial ideology has provided workers with "the symbolic raw material" (Scott 1985: 339) and legitimacy leverage to criticize the discrepancy between the official ideology and the workplace reality. It enables workers to negotiate some concessions from management, who has a stake in maintaining a cooperative workforce and advancing the legitimacy of its own ideology and control.

Culture in action: Labor control by corporate culture

The term "corporate culture" (*qiye wenhua*) was first introduced to China in the 1980s. It has reemerged as a buzz word in Chinese managerial and academic circles since the late 1990s, when the government began to urge Chinese enterprises "to develop advanced corporate culture if they want to compete with their foreign counterparts at the international market" (Xinhua 2003). It has been argued that if properly implemented, corporate culture can be an effective managerial control strategy to promote "loyalty, enthusiasm, diligence and even devotion to the enterprise" among employees, and can "ensnare workers in a hegemonic system" (Ray 1986: 287).

Labor control in China's large automobile factories often began with cultivating workers to internalize corporate cultures, values, and workplace norms – the factors that define workers' behavior toward management and other workers. The orientation and training for new employees devoted substantial time and effort to indoctrinating workers in the corporate culture, values, and normative behaviors, as well as team-building activities and work-safety education, with relatively less time devoted to technical training.[30] Patriotic education was also an essential part of the training curriculum. The state-owned automakers in particular, under the banner of "revitalizing the national automobile industry and making China's own-brand cars," frequently invoked patriotism, self-reliance, hard work, and devotion to motivate their workers.

---

[30] Technical training was usually carried out at new employees' respective departments or shops. The focus on new employees' social and normative aspects resembles the practices of Japanese automakers such as Toyota.

For example, at the state-owned automakers SOE-1 and SOE-2, newly recruited workers were trained by People's Liberation Army (PLA) drillmasters for 2–4 weeks, to learn the virtues of "patriotism, discipline, collectivism, and hard work" before starting in their work positions. Workers at SOE-1 were referred to as "modern industrial warriors," who shoulder the "historical mission of building China's independent, national pillar industry."[31]

I remember one orientation session I attended at SOE-1, along with over 200 new employees, most of whom were college graduates in their 20s. In that session, we watched a documentary titled "SOE-1 Road," to learn the history and corporate culture of SOE-1. The documentary highlighted SOE-1's "miraculous success" as China's leading domestic automaker and its history as a pioneering builder, starting from scratch without sufficient capital and technology, but vigorously competing against mighty JVs with multinationals. After the documentary, a senior manager who was a founding member of SOE-1 came to talk to the new employees about those "hard pioneering days" they had experienced at SOE-1. He described vividly how managers and workers worked shoulder-to-shoulder, seven days a week, 15 hours a day, to build China's own-brand cars – the so-called "7/15 work ethic" at SOE-1. The evocative story of managers and workers working side by side for the common cause and the message of equal opportunity for youngsters to succeed through innovation, a pioneering spirit, and hard work, resonated well among the new employees. "It's like going through a second college education for me," said one of the new employees afterward, "I can feel there is something beyond money...very inspiring." As an HR manager of SOE-1 discussed with me:

It is true that our workers' wages are lower than those of large JVs. But we believe just relying on monetary incentives to motivate employees is insufficient. We need to have the kind of spirit and vision to give our employees a sense of pride and responsibility in their work, to keep their morale up. That way, they can identify with the company and stay longer with the company. I think that's the essence of a successful corporate culture.[32]

Joint ventures, instead, tended to highlight their modern, advanced, and internationalized corporate culture. Meanwhile, they also emphasized their advantage in combining advanced management culture from their foreign partners with the fine SOE tradition inherited from their Chinese parent companies. As an HR manager of the Sino-German JV GER-1remarked:

Our employees have developed a 'GER-1 man' identity – a kind of 'Sino-German hybrid' enterprise temperament. It is the product of our unique corporate culture, the mixture of our own fine SOE cultures that value stability, welfare of workers, and harmonious atmosphere, and our German partner's clear and rational management processes and

---

[31] The author's field notes, SOE-2, June 2004; SOE-1, March 2007. In fact, SOE-1 had an explicit hiring preference for PLA veterans. Similarly, during the early period of Korean industrialization, workers were also called "industrial warriors," part of "the image created by the state in order to exhort workers to hard work, discipline, and sacrifice for the nation" (Koo 2001: 209).

[32] Interview C33, SOE-1, April 2007.

advanced technology. We actually have a lot in common with our German partner, such as dedication to the pursuit of excellence in product quality and caring about employees' long-term welfare. So we don't have a big 'cultural shock' in management at GER-1.[33]

JPN-1 is a good example of a JV integrating the corporate cultures of its SOE parent company and its foreign partner.[34] As mentioned in Chapter 4, JPN-1 followed the lead of its Japanese partner in promoting an egalitarian culture with no visible privileges given to managerial staff in terms of uniform, parking and dining spaces, etc. In order to improve direct communication with workers, the Japanese and Chinese top managers held a monthly open day for workers to walk in to discuss any issues or concerns they encountered at work. The JV also built a "spiritual civilization" (*jingshen wenming*) education center within its 42,864 m² Employee Recreation Center. New employees and Party members were given study tours at the education center to learn the history of JPN-1, its corporate culture and philosophy, its commitment to the public good and social responsibility, the organization and the role of the Party and the union in the company, as well as the various honors it has received through multimedia exhibits. During those study tours, several veteran workers would be present to tell new employees their own experiences of facing layoffs at the company's previous incarnation, which had gone bankrupt before being reborn as JPN-1. The message was clear: as employees of JPN-1, their individual livelihood and welfare was tied to and depended on the growth and success of their employer.[35]

The corporate culture of USA-1 and USA-2 instead centered on lean management principles.[36] As stated in the first sentence of its "Management Philosophy" in USA-1's Employee Handbook, "Lean manufacturing principles are applied across the Company. Every employee is required to contribute to the success of the Company through better efficiency and zero waste at work." Team work and continuous improvement were also emphasized.

Despite some notable differences, I found management in general combined three core values in corporate culture to establish a hegemonic managerial ideology: the market mentality of competition, efficiency, and individual responsibility; the Chinese traditional values of "integrity" (*cheng xin*), being people-oriented, and seeking harmony; and, the socialist rhetoric of enterprise paternalism, egalitarianism, and workers' "sense of being masters of their enterprises" (*zhurenweng jingshen*). Taken together, the main goal is to encourage workers to view themselves as sharing common interests with their companies in a highly competitive market environment.

---

[33] Interview S17, GER-1, November 2006.
[34] The corporate culture of JPN-1 was said to be "people-oriented, respecting personality and talents, valuing communications, and reducing hierarchy." Interview H1, JPN-1, September 2006.
[35] The author's field notes, JPN-1, September 2006.
[36] Interview M13, USA-1, November 2006; interview D10, USA-2, April 2007.

Just how effective is the corporate culture in eliciting hegemonic consent from workers? The answer depends on the distance between managerial rhetoric and workplace reality. At SOE-1, despite its evocative and appealing corporate culture, workers' low pay, short-term contracts, and heavy workload, led to high levels of annual labor turnover – 25–30 percent between 2004 and 2008. At JPN-1, workers seemed to agree that management cared about workers' welfare and that they felt a sense of belonging to the company. Some commented that they liked the "humble and folksy style" of the Japanese and Chinese top managers, who ate in the same cafeteria with workers at lunch and frequented the shop floor to chat with ordinary workers. The interviewed workers were also aware of the monthly open day for employees to meet with the general managers and discuss their issues or concerns directly. At USA-1, by contrast, workers were very cynical about management's claim that it "values every employee," given that most workers were only able to sign short-term contracts. As a veteran worker remarked:

What a joke! If they [management] truly "value every employee," why do they only sign one- to two-year labor contracts with workers? They just don't want to take any responsibilities for workers when they get old. They don't care about workers at all.[37]

Another important factor that influences the efficacy of managerial ideology is the role played by enterprise Party committees and unions.

Ideology at work: The role of enterprise Party committees and unions

My study found that the enterprise Party committees (EPCs) and unions played an important role in building "hegemonic consent" among formal workers at China's large automobile enterprises. This was especially the case in those early-built factories – for example, GER-1, GER-2, and SOE-2 – where a socialist legacy remained strong. On the contrary, where Party committees and unions tended to be less active or less visible – as at, for instance, USA-1 and USA-2 – there seemed to be more contentious labor-management relations, as we will see later in this chapter.

First, the EPCs and unions actively mobilized workers to promote production. At the beginning of each year, the Party committees and unions organized pledging mobilization meetings to boost production workers' morale. At one such pledge meeting at GER-2, for instance, workers were organized into work groups and everyone signed his/her name on a large, red banner representing his/her work group. Each banner had a slogan written in a striking color, such as "to guarantee both quality and quantity, to exceed the production targets," and "gathering the strength of our team, overcoming the equipment repair difficulty." Each work group hung its own banner with workers' signatures in the work block for which it was responsible. Selected advanced Party

[37] Interview M8, USA-1, January 2005.

members – many of whom were model workers – pledged to exceed the production target on behalf of their fellow workers. The Party members also expressed their willingness to undertake urgent, heavy, and difficult tasks. A veteran foreman described the style as "reminiscent of the socialist past," when I chatted with him after the meeting.[38]

The EPCs and unions also mobilized workers by bringing into play Party members' "vanguard and exemplary role," and holding up model Party members and workers as examples. At GER-1, the advanced deeds of Party members, such as volunteering to work overtime on holidays or over-coming technical difficulties to increase production efficiency and reduce waste, were praised and propagated by the Party and the union through storytelling, rap, and other folk art forms in the cafeteria, on the enterprise's television and radio outlets, and in on-site performances in the workshops. At JPN-1, model Party members and workers were promoted by the Party and the union through documentaries, book and journal publications, and social media. It was also common to display photographs and exemplary work of Party members and model workers recognized by the EPCs on public bulletin boards in the entrance areas of workshops, to honor their work and to motivate other workers. The rewards for those put on the "board of glory" – such as bonuses, fringe benefits, and career advancement opportunities – were significant and attractive, but it was also a monitoring mechanism and a means of exerting great pressure on model workers to work harder and perform better.

The EPCs and unions actively promoted worker participation and democratic management on the shop floor. All the studied enterprises implemented "rationalization suggestion programs" (*helihua jianyi*). They also set up programs and measures for "work group democratic management" and "democratic evaluation of team leaders." In order to reach every worker, the EPCs and unions, through their branches at the workshop level, established direct points of contact with each work group, which was the basic unit in organizing daily production and in reaching out to ordinary workers. I observed Party and union cadres at my case-study factories –excepting USA-1 and USA-2 – attending work groups' regular meetings and study meetings of Party members and advanced workers, listening to workers' concerns, helping team leaders resolve practical issues at work, organizing team leader forums or editing monthly work group handbooks for team leaders to learn from and exchange best practices with each other. Some early-built factories also utilized their "revolutionary tradition" to promote lean production and motivate workers. As the Party committee Sectary at SOE-2 remarked:

To promote lean production, we cannot just rely on automation and advanced machinery. We should focus on how to better motivate our workers to become more committed and productive at work. How can we encourage workers to take more responsibility at work, to internalize the '5S' principles and reduce production waste spontaneously?

---

[38] Interview F24, GER-2, October 2006

Our *"Jiefang chuantong"* [liberation tradition] and "thought work" has proved to be very effective in mobilizing workers and boosting productivity since the 1950s. We should develop and carry forward these valuable revolutionary traditions to meet today's new challenges.[39]

The second important function of the EPCs and unions was to build harmonious labor relations and advance employees' welfare through various "care projects" (*guan'ai gongcheng*). The EPCs and unions were known among workers for distributing holiday gifts, giving employees birthday presents, visiting sick employees, assisting workers and their families during times of hardship through donations and "employee caring funds," as well as organizing cultural and recreation activities, such as karaoke events and sports competitions, spring outings, and matchmaking for single workers. Moreover, the Party and the union tried to reach into workers' private lives beyond the factory gate. For example, at GER-1, the union organized *"lao niangjiu"* (peacemaker) teams made up by experienced Party members and workers to help their coworkers resolve work, life, family, and emotional problems through heart-to-heart talks, family visits, and mediation.[40] At JPN-1, the union and the Communist Youth League organized the "New JPN-1" program, which gave financial support to workers' after-work team-building activities, from social gatherings to dance and fitness clubs. The goal was to "enhance enterprise cohesiveness and cultivate bonds among employees."[41]

The EPCs and unions also helped to mediate conflicts between workers and managers through "thought work." For example, during the enterprise restructuring and downsizing that occurred in 2000, SOE-2 managed to reduce the total number of employees from over 4,600 to about 3,000 without overt labor protests or disputes. One important reason for the smooth downsizing was because management relied on the EPC and the union, which in turn relied on the accumulated good will and political commitment of older workers. I was told that the Party and union cadres had visited many older workers'

---

[39] Interview Q17, SOE-2, September 2006. The "'5S' principles" were developed by Japanese manufacturers, referring to a workplace organization method that uses a list of five Japanese words: *seiri* (sorting), *seiton* (stabilizing or straightening out), *seiso* (sweeping or shining), *seiketsu* (standardizing), and *shitsuke* (sustaining the practice). The *"Jiefang"* (liberation) tradition, according to the factory Party secretary, included self-reliance, plain living and hard struggle, dedication, innovation, and a pioneering spirit. It was associated with China's first domestically manufactured automobile, the *"Jiefang"* truck, produced by SOE-1's Chinese parent company in 1956. The brand was named by Chairman Mao, and was meant to embody the moral of the PLA in liberating the Chinese people from the repression of imperialism, feudalism, and bureaucrat-capitalism. The making of the *"Jiefang"* truck marks the birth of China's automobile industry.

[40] Interview S38, GER-1, July 2011. The term *"lao niangjiu"* originally refers to one's mother's elder brothers. In ancient China, when a family or neighborhood dispute would occur, it usually required that *"lao niangjiu"* come forward to mediate. Today, the term is synonymous with "peacemaker," referring to a good mediator (informally) of civil disputes.

[41] Interview H7, JPN-1, May 2007.

homes and talked to them one by one. Those workers who were to be laid off were first praised for their long service, hard work, and dedication to the factory. The workers were then reminded of the factory's *"Jiefang"* tradition, especially the tradition of "dedication to the collective interest of the factory." They were convinced that their sacrifices – in the form of layoffs and early retirements – were in the collective best interests of the factory, and that they would receive guaranteed pensions if they chose to step aside without making a major fuss.[42]

The efficacy of the EPCs and unions in mobilizing workers for production and building harmonious labor relations is made evident in the changing reception of foreign partners. For example, when GER-1 was established in the 1980s, its German partner initially opposed the creation of a Party committee at the JV. But the foreign partner quickly realized that the Party committee would be effective in mobilizing workers and promoting production. Soon it not only welcomed the establishment of the EPC, but also gave full support to its development.[43] Similar stories were told at other Sino-foreign JVs.

On the other hand, the interviewed workers viewed the union as part of management, rather than as an organization that represented the worker. Most of the interviewed formal workers said they would first seek help from their team leaders and fellow workers, or from their foremen and the HR department, in the case of workplace conflicts or disputes. Only five out of the 124 formal workers interviewed reported that they would first turn to the unions for help. Some workers expressed the wish to have a "genuine union" of their own to represent their interests and to be able to deal with their grievances effectively. The lack of effective union representation and grievance resolution procedures, as we will see later in this chapter, often drove aggrieved workers into open or hidden forms of resistance and collective actions.

The pivot role of team leaders

Another important managerial hegemonic control strategy on the Chinese shop floor is to rely on work groups and team leaders to reach out to ordinary workers and defuse direct labor-management conflicts. As mentioned in Chapter 4, every worker is assigned to a work group that is led by a coworker – the team leader, who directly supervises and coordinates his/her fellow workers in a variety of daily tasks. First and foremost, team leaders ensure the timely and reliable completion of production tasks allocated to their groups. They lead the pre-shift meeting and allocate daily tasks, assign posts and set rotations among their group members, check equipment, order supplies, fill in for absent group members, solve on-the-spot production problems, and track production progress and product quality. In carrying out these tasks, team leaders communicate both

[42] Interview Q17, SOE-2, September 2006.   [43] Interview S1, GER-1, July 2004.

horizontally with their coworkers and vertically with management, and help the two groups to communicate with each other (cf. Durand et al. 1999).

Second, team leaders perform a broad range of managerial and record-keeping tasks, including playing a central part in the operation of the merito-cratic system – for instance, conducting performance appraisals and making decisions concerning bonus distributions within their work groups. They also report attendance to their supervisors (foremen), grant group members temporary leave, and recommend group members to their foremen for off-line training opportunities or openings for reserve team leader or skilled-work positions. At GER-2, for example, team leaders spent 50–70 percent of their work time fulfilling 31 managerial functions and 18 record-keeping tasks. As Andrew Walder keenly observed, under the Chinese work group system, "workers do not deal with shop management on a regular basis; they deal mainly with other workers who represent management – their group [team] leaders." By desig-nating a worker as a team leader to perform extensive managerial functions within his/her work group, shop management effectively releases itself "from direct involvement in supervising the workforce," and "bottles up" potential conflict between labor and management within the work group (1986: 103–4).

Compared with the well-documented role of foreman in the U.S. auto indus-try, a role known as "the man in the middle" (Lichtenstein 1989: 153–89), the team leader in the Chinese factory is faced with similar psychological and organizational pressures, a result of their positioning between the conflicting demands and interests of management and workers. Unlike the foreman, however, who has official managerial status, the Chinese team leader is still a worker in spite of his/her extensive managerial responsibilities.[44] As discussed in Chapter 4, most team leaders worked their way up from the ranks and were subjected to democratic supervision and evaluations by their fellow workers. They must gain the support and cooperation of their group members in order to complete the daily tasks smoothly. Thus, the third important function of team leaders is to minimize conflict and build cooperative relations within their work groups. That may suggest team leaders could be more prone to the pressure of their group members' demands.

One of the common strategies that team leaders use to minimize conflict is to play around with some "unreasonable" policies imposed by management. For example, except for GER-1 and JPN-1, the automakers I studied had each implemented an annual evaluation and elimination system (*mowei taotai*), under which an employee would be laid off if he/she scored last or fell into the "elimination range" in the annual performance evaluation.[45] Management

---

[44] Team leaders could earn twice the wages of ordinary production workers, in addition to extra bonuses and allowances. They also had more training opportunities. More importantly, becom-ing a team leader was the first step a line worker could take in order to escape the line and to move up in the factory hierarchy.

[45] The elimination range varied among the automobile factories I studied, from 1 percent to 5 percent of the total number of formal employees.

claimed that this system could raise workers' "sense of crisis" (*weiji yishi*), increase competition among workers, and improve performance. But for ordinary workers, the elimination system caused a great deal of anxiety and antagonism because workers could lose their jobs not over their own faults, but for not being able to compete against their coworkers. Most team leaders and foremen I interviewed considered the system "unreasonable" and "inhuman." As a team leader at GER-2 commented:

> We all know someone has to be at the bottom of the evaluation, but that does not mean that person has to lose his job. If my fellow workers all work hard and do their jobs well, I don't see any reason why anyone should be 'eliminated.' I will just play around with this policy.[46]

One way team leaders would "play around with this policy" was to manipulate performance appraisals and "correction periods." Factory management usually set certain correction periods – ranging from 2–6 months – to give those to-be-eliminated employees a chance to improve their performance before a final layoff decision was made. Team leaders, often under an acquiescent foreman, could first seek to meet the required elimination quota in the performance appraisal within their work groups. They then used the correction period to pull up those who fell into the elimination range by giving them higher evaluation scores to ensure that no one would lose their jobs in the end. By "humanizing" the edge of an "inhumane" company policy, front-line supervisors such as team leaders and foremen could defuse the tension and potential for labor-management conflicts on the shop floor. Meanwhile, by choosing to be less harsh in their treatment than what is prescribed in the formal company rules, supervisors were judged more favorably by workers, seen as "permissive" or "lenient" (Gouldner 1954, quoted in Edwards 1975: 96).

Workers reciprocated with full attendance, by volunteering when overtime was needed, or by being more active in *kaizen* activities and other worker participation programs in their work groups. Everyone tended to understand that the timely completion of production quotas and quality work were the bottom line for any reciprocal relations between team leaders and their fellow workers. In this respect, the function of team leaders for "getting out of production on time and up to standard" is no different from that of the U.S. shop foreman, despite their different styles and techniques (cf. Lichtenstein 1989: 153–89).

At the same time, lean production, which is essentially a designed system of "management by stress" (Parker and Slaughter 1995: 43), puts more pressure on front-line managers and workers with reduced buffers and fewer resources at hand to handle disruptions. Team leaders are increasingly forced to take on more administrative and managerial responsibilities. The interviewed team

---

[46] Interview F17, GER-2, October 2006. The HR managers of GER-1 and JPN-1, who opposed the elimination system, made similar arguments in explaining their decisions not to adopt the system. Interviews H1, JPN-1, September 2006; S17, GER-1, November 2006.

leaders reported that they felt "overburdened," and "stressed," and that they were "the busiest person on the shop floor." I also frequently heard team leaders complain about "inconsiderate upstairs management" decisions that put them in a difficult situation.[47] For instance, a team leader at SOE-1 complained about the excessive compulsory overtime that evoked workers' resentment, making it hard for him to carry out daily tasks:

> We have to follow the words of those 'upstairs'. But it is us who have to implement those decisions, calm down pissed-off workers, and keep the line moving. It is not an easy job. I have to constantly assure my buddies that we will get extra bonus for working those "extended regular hours." But to be honest, I myself have no idea how those HR people actually counted our overtime. The pay slips are always confusing and hard to understand.[48]

The above quote suggests that team leaders tend to stand in solidarity with their fellow workers when they are faced with excessive or unreasonable management demands. On reflection, work group-centered production organization and standardized production quota systems tended to lead to group-based solidarity and worker resistance in the U.S. automobile industry between the 1940s and 1970s (Zetka 1995). Similarly, I found evidence of growing group-based solidarity and worker resistance on the Chinese shop floor, as we will see in the next section.

In sum, management labor control at China's leading automobile factories was sophisticated and "hegemonic" in nature, to some extent working to defuse overt conflict between formal workers and management. However, I also witnessed growing discontent among formal workers. As we will discuss in the next section, the discrepancy between managerial ideology/rhetoric and the reality of workers' lived shop-floor experiences has, in effect, generated cynicism and defiance against management prerogatives.[49] Rather than manufacturing consent, the shop floor is instead a contested terrain of resistance and negotiated compliance.

CONTESTED TERRAIN: FORMAL WORKERS' RESISTANCE AND COMPLIANCE

Formal workers' resistance

Over the course of my fieldwork, I found various incidents of formal workers' resistance, ranging from "everyday forms of resistance" (Scott 1985) in acts of effort bargaining, manipulation of worker participation programs, pilferage and sabotage, to open protest, and, in extreme cases, sit-down strikes.

---

[47] Workers used the term "upstairs" to refer to factory-level management.
[48] Interview C12, SOE-1, March 2007.
[49] For examples of excellent ethnographic studies on how the discrepancy between managerial ideology and shop-floor reality affects workers' consciousness, resistance, and solidarity, see, in particular, Burawoy and Lukacs (1992), Graham (1995), and Vallas (2003; 2006).

Effort bargaining

Under the strict disciplinary rules and tight technical control of the labor process in automobile assembly production, the most common tactics formal workers used to regulate the amount and intensity of their work was through "effort bargaining" – that is, workers would refuse to give full effort during work by ignoring the correct procedures and making careless or intentional mistakes (Edwards 1986, cf. Hodson 1995b: 89–92). This tactic is understandably preferable among workers given that direct defiance of management can put at risk workers' jobs and subsistence, and is thus less common.

For instance, despite the detailed job descriptions and strict requirements to adhere to standard operating procedures, some experienced workers were able to use alternative procedures that were easier on workers physically, or allowed them to "work ahead" so that they could gain some extra break time.[50] A common practice workers used on assembly lines is what is called "doubling up," with one worker working ahead to finish both their own and a co-worker's tasks within the specified time, so that the other could take a short break. As a former worker employed at the body shop of GER-2 for four years before leaving for a car sales job described:

When I worked at GER-2, my job was to polish the front left body side. It was simple and repetitive work and you don't have to work with your brain. After years of doing the same thing over and over again, I was able to finish ahead of time. I tried to help my buddy standing next to me up to two sedans so that he could take a short break. He would do the same thing for me so that I could have a break. Of course, our team leader knew about that, but he would not say anything so long as we got the work done in time without causing any quality problems. Workers in other work groups did the same thing. You know, it was a tough, boring job and we had to find some way to make it a bit more bearable; we had to help each other to make it through.[51]

The various "tricks" that skilled operators learned over time not only helped them get work done with less effort and in a shorter period of time, they also gave them some sense of control. As Randy Hodson (2001: 121) observed:

This practice [of working ahead] allows them to take pride and pleasure in momentarily being ahead and to have a few seconds rest as the moving line catches back up. Working ahead also gives workers some sense of control over their activities. Most importantly, however, is the fact that working in short energetic bursts followed by slower periods gives some relief from the grindingly steady pace of the assembly line.

In this regard, Burawoy's (1979) "game" metaphor – which describes the shop-floor "making out" accompanying work and exploitation – remains relevant to understanding work on automobile assembly lines. But the room for autoworkers to "make out" has certainly been shrinking in the face of management's

---

[50] The practice of assembly-line workers "working ahead" has been widely observed and documented in ethnographies of assembly work in different industrial and country settings. See, for instance, Hodson (2001: 121)

[51] Interview F38, Guangzhou, June 2007.

vigorous push for lean production methods and standardized operations. The continuous speed-up of the line also makes it harder and harder to "beat" the fast-moving lines, even for the most skilled and experienced line operators.

In fact, the practice of "doubling up" was strictly forbidden by management due to concerns about the increased potential for defects or accidents. All of the auto factories I visited installed cameras around production areas to catch "nonstandard operations," but it did not take too long for workers to figure out the blind angles of the cameras that would allow them to engage in "effort bargaining" in their daily production, one way or another. Thus management was relatively powerless in the face of workers' effort bargaining in the labor process.

Manipulating the worker participation program

To most interviewed workers, worker participation programs did not grant them any greater workplace autonomy. Instead, it put added pressure and increased burdens on workers who were "forced to participate."[52] For example, the rationalization suggestion program was limited to fine-tuning the production process, focused on how to increase productivity and reduce waste, which resulted in more pressure on workers to "get more out from less." Workers also complained about requirements that they meet the monthly "suggestion quotas." For instance, USA-1 and USA-2 required every employee to submit at least two suggestions per month. When forced to participate, some workers manipulated the rationalization suggestion program and made fun of it. As an assembler at USA-2 described:

When they first asked us to submit suggestions for improvements, many of us took it seriously, and we raised questions about scheduling of overtime, wages, the food quality of the cafeteria, shower facility, etc. But nothing has ever changed. We doubt whether they actually read our suggestions. It is a "paper-wasting" program. Even worse, it has become an obligation that we have to submit at least two suggestions each month. So we write things like "we should limit the quantities of toilet paper to reduce waste." (Laughing)[53]

Collective acts of defiance

Workers' resistance also took the form of collective acts of defiance toward management, such as the collective refusal to participate in factory rituals. For example, in March 2007, after several months of working 12-hours a day with only one day off per month, workers in the assembly shop at SOE-1 were all exhausted and they were expecting a big bonus in their upcoming monthly paychecks. On pay day, however, the workers found out that they were not to receive any bonuses for the month of March. Workers were very disappointed and resentful. On the following two mornings, about half of the assembly shop workers did not participate in the company's morning exercises

---

[52] Interview H5, JPN-1, May 2007.   [53] Interview D3, USA-2, August 2006.

and pre-shift meetings to show their discontent. Many team leaders stood in solidarity with their fellow group members by not recording their lateness. In the "demonstrative" collective acts of defiance, workers were united by their work groups. Workers did not return to the morning routine until the shop manager promised that workers would receive extra bonuses in April to make up for the month of March.[54]

Legitimacy leverage and "normal" resistance

Another common form of resistance was workers' organized negotiations with management, in which they utilized their legitimacy leverage and sought to turn managerial ideology on its head. This form of resistance often followed the normal channels, for instance by appealing to EPCs and unions to protect the legitimate rights and interests of workers. For example, in 2006, workers at the assembly shop of GER-1 wrote a complaint letter to the Party committee Secretary and the union Chairman over the new rule instituted by the new shop manager that forbade line workers to talk to each other during work. According to a formal worker involved in drafting the letter, the workers invoked the same rhetoric used by the Party and union in the letter to denounce the "inhumane" rule as going against "the Party and union's genuine efforts to care for workers' welfare and to create a harmonious and pleasant working environment," and by noting that the rule "has seriously dampened workers' enthusiasm and motivation at work." I was told that the shop manager soon thereafter removed the rule, following the intervention of the Party committee and the union.[55]

Another good example occurred at GER-2, when management implemented a wage reform in late 2005 and 2006, in order to transform the position-grade wage system to a position-merit wage system. About 150 veteran workers whose incomes were negatively affected by the wage reform signed a petition letter addressed to the EPC Secretary and the union Chairman. In the letter, the workers complained about the reduction of their wages and emphasized their loyal, long-term service and contributions to the factory. The result was symbolically meaningful. The wage reform continued to be implemented, but with a supplementary policy that stipulated that veteran workers hired before 1995 would receive compensatory wages to counterbalance any reduction to their wages caused by the wage reform. At the same time, the new merit wage system "allowed a twenty-something college graduate to earn as much as a veteran worker with twenty years seniority."[56] The outcome was a negotiated compromise between management and veteran workers that afforded some protection to veteran workers, while allowing the system to continue to move in a profitability-oriented direction that would further reduce veteran workers' privileges.

---

[54] The author's field notes, March 2007. Laurie Graham (1995) observed similar practices of worker resistance at a Japanese automaker's nonunion U.S. plant located in Indiana.

[55] Interview S18, GER-1, November 2006.   [56] Interview F15, GER-2, October 2006.

Pilferage and sabotage

Theft and pilferage were also common tactics workers used to express their discontent. For example, at a newly built Sino-Japanese auto assembly plant, there were frequent reports of "missing" auto parts from deliveries from the factory's warehouse to the assembly shop in early 2005.[57] The widespread pilferage, according to a team leader I interviewed, were workers' intentional acts, through which they vented their smoldering resentment over the newly introduced "Toyota Production System," as well as the speed-ups, frequent layoffs, and low wage policy. In late 2004, when the Japanese partner of the JV made very pessimistic predictions about the prospects of the auto market in China in 2005, the factory started dismissing workers beforehand, including one-third of skilled workers. This move aroused intense resentment among workers. As the team leader explained:

> Why are there so many missing parts? Because workers were resentful about the new system and they wanted to vent. Because the new system always tries to get the most out of us while only giving back the minimum. For example, in my work group, we used to have fourteen people. In late 2004, they let six go. Now we only have eight left doing the same amount of work, which means the workload of each of us has almost been doubled, but we are still getting paid the same. Here, the so-called "Toyota miracle" is simply to lay off workers and keep workers' wages low. How can you expect workers to be committed to their work if they don't know whether they would be the next to be sacked when another downturn or cut comes? This is stupid![58]

Unable to identify individual workers who stole the parts, in the end, in order to keep production flowing smoothly, management was obliged to eliminate their experiment with the JIT production model, and returned to the old system with greater built-in supply buffers. In other words, when faced with resistance by workers with strong workplace bargaining power, management had to abandon – or rely less upon – the lean production system, as they were unable or unwilling to find a way to gain workers' cooperation in the implementation of the most advanced and efficient forms of production.

Workers also used sabotage to vent their grievances. During my fieldwork at the Sino-American JV USA-2 in the summer of 2006, the company's repair shop was filled with newly-made cars with all sorts of defects caused by workers' acts of sabotage, such as scratches, dents, loud-running engines, and faulty signal light controls. I was told by the workers that the sabotage was fueled by workers' discontent over speed-ups, arbitrary management decisions, and the fact that workers' wages at USA-2 were much lower than those of workers at the other two assembly plants of the same automaker elsewhere (one of the two plants was located in Shanghai). According to a manager who had worked at both USA-2 (located in a smaller city) and in

---

[57] This plant was not included in the seven cases analyzed in this study due to the limited number of interviewees.
[58] Interview T1, Tianjin, August 2005.

the Shanghai plant, workers at USA-2 were considered more hardworking and obedient than those in Shanghai, and they were also willing to work for a significantly lower wage.[59] The allegedly cheap and docile workforce was an important reason why the automaker had expanded its production base in this new location. However, shortly after USA-2 started operating, the allegedly docile workers carried out acts of sabotage and strikes to protest the arbitrary management decisions and unfair wage policies of the parent company.

Sit-down strike

The most visible manifestation of formal workers' discontent during my field research was a sit-down strike that shut down production at USA-2 for 10 hours in June 2006. The strike started on the Chevrolet line in the general assembly shop during a morning shift. Over 400 formal workers in the general assembly shop went to work as usual, but stood by the line and refused to work when the line started running at 8:00 a.m. Following the stoppage in the general assembly shop, workers in the press, body, and paint shops soon stopped working as well, and the whole plant came to a complete halt. At the same time, leaflets stating workers' demand for a 500 *yuan* (25 percent) wage increase were distributed throughout the factory. June was part of the peak production season, and USA-2 was making several of the company's best-selling compact car models. The last thing management wanted was any stoppage in production. The deputy general manager and the HR manager of the parent company flew from Shanghai that afternoon and promised to raise workers' wages if they went back to work immediately. But management only agreed a raise of 300 *yuan* (15 percent), instead of the 500 *yuan* the workers had demanded. Without any support or representation from the enterprise union to negotiate with management, and under the threat of being fired if they did not go back to work, the striking workers accepted the offer of a 300-*yuan* raise and production resumed at 6:00 p.m., after a 10-hour stoppage.[60]

Although the workers at USA-2 earned more than twice the local average wage, my interviews with workers suggested the strike was directly fueled by workers' indignation about the discriminatory wage policy based on regional differences. It gained wide support from both workers and local managers based on the shared localism and the anger at "being bullied by Shanghai managers." An assembler at USA-2 indignantly commented:

Why should we only get paid one third or less than those Shanghai workers while we are doing heavier work? They [Shanghai managers] say that is because living costs in Shanghai are much higher. But the living costs at the other plant [in another smaller city] is similar to us, why are their wages higher than us as well? They [Shanghai managers] say that is because there are many carmakers there [in the smaller city], and they have

---

[59] Interview D5, USA-2, August 2006.
[60] Summaries from the author's field notes, August 2006.

to offer a more competitive salary to keep workers from leaving. This was bullshit! They just think workers here are docile and easy to bully. That really pissed us off![61]

The interviewed workers also expressed their frustration with the lack of any formal channels through which they could seek redress for their grievances and demands. They complained about the "uselessness" of the factory union to speak for workers and to represent workers' interests. As the following quote from an assembler indicated:

We know those actions [sabotage and strikes] are extreme. But why would we take such radical actions and break the cars that we made with our own sweat? Because there is no other way for us to get our voices and complaints heard! We have tried many times through formal channels to request for a reasonable wage increase – we wrote letters and signed petitions to the factory union and the HR department. But no one has ever responded to us. The union here is useless. Our dear union chairman is our deputy general manager. How can you expect him to speak for us workers and fight against his own interest? No one speaking for us, the only way we can catch attention and have our grievances heard is through those more radical actions![62]

Although no details were available as to how the strike was actually organized,[63] it was clear that there had been some planning and organizing work done prior to the strike, and that it was not merely the spontaneous action it appeared to be. A former team leader who participated in the strike told me that it had been incited by an online post that listed all the harsh working conditions and the unfair treatments that workers at USA-2 had to endure.[64] The article was first posted on the online forum of USA-2 workers and soon spread throughout the plant. It evoked strong repercussions and indignation among workers. Shortly thereafter, a small group of workers in the final assembly shop set up a "dare-to-die squad" that played a leading role in planning and initiating the strike.

The interviewed workers also indicated that the strike was secretly assisted by some local foremen and team leaders who were also dissatisfied over having been snubbed by senior and middle managers from Shanghai. Some interviewed local managers at USA-2 complained that the strike did not bring any significant changes in the personnel policy and the attitude of the Shanghai-based management of the parent company. As a local team leader remarked:

The problem has not been solved yet. Many Shanghai managers don't trust us. Neither do we trust them. This is a big obstacle for the healthy growth of USA-2. To be honest, I think as long as the general company still assigns senior and middle

---

[61] Interview D4, USA-2, August 2006.   [62] Interview D6, USA-2, August 2006.
[63] At the time of my fieldwork, workers were open to talking about the strike, but they were wary of discussing any specific details about how the strike was organized. Indeed, management was still investigating and trying to identify the organizers of the strike but had found very few clues and little evidence, as both workers and local shop-floor managers remained silent, in solidarity.
[64] The team leader in question resigned shortly after the strike. Interview D1, USA-2, August 2006.

managers [of USA-2] from Shanghai, the problem will remain. They would have more troubles in the future if they did not change the personnel policy.[65]

The fact that the strike at USA-2 was fueled largely by the unequal wage policy and the regional conflicts between local managers and workers versus Shanghai managers suggests that the divides and distinctions within the Chinese working class – rather than leading to passivity – have been concrete and continuing sources of irritation and activism, an important point we will elaborate on in Chapter 6.

Another relevant point is that automakers in China have been aggressively establishing and expanding production bases in new regions in recent years. Among the many factors considered, auto companies are clearly responsive to both competition among local governments seeking to attract auto sector investment and differences (whether real or perceived) in the cost and docility of labor in different areas of China. Yet as the USA-2 case demonstrated, the allegedly "cheap and docile" workers employed at the new investment site soon carried out struggles against management arbitrary and unequal treatment. Instead of producing a straightforward "race to the bottom," the evidence lends support to the thesis "Where capital goes, conflict follows" (Silver and Zhang 2009; cf. Silver 2003: Chapter 2). Furthermore, a relatively small number of autoworkers are able to obstruct the entire production system by blocking the delivery of necessary auto parts to the assembly shop, or to shut down the entire plant by stopping work at one shop, indicating autoworkers' strong workplace bargaining power on which their resistance is based.

Formal workers' calculated compliance: "Exit" or "Voice"

I have so far shown evidence of growing grievances and resistance among formal workers. However, it should be made clear that the majority of formal workers I interviewed tended to resort to individualized coping strategies rather than seeking collective action or open defiance to challenge management authorities.

Hirschman's (1970) categories of "exit" and "voice" are useful in understanding the respective coping strategies of young and veteran workers. According to Hirschman, in a declining organization, both "voice" and certain forms of "exit" play a "recuperative role," as they make employers aware that changes in the way of doing business are necessary if they are to survive. Exit is a viable solution for members as long as there are some outside options available to them. However, when exit is no longer a viable solution to workers, they are more likely to express their discontent directly to management. Hirschman calls this way of catching management's attention "voice," which he defines as any "attempt to change, rather than escape from an objectionable state of affairs" (1970: 30). When both exit and voice options are available, workers are more likely to choose exit over voice, as doing so

---

[65] Interview D2, USA-2, August 2006.

only requires that they search for better alternatives. Once a better alternative is found, exit would certainly lead to increased welfare. On the contrary, voice involves calculated decisions and uncertainty. Workers therefore would choose voice only if they consider exit not to be an option and if they believe that management would seriously consider their voice, and that the chances that the ailing organization will be revived are good.

The "exit" category might describe the current attitude and coping strategy of young formal production workers, especially those in their 20s with relatively high qualifications and short-term labor contracts. As discussed previously, these youngsters were hopeful that they would be able to "exit" from the line and move up in the factory, or to get out of the factory completely. Such an "exit" option – whether it was realistic or imaginary – made the harsh working conditions a bit more tolerable by allowing workers to view them as temporary. For example, when asked if he could keep up with the current line speed in his 30s and 40s, a 23-year-old assembler at JPN-1 responded:

It doesn't really matter whether or not I can keep up with the lines when I reach my 30s or 40s, because I won't stay in this line job that long anyway. I will probably work here [on the line] for another 3–5 years before I move on to better things. There is no future to work on the line.[66]

The seemingly viable alternative to "exit" from the line, combined with the meritocratic rhetoric, tended to keep young formal workers from openly "voicing" their discontent. Instead, many young workers focused on working hard to impress their team leaders and foremen, in order to secure recommendations for off-line, skilled positions or to become team leaders.

The "voice" category might *partially* describe the current attitudes and coping strategies of veteran workers in that they complained and made "noise" to management but did so without much faith in management to make changes. On the one hand, veteran workers were increasingly dissatisfied and cynical about management as their privileges and protections were reduced, and their chances for further advancement in the factory became slim. But they were less likely to "exit" from the factory because their established benefits and privileges – although declining – were based on seniority, and therefore made it too costly to exit. On the other hand, veteran workers had more bargaining power and job security based on their skills and experience, which made them more likely to "voice" their dissatisfaction to management without worrying too much about being sacked. Whereas veteran workers grumbled a lot, most of them had no intention of taking collective, radical actions against management. Their "voice" was more a way of "venting" their discontent than a concerted effort toward change.

It is worth keeping in mind, however, that both "exit" and "voice" strategies are subject to change over time. For those young workers who aimed to exit

---

[66] Interview H3, JPN-1, May 2007.

from the line and to rise through the ranks, a common strategy was through further education by earning college diplomas and other qualifications in their spare time. However, it was a big challenge for workers to sit in a classroom after working 10-12 hours a day, 6-7 days a week. The following comments from a 25-year-old assembler at USA-1 were representative:

I have been attending night classes to get a college diploma in computer programming for about a year – I hope it can help me get an office job. But time is the biggest challenge for me. The classes are from 6:30–8:30 p.m., so if I am on day shift, I can go to school directly after getting off. But I have to miss the classes when I am on night shift. So I just have to spend [a] longer time to get the diploma. Even during those nights when I could attend the class, it was very difficult to sit in the classroom after a long, exhausting working day. I was nodding off all the time.[67]

To those youngsters who planned eventually to exit the factory, the gap between their aspirations and reality was even larger. Financial constraint was one of the biggest concerns. For example, a 26-year-old line operator at JPN-1 told me about his constantly postponed plans to get out of the factory:

Hard to believe I have been working here for five years. When I first came here, I kept on telling myself that I would not do this job for long. I just wanted to save enough money and open a small business with my girlfriend. But things have kept on coming up. I need to support my younger sister who got admitted to a top college. The tuition is very high and my parents are both retired workers with meager pensions. So I have to be the breadwinner for my family. Now, my sister has graduated, but I need to buy an apartment for my own marriage. I am not sure how long I will hold on to this job.[68]

Between 2004 and 2009, only 5 of the 26 young workers who had planned to exit from the line by moving up within the factory had achieved their goal – three had been promoted to team leader positions, and two had become technicians. Among the 12 who had intended to leave the factory altogether, only two did so – one became an auto salesman and the other took a technician job at a newly built automobile plant in another city.[69] The evidence, again in echo of Chinoy's study of American autoworkers and their blocked aspirations for upward mobility, suggests that it was rare and difficult for blue-collar workers to move up from the bench – either within the factory or outside it – in a hierarchically structured society, despite the meritocratic rhetoric.

Over time, if young workers were to find that, in reality, "exit" was hard to achieve, and if veteran workers found that their "voice" was consistently ignored and their privileges were continuously eroded, it is possible to envision formal workers becoming more radicalized.

---

[67] Interview M12, USA-1, November 2006.　　[68] Interview H4, JPN-1, May 2007.

[69] It should be noted that I was likely to interview the more successful types of workers because they also tended to be more willing to talk about their aspirations. In the other words, the actual opportunities available for the majority of blue-collar workers to exit from the assembly line could be even fewer.

CONCLUSION

In this chapter, I detailed the contradictory positions and attitudes of the core segment of formal autoworkers and their changing relations with management. On the one hand, we have seen growing grievances among the formal workers, derived from an authoritarian and exhausting workplace, as well as from their inferior status as blue-collar workers in a hierarchical factory setting. Moreover, the cut-throat competition and the profitability pressure have driven management to further reduce the privileges and protections afforded to formal workers. As a result, formal workers' consent to management on the basis of promised job security and material benefits is declining. The growing resistance among formal workers signals the gradual radicalization of the "core" segment of workers.

On the other hand, most formal workers have tended to refrain from openly challenging management. Four main factors could explain formal workers' compliance. First, the perceived oversupply of the labor market, coupled with the difficulty in finding better alternatives, inhibit formal workers from engaging in overt protest against management. Second, the practice of labor force dualism and the existence of a large number of temporary workers provide formal workers with some sense of job security. Third, management labor control strategies over formal workers are sophisticated and hegemonic in nature. In particular, by relying on cultural and ideological means of control and the mediating role of EPCs, unions, and team leaders, management has so far been able to defuse direct and intense confrontation and contain labor militancy. Fourth, the seemingly viable alternatives for young workers to "exit" from the line and for veteran workers to "voice" their discontent have inhibited formal workers from organizing overt challenges to management prerogatives.

However, far from "manufacturing consent" (Burawoy 1979), my evidence suggests that formal workers' current compliance can best be understood as a process of negotiation, not consent. As documented in this chapter, through various hidden and open forms of resistance at the point of production, formal workers have been able to exploit their strong workplace bargaining power and management concerns with maintaining peaceful and cooperative labor relations to win specific concessions from their employers.

To fully understand labor politics in the Chinese auto industry, however, we will need to consider the other "flexible" segment of temporary workers, and to examine their group characteristics, grievances, bargaining power, collective actions, and their relations with management and formal workers, respectively. These are the questions that we will explore in Chapter 6.

6

Temporary workers' struggles and the paradox of labor force dualism

> In China, labor fragmentation has not implied passivity. Despite, indeed in large part because of, important distinctions along lines of native-place origins, age, and skill level, the Chinese working class has shown itself to be remarkably feisty... Worker activism during the Hundred Flowers Movement, the Cultural Revolution, the strikes of the mid to late 1970s, the uprising of 1989, and the explosion of industrial disputes in the 1990s can all be linked to splits within the working class.
>
> ——Elizabeth Perry (2002), *Challenging the Mandate of Heaven*, 223

In mid-June of 2004, when I arrived at the state-owned truck maker SOE-2 to start my fieldwork, the first thing I heard from workers was about a wildcat strike that had just happened at the factory a week before my arrival. Over 300 student workers employed at the assembly shop stayed in their dorms and refused to go to work to protest the delay in receiving their monthly pay. With the support of formal workers, the whole assembly line stopped for 15 hours before workers returned to work upon receiving their delayed wages. In November 2004, around 350 laid-off temporary agency workers at the Sino-German JV GER-2 filed a collective labor dispute case against the automaker and the labor agency for the arrears in their social insurance premiums for the time they had worked at GER-2. In March 2005, more than 500 temporary agency workers and student workers at another state-owned carmaker, SOE-1, walked out during a morning shift to protest excessive compulsory overtime and to demand wage increases. In February 2006, right after the Chinese New Year holiday, about 400 temporary agency workers at SOE-1 did not return to work, and management had to send out its office staff to work on the shop floor before it was able to find enough workers. In October 2006, more than 300 student workers at SOE-2 went on strike again, this time to protest the exclusive wage raise for formal workers and other unequal treatment between formal and temporary workers.

Over the course of my fieldwork, I witnessed ongoing struggles by temporary workers against unequal treatment in the workplace and management arbitrary control in the form of sabotage, slowdowns, absenteeism, wildcat strikes, the filing of labor dispute cases, and by quitting jobs en masse. Temporary workers, who were often perceived as weak, vulnerable, and thus more docile and obedient due to their lack of job security, took management by surprise with their activism. How to explain the unexpected resistance among temporary workers? What was the extent and nature of their grievances and bargaining power? What rhetoric and strategies did temporary workers use to protest and to make their claims to employers? How did formal workers and management respond to temporary workers' protests, and how did those responses, in turn, affect the outcome of temporary workers' struggles? What were the implications of temporary workers' struggles for the direction of labor force dualism and the dynamics of labor politics in the Chinese automobile industry?

This chapter aims to address these questions by using ethnographic and interview data to describe the lived shop-floor experiences and collective actions of the "flexible" segment of temporary workers under labor force dualism. Two arguments are central to this chapter. First, although labor force dualism has so far kept formal workers from actively supporting temporary workers, the same dualism has become the major source of temporary workers' grievances, and the catalyst sparking temporary workers' resistance to the unequal treatment they experienced in the workplace.

The second main argument is that Chinese labor politics is not a settled fact; instead, it is better understood as a dynamic process that unfolds through contestation and negotiation among multiple actors – workers, capitalists/managers, and the state. The result is a "contested terrain," and one that is constantly being made and remade. The underlying force driving this process is the unresolved contradiction between increasing profitability and maintaining legitimacy – that is, keeping a peaceful and cooperative labor force – and the efforts of both firms and the state to strike a balance by drawing boundaries within the workforce.

COLLECTIVE CHARACTERISTICS OF THE NEW GENERATION OF TEMPORARY WORKERS

I found three notable collective characteristics common to the new generation of temporary workers that have contributed to their rising labor activism. First, as discussed in Chapter 3, the "new temps" – agency workers and student workers – are increasingly urban, with higher levels of education and a fuller sense of rights as compared with the "old temps" of peasant workers. As a result, the boundary between temporary and formal workers based on their rural-urban *hukou* status has become blurred. Moreover, the rural temporary workers I interviewed had strong desires to stay in the city, and they longed for economic and social advancement as well as workplace equality and dignity. For instance, temporary workers with both urban and rural *hukou* statuses at the Sino-German JVs GER-1 and GER-2 mentioned that they cherished the opportunity to work at the "well-known," "modern," and "advanced" automobile factories, for the opportunity of "learning and self-advancement," rather than just for the money. But the harsh reality of being treated as "second-class" workers and the slim chances of becoming formal workers led temporary workers to feel frustrated and resentful. There was a strong sense of injustice and resentment among the new temporary workers over the unequal treatment they received at work.

The second notable collective characteristic of the new temporary workers that facilitated workers' collective mobilization was their concentrated residence in dormitories close to their workplaces. As noted in previous chapters, the central government's desire for large scale and concentrated automobile production has created gigantic automobile production complexes and factory towns, mostly located in the suburbs of major Chinese cities. While local workers – including both formal and temporary workers – use the company-provided shuttle buses to commute daily between home and the factories, most student workers and some agency workers were not from local areas and lived in factory-subsidized dormitories adjacent to the production complex. Some local workers, especially those who were still single, also chose to live in the factory dormitories or to rent housing close to the factories rather than commuting 3–4 hours roundtrip every day. As a result, a large number of young, male workers with similar backgrounds and workplace experiences concentrated in factory dormitory residences close to their workplace. This pattern of residing in company-provided dormitory residences, as will be shown in the next section, enabled temporary workers to stay close and connected with each other and helped them to foster the group solidarity necessary to effectively mobilize.[1]

The third salient group characteristic of the new temporary workers, similar to one shared by the young generation of formal workers, was that they were technologically-savvy and adept at using social media, including social networking sites, internet forums, blogs, and instant and text messaging, to spread information and initiate collective action. This was especially the case among student workers, who were often connected through the social networking sites of their schools. About three-quarters of the interviewed temporary workers identified themselves as active participants on online forums and social networking sites, and about half mentioned that they had at some point posted online comments about their wages, overtime, work assignments, company policies, or management styles. This group characteristic contributed to the wide use of online organizing strategies among temporary workers, as we will see later in this chapter.

---

[1] Pun and Smith (2007) described a "dormitory labor regime" in China's labor-intensive, export-oriented industrial zones that features teenage, female, migrant workers from the countryside out of province. I found the dormitory residences of autoworkers were characterized by young male workers between the ages of 18–24, with relatively higher education. Most were from the local area or the surrounding countryside.

WORKPLACE GRIEVANCES AND BARGAINING POWER
OF TEMPORARY WORKERS

Intense workplace grievances

Temporary workers had good reason to feel aggrieved and resentful. Besides sharing similar workplace grievances with formal workers under an exhausting and authoritarian work regime (see Chapters 4 and 5), temporary workers also had more intense grievances derived from the unequal treatment they received as second-class workers. The first set of major complaints among the interviewed temporary workers centered on unfavorable job assignments. Temporary workers were often assigned to the least desirable positions. As one worker recounted:

Although we work side by side with formal workers, they have preference over the job assignments, and they usually work at the same position as long as they want. But we have no choice, and we are, with almost no exceptions, to be allocated to the least desirable positions – those tiring and dirty jobs, most at the welding shop. We are also frequently transferred among different lines depending on the production orders and the sales of certain models.[2]

Temporary workers also suffered from discriminatory decisions over daily production issues, such as working hours and compulsory overtime. As a student worker complained:

My team leader always asks us to do overtime on the weekends and holidays, because those formal workers always come out with some reasons and the team leader usually does not get them to work against their will. So, we poor student intern workers have to fill the vacancies, regardless of whether we have our own plans. They just think we dare not say no or bargain as many formal workers do.[3]

Despite the fact that temporary workers had to shoulder heavier workloads and perform less desirable tasks, they received only between half and two-thirds the pay of formal workers, with fewer benefits and little job security. The unequal treatment led temporary workers to feel deeply aggrieved and resentful. The following quote from an agency worker who had worked at GER-1 for three years is very telling:

On the C line at the engine shop where I work, almost all the line operators who are actually doing the work are us *laowu gong*. I have to work on four machine tools continuously during the day, except for a half-hour lunch break and two 10-minute breaks in the morning. My legs and arms always go to numb when I finish my daily work. I feel I've become a robot. Those formal workers, instead, have [a] much lighter workload than ours. But at the end of the month, we only get 2000 RMB, half of those formal workers' – simply because we are *laowu gong*. If you were in my shoes, wouldn't you feel resentful? It is really unfair![4]

---

[2] Interview S14, GER-1, November 2006.   [3] Interview C7, SOE-1, August 2005.
[4] Interview S15, GER-1, November 2006.

To be sure, according to China's Labor Law, workers should be paid equally for doing the same work. The "equal pay for equal work" (*tong gong tong chou*) maxim was frequently cited by the interviewed temporary workers, to denounce the "illegality" (*bu hefa*) and "illegitimacy" (*bu heli*) of paying them less than formal workers for doing the same work. Apparently, the interviewed managers were aware of the "illegality" of the differential wage policy between formal and temporary workers. They responded by emphasizing that formal workers had better education and higher skills, and they performed better jobs and took on more responsibilities than did temporary workers. In the managers' words, formal and temporary workers were doing "similar but qualitatively different" work. This was far from temporary workers' lived shop-floor experiences, and it served to intensify the anger and the sense of injustice among temporary workers.

Temporary workers also complained about the lack of training and learning opportunities at the automobile factories where they work:

Let me tell you, here, *laowu gong* do not have any training and learning opportunities to get improvement. After working here for two years – continuously working day and night shifts as an assembler – I now always tell folks don't come to work here if you are hired as a *laowu gong*. You will learn northing. It is a waste of your youth and energy.[5]

Temporary workers were most indignant about their frequent dismissals as they were used as buffers against market fluctuations. This topic always aroused the most heated feelings during interviews. An agency worker who used to work at GER-1 described his bitter experience as a *laowu gong*:

I used to work on the P assembly line. In 2004, the P model did not sell well. So beginning in 2005, the managers either asked those formal workers on the P line to stay at home or transferred them to other lines. But even the formal workers who stayed at home could still earn 2000 *yuan* per month. We *laowu gong* were not that lucky. Most of us were simply kicked out with a compensation of one-month pay for one-year work at the factory. I contributed my youth and energy to GER-1 for four years, but I got almost nothing in the end. I think this dual system is so wrong! It is really unfair![6]

Moreover, agency workers had little chance of becoming formal workers at the automobile factories where they worked. In other words, temporary workers were faced with social exclusion through what Max Weber called a "closed social relationship."[7] A relationship is closed insofar as the "participation of certain persons is excluded, limited, or subjected to conditions." Closed relationships are often used to "guarantee the monopolized advantages" (Weber 1978: 43–4). It is worth noting that GER-1 used to offer temporary

---

[5] Interview S21, GER-1, November 2006.   [6] Interview S20, GER-1, November 2006.

[7] Exclusion is a mechanism by which social groups (status groups) monopolize goods and opportunities to exclude outsiders from access, and restrict them from free market exchanges (Weber 1968: 190–3). Exclusion can be carried out through maintaining boundaries according to group attributes, such as race, language, religion, party membership and locality; exclusion also can be carried out by social groups, through the function of "closed social relationships" (Weber 1978: 43–4).

workers the opportunity to become formal employees by obtaining the "five-star" award – earned by receiving the annual award for best work performance for five consecutive years. In early 2005, GER-1 granted 65 (out of 5,000) agency workers formal worker status. My interviews with agency workers at GER-1 in the summer of 2004 suggested that the "five-star conversion" policy, despite being criticized by agency workers as too demanding, at least gave agency workers some hope that working hard would help them become regular workers. After more than 2,000 agency workers were laid off during the market downturn in late 2005, however, GER-1 suspended the five-star conversion policy.[8] The agency workers hired after 2005 spoke bitterly about their disillusionment with the prospect of becoming formal workers:

I just wonder why they stopped the policy and why they won't even give us some hope – the hope that there is a chance to become formal workers if we try our best and if we work extremely hard. Now I feel I am in a dead-end job. I just work for the money. There's no hope, no future in this job.[9]

Finally, the triangular employment and the lack of regulation – especially before the LCL took effect in 2008 – often led to fraud in agency workers' social insurance payments, as both labor dispatch agencies and user companies tried to evade their responsibilities to agency workers. The interviewed agency workers generally did not trust the labor agencies with which they signed labor contracts. Many agency workers called the labor agencies "paper companies," who just wanted to skim commission fees from their hard-earned wages without taking any responsibilities for them. The following extract from a group interview with agency workers at SOE-1 illustrates this point:

When we applied for the jobs as operators at SOE-1 through the labor agency, we thought we were hired by SOE-1. Until we were asked to sign labor contracts with that agency, we were then told that we were just hired as agency workers, not formal employees of SOE-1. They charged 25-percent commissions from our monthly earnings at SOE-1. The social insurance package we received from the agency was also much thinner compared to SOE-1 formal workers'. We felt we were cheated.[10]

From what we have discussed so far, we can see that the agency workers' grievances were derived from the multiple oppressions of having "double employers" – the automobile firm and the labor agency or vocational school – as well as their second-class worker status, rather than simply from lower wages and poorer working conditions. During the interviews, temporary workers frequently used the words "injustice" (*bu gongzheng*) and "unfair" (*bu gongping*) to denounce labor force dualism and temporary agency employment. Thus temporary workers had a keener sense of injustice and felt deep resentment, and their claims and protests were often explosive and morally-based.

---

[8] GER-1 restored its five-star conversion policy in 2008.
[9] Interview S22, GER-1, November 2006.   [10] Interview C17, SOE-1, March 2007.

Growing workplace bargaining power

At the same time, growing numbers of temporary workers concentrated on assembly lines and throughout the JIT production system enabled temporary workers to shut down entire shops by acting suddenly and collectively at the point of production. As the following quotes from a temporary agency worker at GER-2 recount:

In our work group, there are 21 workers, and 12 of us are *laowu gong*. The whole assembly shop has 500 workers, and almost half are now *laowu gong*. If we [agency workers] stop working all together, the whole shop will stop.[11]

Moreover, a growing number of temporary workers who had worked at the automobile factories for long tenures had become the backbone of the production workforce; some even had become team leaders.[12] Thus, in both numerical and functional terms, temporary workers had gained growing workplace bargaining power. This, combined with their intense grievances, has led to rising resistance among the temporary workers.

TEMPORARY WORKERS PUSH BACK

The aggrieved temporary workers pushed back by using various forms of resistance to cause stoppages and interruptions of regular production and major losses in output. The most common strategy temporary workers adopted was to use small-scale, less-open, but highly disruptive forms of everyday resistance, such as sabotage, slowdowns, absenteeism, and collective quitting of their jobs. For example, when over 300 student workers at the welding shop of SOE-1 did not return to work after the traditional Chinese New Year holiday in 2006, the whole welding shop was forced to shut down for three days before enough replacements could be hired. In fact, at SOE-1, about 20 percent of line operators quit every year. Among them, most were student workers.[13] High labor turnover and a lack of commitment in production among temporary workers caused slowdowns of production and had a negative impact on product quality. This issue had become a major concern of management. During the interviews, some shop floor managers complained about the lack of commitment and the "careless" work done by temporary workers. On several occasions, agency workers were accused of abusing production tools like welding torches, thereby incurring higher maintenance costs.

The most effective means of voicing their grievances and demands to employers were strikes at the point of production. The important question is: when, where, and how did temporary workers organize and develop collective

---

[11] Interview F14, GER-2, October 2006.
[12] Among the 88 temporary workers I interviewed two were team leaders, each heading work groups of 10–15 workers.
[13] Interview C10, SOE-1, March 2007.

actions such as strikes? My fieldwork found that temporary workers were more likely to take collective actions, and to wring more concessions from management, when formal workers shared their discontent and grievances. Then, the question becomes: under what conditions did formal and temporary workers share discontent and grievances, and what could make them more likely to engage with each other in collective actions?

The June strike

It was a big surprise to everyone when the temporary workers at SOE-2 went on strike. Not only had there not been a single open protest at SOE-2 since 1993, when the factory carried out its first enterprise restructuring,[14] it was also a surprise because no one expected the temporary workers – who were commonly perceived as vulnerable, and thus more docile and passive – would be willing to risk striking and potentially losing their jobs. Both formal and temporary workers spoke with amusement about how managers had rushed around trying to find workers, and how the seemingly never-ending assembly lines had suddenly stopped and the whole assembly shop had been shut down. A formal worker recalled the dramatic scene he encountered when he arrived at work on the day shift after the night shift had gone on strike:

When I entered the shop that morning, I immediately noticed something unusual happened. It was so quiet in the entire workshop, and the night shift folks were not there. We stood there chatting, and no one started working. Then suddenly someone said, 'They [temporary workers] were on strike!' I thought it was cool! It was fun to watch managers running around and trying to find workers to get the line to start running again. But it was impossible when 3/5 of the line workers [temporary workers] went on strike. It was seven in the morning.[15]

The strike was initiated by the night-shift student workers in the assembly shop. Sitting in their small and simple dorm room, four student workers who had participated in the strike described to me the vivid picture of the strike and their unforgettable experiences from it. Hai, an 18-year-old student worker, explained to me how the strike came about:

It [the strike] happened on the payday in June. We had continuously worked 10–12 hours a day without any day off for two months. We were all exhausted but stuck at the work only in hope to get a high bonus for the excessive overtime. Besides, we had not gotten paid for the month before because the school changed its computerized payroll system and we were expecting to get paid together. So everyone was counting on the pay day. We waited until that afternoon, but still, no payments were deposited to our bank accounts. We were all outraged. That night, we over 300 student workers living in the

---

[14] Veteran state workers who were forced to take early retirements when SOE-2 was acquired by another large truck maker in 1993 organized several petitions. Interview Q3, SOE-2, June 2004
[15] Interview Q4, SOE-2, June 2004.

West Dormitory Residence decided not go to work until we got paid. We stayed in our dorms sleeping. The whole assembly line B stopped.[16]

I asked, "Were you worried about being fired for participating in the strike?" After a short silence, another student worker named Lei responded:

Honestly, at that moment, we did not think that much. We were so angry, and it [the strike] just happened like, you know, spontaneously, and we came together and got organized! You know, we were hardly able to sustain our daily lives without getting paid for two months! We didn't know who first called for the strike. It's like someone on the third-floor shouted that we should not go to work until we got paid. We all responded to the call. I think everyone at that moment would do so.[17]

The others nodded. Xing, a 19-year-old student worker, described how the strike evolved:

The shop manager came to our dorms one hour later and asked us to go back to work. We said not until we got paid our wages in arrears. The manager said they would discuss the issue with our school but we must go back to work first. No one responded. That was almost 10 p.m. And we learned that our co-workers, the formal workers, went back home without working as well. The whole assembly shop was shut down. The following morning, the production manager and the HR manager came to our residence – I bet it was the first time they paid attention to us and visited our dorms. They promised to solve the problem, but we must go back to work immediately. They threatened to fire those who didn't go back to work. Many of us were frightened, but we insisted on getting paid first.[18]

Another silence ensued. Everyone seemed to be brought back to the intense moment of strike. Then Shui, an 18-year-old student worker, broke the silence:

Our brothers in the day shift stayed with us and no one showed up at work. We all insisted to get paid first. The vice principal of our school came after receiving the phone calls from the factory. He apologized and said the delays were caused by an upgrading of the school's payment system. He said that the new system had been fixed and we should see our paychecks in our banking accounts by noon. And we did. Most of us went back to work shortly afterwards.[19]

Even though the strike was short-lived, having engaged in the strike and experienced the intense pressure from management, the student workers came out of the strike with a stronger sense of group solidarity and collective power. The strike brought student workers out of their isolated daily work experience and enabled them to see their potential to "achieve something" by staying united and acting collectively. As Hai and Lei reflected:

It used to be, you went to work, worked hard through your shift, went back to your dorm to sleep, and got back to work again. When you did not receive your paycheck on time, or only earned half of those formal workers for the same work, you just thought

---

[16] Interview Q6, SOE-2, June 2004.   [17] Interview Q7, SOE-2, June 2004.
[18] Interview Q8, SOE-2, June 2004.   [19] Interview Q9, SOE-2, June 2004

there was nothing you could do about it. But suddenly, you realized that you could actually achieve something by coming together and acting together![20]

At that moment [of the strike], you feel like we are all staying together, we are all supporting each other. You realize at least I am not alone... That makes you feel stronger. It's a great feeling![21]

The workers perceived the June strike as a success. As Xing commented:

I think the strike was successful even though it did not last long. The factory managers paid attention to us. We received our delayed payment, and no one got in trouble for participating in the strike. Seven of us returned to work in the afternoon, but the managers just let us get by. No one got fired in the end.[22]

From the interviews, we can identify several factors that may explain the success of the June strike. First, the increasing number of student workers deployed on assembly lines enabled them to shut down the entire shop by acting suddenly and collectively.

Second, the closely connected dormitory residences of student workers, many with similar backgrounds and workplace experiences, facilitated effective organizing and collective action on the spot.

Third, from my interviews with the managers, it is clear that they saw the strike as "a spontaneous and natural response of workers" when their subsistence was jeopardized, and thus managers responded "softly" to the striking workers. For instance, when asked about the strike, the production manager responded, "The strike was an incident caused by the mismanagement of the vocational school. We need to find a better labor agency."[23] Thus, instead of punishing student workers for participating in the strike, SOE-2 set up a "no-delay policy" to guarantee that student workers would receive their monthly pay on time. Also, SOE-2 requested that the vocational school send a representative to reside at the factory in order to better "communicate" with and control student workers.

Fourth, the timing of the strike played an important role as well. Prior to the June strike, workers had been constantly working 10 hours a day, day and night shifts in turn, without a single day off for two months straight. A team leader made this point clear:

Between May and September, when production orders all come in and the factory is in its peak season, management is under great pressure to get the production quota out as much as possible. They are reluctant to lay off workers when the factory is desperately in need of workers to make the targeted output within the deadlines.[24]

Perhaps more importantly, the "silent support" from formal workers played a key role in magnifying the disruptive effects of the temporary workers' strike. After learning that the night shift temporary workers went on strike, formal

---

[20] Interview Q6, SOE-2, June 2004.   [21] Interview Q7, SOE-2, June 2004.
[22] Interview Q8, SOE-2, June 2004.   [23] Interview Q1, SOE-2, June 2004.
[24] Interview Q10, SOE-2, June 2004.

workers at the assembly shop stood aside the production lines, chatting and resting without working. They claimed that they were unable to keep the line moving when three-fifths of the workers were absent. As the team leader explained to me:

Right before the strike, workers were all exhausted and complained about such excessive overtime. Everyone was expecting a big bonus on their paychecks. But they only found a slight increase in their monthly bonus on the pay day. Folks were very disappointed and resentful. So the strike by student workers was an outlet for formal workers to vent their discontent as well.[25]

This was in sharp contrast with the detachment of formal workers toward the October strike by temporary workers, which I will discuss below. As we will see in the following sections, the outcome of temporary workers' struggles were largely influenced by whether or not formal workers acted in support of temporary workers.

The October strike

On October 10, 2006, the temporary workers at SOE-2 went on strike again. That morning, I received a phone call from Hai and Lei, whom I had interviewed at SOE-2, "We are on strike! We are on strike! We want the same wage increase as those formal workers!" This time, the temporary workers at SOE-2 demanded an equal wage increase after the company raised the wages of formal workers exclusively. The strike broke out in a similar pattern, originating from the West Dormitory Residence: over 300 student workers working in the assembly shop stayed in their dorms and refused to go to work during a morning shift. At that time, I was doing fieldwork at another automobile factory in northern China. I rushed back to the eastern coastal city where SOE-2 is located the next morning, only to find that the strike was over and eighteen striking workers had been fired.

This time, management took a hard line – the factory director sent out an ultimatum stating that those who did not go back to work by noon would be fired. Managers asked the striking workers to send a representative to talk but no one would step up. The strike ended shortly before noon, with eighteen workers fired for not having returned to work by then. Management considered the strikers' demand for an equal wage increase as an "intentional confrontation" challenging their authority. Concerned that such "trouble-making" actions could cause further disruptions to production in the future, management decided to fire the "black sheep," as well as those who did not obey the order to return to work on time in order to intimidate workers from taking similar actions in the future.[26]

It is worth noting that one month after the October strike management raised temporary workers' wages. There was a 200 *yuan* raise for those who

---

[25] Interview Q10, SOE-2, June 2004.   [26] Interview Q28, SOE-2, October 2006.

didn't participate in the strike, while strike participants only received a 100 *yuan* raise – as a way to punish those who went on strike but nonetheless returned to work before noon.

Notably, in contrast to their supportive attitude toward temporary workers during the June strike, formal workers showed little support for temporary workers in the October strike. The following quote from a formal worker explains why:

You know, the market is not that good these days, and the factory is struggling. I am happy that they [management] still raised our base wages, which are not linked to the market sales under the current situation. You know, it is just impossible to pay everyone the same. Otherwise, why would the factory even bother to hire temporary workers? Because it needs cheap and flexible hands. I also think this is unfair. But look, there are so many people who don't even have a job. I am sure they are more willing to take those temporary jobs. They [temporary workers] should feel lucky to even have a job and work here.[27]

In the June strike, the shared workplace grievances motivated formal workers to stand alongside temporary workers. In the October strike, however, the divisive wage policy kept formal workers from supporting temporary workers. Also, temporary workers were frequently reminded by management about the oversupplied labor market and their weak marketplace bargaining power in finding formal employment. In fact, management constantly conveyed to workers the message that the labor markets were oversupplied and anyone – including formal workers – could lose their jobs if they did not work hard. The hard line that the managers took in firing the eighteen striking workers who did not resume work within the given time reinforced temporary workers' feelings of "insecurity" and "powerlessness." As the following responses from a group of student workers indicated:

You know, at that moment, we really didn't have any other options other than going back to work. The manager told us there were so many people waiting outside the factory to try to get a job, and they would fire those who did not come back to work by noon. We were all afraid to lose our jobs, because it also meant that we could not receive our diplomas from the school. Honestly, although we were not treated fairly, we are still better off than many of my schoolmates working in electronics and textile factories.[28]

But instead of viewing the October strike as a failure, the interviewed temporary workers tended to think that the strike at least got management to pay attention to their grievances and demands, which led to the 100–200 *yuan* pay increase a month later. The main problem, according to the temporary workers I interviewed, was that they did not "have a representative to step up and to speak for" them:

[27] Interview Q27, SOE-2, October 2006.
[28] Interviews Q29, Q30, Q31, Q32, SOE-2, October 2006.

They [managers] would not listen to you unless you cause them trouble and make loud noises. But the problem was that we didn't have a representative to step up and to speak for us about our demands when the managers asked us to send a representative to talk with them. We didn't have any experience, and individually, everyone was scared to be identified as black sheep and get fired. If we could have a union or an organization that can genuinely represent us and speak for us, things could have been different.[29]

By comparison, we can see that both strikes broke out in an unexpected manner as several hundred student workers stayed in their dormitory rooms and refused to go to work at the start of a shift. Both strikes were wildcat strikes, without the official support of a trade union. Both strikes were fueled by the sense of injustice, with a direct goal of economic gain. The June strike was incited by the threat to workers' livelihood – in the form of the delay of workers' monthly wages – and it was reactive and defensive in nature. In the October strike, temporary workers had begun to target equal treatment with formal workers, and the strike was initiated and planned in advance. The June strike was perceived as a success given that temporary workers received their delayed payment, and no one got in trouble for participating. But in the October strike, management took a hard line and fired striking workers. There were several factors that accounted for the different outcomes of the two strikes, including timing, management's perceptions of the strikes, and, perhaps most important, whether or not formal workers had supported temporary workers' struggles. In the June strike, the shared workplace grievances motivated formal workers to stand alongside temporary workers and magnified the disruptive effects of the strike. In the October strike, however, the divisive wage policy succeeded in keeping formal workers from supporting agency workers' demands.

While both strikes were short-lived, small-scale, and did not go beyond economic demands, the "moments of madness" (Zolberg 1972) in the heat of strikes enabled temporary workers to see their ability to achieve goals if they acted collectively. This is the first step toward overcoming their perceived "weakness" and developing a collective consciousness. Temporary workers also began to demand a genuine organization representative of their interests as a result of the strikes.

Enterprise union response

Apparently, temporary workers did not consider the enterprise union to be their representative. In fact, it was not until the implementation of the LCL in 2008 that agency workers were allowed to join the unions of the automobile enterprises at which they were working. Student workers were still not qualified to join the unions due to their lack of *de jure* worker status. Among the temporary workers I interviewed, only two responded that they would seek

---

[29] Interview Q26, SOE-2, October 2006.

the union's help in handling grievances.[30] Most temporary workers would rather turn to their co-workers, team leaders, or school representatives (for student workers) to resolve workplace issues. Union officials, on the other hand, responded passively to temporary workers' grievances and demands. Most interviewed union officials held negative attitudes toward temporary workers' "trouble-making" actions. The following response of the union chairman at SOE-2 is illustrative:

> The factory union represents the collective interest of the majority of workers, not the individual demands of a handful of trouble-making workers. If workers were allowed to go on strike whenever they had grievances, it would bankrupt our enterprise and eventually hurt workers' own interests. Therefore, we union will not support any strikes, sabotage or absenteeism that could interrupt daily production. We believe regular communication and open dialogue between workers and management through the factory Party committee and the union is a much better way to solve problems.[31]

Such views were widely held among the interviewed enterprise union leaders. This is not surprising given the subordinate position of unions to the Party and the dependence of enterprise unions on management in the Chinese workplace. In fact, both formal and temporary workers considered factory unions as part of management, rather than a labor organization able to represent them and stand up for their rights and interests. But with the pressure of rising labor unrest and the danger of being bypassed completely by temporary workers in favor of other underground or informal organizations, the unions have begun to change their attitudes and strategies toward temporary workers, from exclusion to "incorporation," as we will discuss later in this chapter.

New organizing strategy

Another salient feature of the October strike was the new strategy of organizing through web-based and mobile-based social media technologies. According to my interviews with some striking workers at SOE-2, the strike was initiated and planned through a social networking site created by the student workers from the same vocational school working in different cities and sectors. Over three-quarters of student workers at SOE-2 – about 300 in number – were active on this social networking site, sharing information on jobs and wages as well as venting their discontent and resentments at work. The mobilization started from an online post on the discussion forum about an exclusive wage increase for formal workers at SOE-2. During a week of extensive online discussions,

---

[30] The two temporary workers were both model agency workers introduced to me by management at the time of my interviews with them. One was a team leader who had been working at GER-1 since 1999; the other had been working at GER-2 since 1998, and had become a formal worker of GER-2 in March 2011. He was the first agency worker to be granted formal worker status at GER-2. Interviews S11, GER-1, July 2004; F8, GER-2, August 2004, July 2011.

[31] Interview Q25, SOE-2, October 2006.

over 200 student workers expressed their indignation and support for "taking action" in the act of protest. The involved student workers then progressed into "real" world organizing through their closely connected dormitories, eventually bringing about the October strike.[32] Similarly, before and during the strike at USA-2 (see Chapter 5) and the Honda strike, workers used various social media technologies, such as *weibo* (MicroBlog) and online discussion forums, instant messaging services such as QQ, and text messages to disseminate information, initiate collective action, and stay connected with each other. This new organizing strategy provided temporary workers – who are often perceived as "unorganizable" due to their frequent changes of workplace – with new opportunities and potential to organize and stay connected. In fact, there has been a growing trend of utilizing social media to facilitate collective action in China more broadly. As the Director of the China Internet Project, Xiao Qiang, observed:

Information and communication technologies are playing a critical role in facilitating social and political action in China. The Chinese internet is still a highly contested space. The authoritarian regime is learning to be more responsive and adaptive in this new environment. Likewise, the internet has also become a training ground for citizen participation in public affairs.[33]

"Using the law as the weapon"[34]

Until the implementation of the Labor Contract Law in 2008, the lack of regulations on labor dispatch often led to fraud in agency workers' social insurance payments, as both labor agencies and user firms attempted to evade their responsibilities for agency workers. As a result, there had been growing numbers of collective labor dispute cases filed by agency workers.[35] One such example was a collective labor dispute case filed by 300 laid-off agency workers at the Sino-German JV GER-2. During the auto market downturn in late 2004 and 2005, GER-2 dismissed over 1,000 agency workers. The laid-off agency workers found that neither GER-2 nor the labor agency had made the contributions to their social insurance premiums required by the government during the time when they had worked at GER-2. Indignant workers turned to the

---

[32] Workers were wary of, and skilled in, keeping their online activities and identities secret from management.

[33] Comments delivered in a speech at the Congressional Executive Commission on China (CECC) Hearing, "What Will Drive China's Future Legal Development? Reports from the Field." Washington, D.C., June 18, 2008.

[34] The strategy of "using the law as the weapon" have been discussed in the works of Gallagher (2005b), Lee (2007), and Michelson (2008), among others.

[35] This statement is based on the author's piecemeal interviews with district LDMAC officials and labor arbitrators in Guangzhou, in September 2006; and in Shanghai, in February 2007. So far, there have been no systematic statistics on the collective labor dispute cases filed by dispatched employees in China.

district Labor Dispute Mediation and Arbitration Committee (LDMAC), and filed a collective labor dispute case. At that time, there was no legislation in place that clearly defined the responsibilities of labor agencies and client firms for agency employees.[36] The district LDMAC arbitrator tried to settle the case by requiring that GER-2 and the labor agency each pay half of the premiums in arrears for the dismissed agency workers. GER-2 complied, but the labor agency filed for bankruptcy after the district LDMAC made the arbitration decision. GER-2 eventually agreed to pay all of the social insurance premiums due for the dismissed agency workers in order to settle the dispute. The whole process lasted almost a year, and most of the involved agency workers had already left the city by the time the final settlement was reached. Just imagine how hard it would be for the unemployed temporary workers to survive such a long period in the city. It was unclear how many of the laid-off agency workers in fact received the back social insurance payments owed to them in the end.[37]

The GER-2 case revealed that, on the one hand, temporary workers had rising legal consciousness and they were willing to "use the law as the weapon" to fight against violations of their rights and interests. On the other hand, the existing labor dispute resolution system was not effective in addressing workers' grievances.[38] Although the interviewed agency workers were cynical about the labor laws and the labor dispute resolution process handled by local officials, they had developed good strategies as to how to leverage the aspects of the law that could be used to their advantage. As one veteran agency worker who witnessed the collective labor dispute case at GER-2 commented:

We know that the law often does not work the way it says. But even if that does not work, it is good to have the labor laws on our side – we can at least file labor dispute cases when they [employers] violate the law! Employers, especially those high-profile large ones like GER-2, are more worried about getting into trouble with labor disputes that could attract bad publicity. If we workers can catch public and media attention to our grievances, the companies will be more likely to compromise in order to get out of trouble quickly. Social media can be very useful to spread the word.[39]

The comments also reflect the empowerment effect of the labor laws in motivating ordinary Chinese workers to stand up and defend their legitimate labor

---

[36] The LCL, which took effect on January 1, 2008, contains specific clauses designed to regulate labor dispatch, and stipulates the responsibilities of both labor agencies and client firms in regard to agency workers. See the discussions in Chapters 3 and 7.

[37] When I revisited GER-2 in October 2006, I was unable to find and interview workers who had directly participated in the collective labor dispute case, because most had since left the plant. The descriptions of the case were provided by workers – both formal and temporary – who had witnessed the dispute but who were not directly involved.

[38] On May 1, 2008, the Labor Dispute Mediation and Arbitration Law went into effect. The law aims to facilitate quicker, cheaper and easier access for workers to the labor dispute mediation and arbitration system.

[39] Interview F19, GER-2, October 2006.

rights through the courts. This point is further illustrated by the dramatic increase in the numbers of labor dispute cases filed by workers after the LCL was passed in 2007 (see Chapter 7). As the IHLO observed, "the awareness of the new law and what it may mean for workers has been one of the most important and immediate impacts of the new law – regardless of whether or not it is implemented properly."[40]

So far, we have witnessed rising activism among the new temporary workers against unequal treatment at work. Temporary workers have demonstrated their potential and ability to push back through small-scale, less-open but highly-disruptive forms of everyday resistance, such as wildcat strikes, as well as through formal legal channels. Before we draw conclusions, however, it is important to examine the intergroup relations between formal and temporary workers under labor force dualism. How have formal workers responded to temporary workers' resistance? And, whether and under what conditions are formal workers more likely to use their strong workplace bargaining power in solidarity with temporary workers?

INTERGROUP RELATIONSHIP BETWEEN FORMAL AND TEMPORARY WORKERS

One of the persistent themes in studies of labor movements is that intra-class divisions among workers impede working-class solidarity and lead to weak labor movements (Aronowitz 1991; Gordon et al. 1982; Oestreicher 1986; Sabel 1982; Wright 1997). Workers also have "an endemic tendency to draw nonclass borders and boundaries," to protect themselves from labor market competition (Silver 2003: 22; cf. Arrighi 1990b). Bonacich's "split labor markets" (1972, 1976) approach undergirds these presumptions. It argues that when there is a large differential in the price of labor for the same occupation, labor market competition is split between higher-paid labor drawn from the dominant ethnicity and low-cost, usually ethnic-minority labor. When confronted with employers' attempts to displace higher-paid labor with cheaper labor, the higher-paid (white) workers tended to take antagonistic and collective exclusionary action toward the lower-paid, racial/ethnic workers to prevent the latter from entering the higher-paid labor market and/or to try to maintain their aristocratic position (Bonacich 1972). The "split labor market" approach that developed in the U.S. context in the 1970s highlights race and ethnicity as central to the divide in labor markets and within the working class. In China, as noted in Chapter 3, one of the most salient and persistent labor market divides is the urban-rural *hukou* system established and institutionalized by the Communist state. The *hukou* system is also known to have created a clear boundary between urban and rural workers in the workplace.

[40] IHLO, 2008. The IHLO is the Hong Kong Liaison Office of the international trade union movement.

My field research found that the intergroup relationship between formal and temporary workers at China's major automobile factories was better characterized by "detachment" rather than "antagonism." The explanation is threefold. First, labor force dualism tended to divide formal workers from temporary workers, creating an unequal workplace and visible social distance between the two groups of workers. At the same time, however, formal workers had little incentive to pressure management to exclude temporary workers – given that management had up until then mainly used temporary workers as a buffer to counter the fluctuation of markets and production demand rather than as an open replacement of formal workers. Moreover, close daily cooperation within the same work groups at the point of production, as well as the blurring of boundaries between formal and temporary workers based on their rural-urban *hukou* statuses, moderated the degrees of division between the two groups of workers. As such, the social distance – the degree of "detachment" – between formal and temporary workers was largely contingent on management employment policies and labor control strategies, as well as local and shop-floor cultures.

My interviews with formal and temporary workers suggested that the divisive effect of labor force dualism created visible social distances between formal and temporary workers. The two groups viewed each other as "them" rather than a collective "us." This was especially the case when differences in formal-temporary worker status were associated with urban-rural *hukou* status. As illustrated in the following comments from an agency worker with a rural *hukou*:

We [agency workers] have different social circles from them [formal workers]. We don't hang out with them [formal workers] after work. It especially hurts when some formal workers from the city call us "those from *Nongcun*" [countryside].[41]

Temporary workers were also very sensitive to some of the "show-off" practices of formal workers that reinforced their awareness of their own second-class worker status:

I get very depressed whenever formal workers boast about their high wages, bonuses, and fringe benefits in front of us, as if showing off their superior status to our inferior temporary status. I would rather just stay away from them.[42]

Formal workers' attitudes toward temporary workers were more contradictory and ambiguous. On the one hand, formal workers tended to downplay the differences between them and temporary workers at work. For example, more than two-thirds of the interviewed formal workers said they did not look down upon temporary workers, and that they did not see much difference between them and temporary workers when they all worked side by side on assembly lines. On the other hand, many formal workers did not think they had much in common with temporary workers beyond the factory gate. About one-third of

[41] Interview S8, GER-1, July 2004.   [42] Interview S9, GER-1, July 2004.

the interviewed formal workers mentioned that "temps had lower education and bad manners," and reported having little contact with temporary workers after work. The following quote from a formal worker in the assembly shop at GER-2 is representative:

I don't think they [temporary workers] are different from us [formal workers] when we all work together on assembling lines. After all, we come to the factory to work for a living. Why should we treat our worker brothers differently? But after work, we don't have much contact. You know, we have different social lives and circles. We don't have much in common.[43]

The social distance between formal and temporary workers was made greater by the two groups' segregated living spaces and unequal living conditions. Formal workers and temporary workers lived in separate factory dormitories provided by the company. For example, at SOE-2, student workers lived in the West Dormitory, formal workers with junior college degrees lived in the South Dormitory, and formal workers with Bachelor's degrees lived in the University Apartments. Formal workers had much better living conditions than temporary workers. At the West Dormitory, 5–6 student workers shared a dorm room with bunk-beds, a TV set, and an electric fan. There was only one public toilet at the end of the corridor on each floor, shared by about 60 people. The biggest complaint was the lack of shower amenities. There was only one shower room, with 16 showers for the over 300 student workers living in the West Dormitory. By contrast, in the South Dormitory, four people shared a furnished room with a private bathroom, color TV, and electric fans. At the University Apartments, two people shared a furnished, 2-bedroom apartment with a private kitchen and bathroom. Workers living in different dormitory residences had little contact.[44]

It is worth noting that young formal workers, especially those with one- to two-year labor contracts, tended to be more empathetic toward temporary workers. More than three-quarters of the interviewed formal workers under the age of 30 strongly agreed with the statement that "temporary workers should be treated equally for doing the same work." By contrast, veteran formal workers seemed to have more negative views of temporary workers. Some veteran workers commented that temporary workers were of "low quality" (*di sushi*), and lacked work ethic. As a 34-year-old mechanic at GER-2 commented:

I don't think they [temporary workers] should be put on important positions in production. I don't mean to look down upon them. But I saw many times those temps misuse the tools. They just don't care. Many temp workers have low education and little skill training. You know, they are not the kind of workers that we can count on.[45]

---

[43] Interview F4, GER-2, August 2004.
[44] The author's dormitory visits and group interviews, SOE-2, June 2004.
[45] Interview F9, GER-2, August 2004.

Such differences in formal workers' attitudes might be explained by the growing homogeneity in the social composition of the young generation of formal
workers and temporary workers, as discussed in Chapter 3. It might also have
to do with the fact that, in comparison with veteran formal workers, young
formal workers had less job security and fewer privileges. They were thus more
likely to share similar feelings of "insecurity" and "disempowerment" with
temporary workers.

In spite of the clear divisions and the social distance between formal and
temporary workers, my fieldwork found few instances of direct confrontation
between the two groups. Instead, there was a sense of "fellow workmates"
between formal and temporary workers on the line. This first had to do with the
work group system that required close contact and cooperation between formal
and temporary workers within their work groups. As a temporary worker who
worked as a welder at GER-2 noted:

At work, I don't feel they [the formal workers] treat us differently. We work side by side
and we help each other to get daily production tasks done.[46]

A formal worker from the same work group expressed a similar view about the
cooperative workmate relations between formal and temporary workers on the
line:

In my work group, we have eight temporary workers and six formal workers. You
cannot get work done without temporary workers. Cooperation makes everyone's life
easier. I don't see much difference between us at work.[47]

More importantly, despite the wide use of temporary workers on assembly
lines, there had not been instances in which formal workers were openly
replaced with temporary workers. Rather, temporary workers were used as a
buffer to counter fluctuations in production. Therefore, there was little direct
confrontation between formal and temporary workers as a result of the two
groups competing for jobs. In fact, as mentioned in the previous chapters, the
presence of temporary workers provided formal workers with some sense of job
security.

This point is made clearer when viewed in comparison to the adverse social
relations between temporary workers and regular (formal) workers at a large
Korean auto company. Lee and Frenkel (2004) found a "moral exclusion"
existed between regular employees and temporary workers. One of the main
reasons for the increasingly adversarial relationship between the two groups of
autoworkers in South Korea was management's decision to substitute temporary workers for regular workers as the strength of the regular workers' union
declined. As such, regular workers viewed temporary workers as a threat to
their own employment. The contrast between the Chinese and South Korean
cases suggests that different management employment policies and labor

---

[46] Interview F6, GER-2, August 2004.   [47] Interview F7, GER-2, August 2004.

control strategies can play a key role in determining the nature of intergroup relations between formal and temporary workers and, correspondingly, the outcomes of workers' struggles.

Another important factor that moderated social divisions between formal and temporary workers on the Chinese shop floor was the socialist egalitarian legacy that was still relevant to both workers and managers, especially at those early-built factories. For example, at GER-2, the Sino-German JV located in an old industrial base in Northeast China, socialist legacies and SOE culture remained strong. More than two-thirds of the interviewed formal workers considered that it was "not right" to pay temporary workers less for doing the same work. Management tried to obscure the divisions between formal and temporary workers, and promoted organizational integration. Formal workers and temporary workers wore the same uniforms, ate at the same cafeterias, and took the same company buses free of charge. Temporary workers also received gifts during the Chinese traditional festivals. Moreover, most workers, both formal and temporary, were locals and thus spoke the same dialect. As a result, the divisions between formal and temporary workers were less visible, and the social relations between the two groups tended to be closer and more cooperative than at the other studied factories that had adopted labor force dualism. When the factory dismissed around 1,000 agency workers in late 2004, most of the interviewed formal workers expressed their sympathy to those agency workers. One of the interviewed formal workers commented that the apparent callousness of GER-2 in letting go of a large number of agency workers without any compensation "chilled formal workers' hearts as well." The fact that agency workers with long tenures were let go first made it clear that the company only cared about cutting costs and shaking off responsibilities for workers, rather than valuing workers' loyalty and long-time service.[48] When nearly 300 dismissed agency workers filed a collective labor dispute case against GER-2 and the labor agency for unpaid social insurance premiums, some formal workers provided financial support for the involved agency workers who had lost their jobs and income during the lengthy legal process.[49]

These factors all acted to moderate the degree of the divisions and social distances between formal and temporary workers, indicating that there was the potential for developing a more engaging and cooperative relationship between formal and temporary workers.

At the same time, management explicitly employed "divide and control" strategies to keep different groups of workers from coming together and forging a sense of solidarity. For example, at another Sino-German JV GER-1, the factory organization was very hierarchical. Management adopted a "visual control method," making the distinctions between formal and agency workers visible in almost every possible aspect. Formal workers and temporary workers

[48] Interview F13, GER-2, October 2006. [49] Interviews F27, F30, GER-2, October 2006.

wore different-colored work uniforms – in fact, even among formal workers, the uniform color of skilled workers and team leaders was different from that of semi-skilled operators. As the Secretary of the factory Party committee explained:

We use different colors of uniforms to easily identify different types of workers. You can see that technicians and team leaders wear gray uniforms. Ordinary formal workers wear dark blue uniforms. Those in sky blue color are agency workers. But there are two different "sky blues" – those in uniforms with a company name stamped on their uniform pockets are the 'new' agency workers hired through the labor agency company after 2005; those in sky blue without characters are 'old' agency workers recruited before 2005 through labor bureaus in the surrounding districts and townships.[50]

Moreover, temporary workers at GER-1 were mostly rural youths from the suburbs of Shanghai, while formal workers were Shanghai urban residents. As a result, the divisions between formal and temporary workers were salient and visible at GER-1, and the different groups of workers tended to be more detached from each other. This can be seen in the indifferent attitude of formal workers toward the layoffs of a large contingent of temporary workers in 2005. When GER-1 dismissed over 2,000 agency workers in 2005, formal workers just stood by in silence. The formal workers I interviewed were either reluctant to talk about the layoffs, or responded by saying, "I don't know much about it because I don't have much contact with them [agency workers]."[51] A team leader commented that it would not be difficult for the laid-off agency workers to land other jobs through their labor agencies, "but it is certainly not easy to find the same well-paying jobs as they had here at GER-1."[52] This was in direct contrast to the sympathetic and supportive attitude formal workers exhibited toward the dismissed temporary workers at GER-2.

From the critical Marxist perspective of a segmented labor market approach, such "divide and conquer" strategies as used by employers have made the micro-level relations among workers complex and variegated, and in many cases have pitted workers against one another, undermining the likelihood that workers of all statuses would take a stance in solidarity against capital and management. Yet a divided labor force does not necessarily preclude robust and continuing labor activism that can lead to significant change. As this chapter has shown, the paradox of labor force dualism is that this management-constructed division among workers has at the same time become a continuing source of irritation and an impetus to rebel among temporary workers.

How these struggles are likely to develop depends in large measure on how management and the state respond – that is, how management and the state choose to balance the tension between the drive for profitability and the need for legitimacy with labor. Thus, in the next section, I will examine

---

[50] Interview S16, GER-1, November 2006.   [51] Interview S18, GER-1, November 2006.
[52] Interview S19, GER-1, November 2006.

how management and the union have responded to the rising resistance by temporary workers. In Chapter 7, I will analyze the state's response.

MANAGEMENT AND UNION RESPONSES AND THE LIMITS OF LABOR FORCE DUALISM

The rising resistance of temporary workers, albeit small-scale and short-lived, did cause interruptions of regular production and losses in output, and raised management concerns about the limits of labor force dualism in regard to labor control. In response, management and unions took various measures and made some compromises to better accommodate and manage temporary workers.

The first strategy management adopted was to raise temporary workers' wages and grant them more equal access to the companies' facilities, resources, and fringe benefits, such as free shuttle buses, meal subsidies, allowances for work in high temperatures, holiday gifts, and company car purchase discounts.

The second strategy was to open a channel for a handful of selected temporary agency workers to become formal employees. For example, GER-1 restored its "five-star conversion policy" in 2008. The two Sino-US JVs, USA-1 and USA-2, established a similar conversion mechanism in 2011, as required by SAIC, their Chinese parent company. Two others, GER-2 and SOE-2, also began to recommend a very few top-performing agency workers to be granted formal worker status in March 2011, following the directive of their Chinese parent company FAW.[53] This strategy could potentially be an effective way to motivate and control temporary workers. As Vicki Smith (1998) found in her study of temporary workers in the U.S., temps can work even harder than regular workers for the chance to be converted to permanent employees. However, most temporary workers I interviewed considered the criteria too demanding to offer them a real chance of becoming formal employees.

The third strategy was to monitor agency workers' grievances and complaints and channel them through formal mechanisms, such as enterprise unions and Party committees. As noted in the previous section, automobile enterprise unions changed their attitudes and strategies toward temporary workers, from exclusion to incorporation. After the implementation of the LCL in 2008, temporary workers were allowed to join the unions of the automobile factories at which they work. The Party committees and unions also made efforts to respond to some of the grievances and complaints of temporary workers. For example, at GER-1, the Party committee and union leaders set up monthly "heart-to-heart" meetings with randomly selected agency workers to listen to their concerns and demands. According to the Secretary of the Party committee at GER-1, many of the issues raised by agency workers were

---

[53] The more inclusive policies and attitudes toward agency workers that China's large automakers have adopted were in part a direct response to agency workers' resistance, and in part due to the new, stricter government regulations on labor dispatch (see Chapter 7).

resolved immediately at the meetings or shortly afterward, such as granting equal access to the company's shuttle bus service, offering temporary workers the same allowances given to formal workers, providing more training opportunities, and improving work meal quality. But the interviewed agency workers were not all that enthusiastic about those meetings. As an agency worker (*laowu gong*) who once attended the monthly meeting satirized:

> Would I tell them my team leader always allocates the heavy, dirty work to us while those formal workers can just stand aside chatting? Would I ask them why we *laowu gong* only get paid half of that of formal workers for doing the same or even more work? Definitely not, if I still want to work here. The real problem is this unequal system, but they won't change the system anyway. But we had to raise some issues at the meeting to let those *lingdao* [leaders] show that they care about us. So I asked why we *laowu gong* do not get the free annual physical examination as those formal workers do. Very soon, we received the free physical examination as well.[54]

Management was aware of the limits of labor force dualism in labor control and eliciting temporary workers' efforts in production. Among the interviewed managerial and union staff, about two-thirds expressed their concerns about the high labor turnover and the lack of commitment among temporary workers, which could have a negative impact on product quality. More than half of the interviewed managers recognized that the unequal treatment between formal and temporary workers was a potential source of conflict, and a factor that could harm the harmonious labor relations of their enterprises. As a result, management became more cautious in deploying temporary workers in direct production. At GER-1 and GER-2, management decided to restrict the use of temporary workers to certain line operating posts that could be relatively easily replaced. At SOE-2, management set a "15 percent" rule, limiting the use of temporary workers to 15 percent of the workforce in its final assembly shop, where any worker stoppages could have amplified disruptive effects.

While recognizing its notable limits, for companies that had adopted labor force dualism it was difficult to pull back completely. As the HR manager of GER-2 explained:

> We want all of our workers to stay happy with the company. But let's be realistic – the company has to first make profits. For that, we need to increase productivity and flexibility, and reduce labor cost. But the government wants us to help on employment and social stability; for that, we need to keep our workers quiet. That's why we brought in temporary workers. But that has created some new problems. It is a dilemma. I think for now, we will have to find a way to improve our management of those temporary workers.[55]

The dilemma faced by management reflected the underlying tension between its need to increase profitability and its concerns with maintaining peaceful and

---

[54] Interview S26, GER-1, April 2007.   [55] Interview F15, GER-2, October 2006.

cooperative labor relations. On the one hand, workers' resistance to the large-scale restructuring and downsizing of many SOEs in the 1990s put the "crisis of legitimacy" ahead of management's concerns. To avoid potential labor unrest, and with substantial resources, China's large automakers chose to protect a segment of formal workers in an effort to obtain consensual and cooperative labor relations. On the other hand, intensified competition and profitability pressures drove automakers to adopt more cost-cutting measures, including using temporary workers and reducing job security for formal workers. Such measures, however, have provoked temporary workers' resistance and caused a decline in formal workers' consent and cooperation, incurring another round of legitimacy crisis. This ongoing tension is crucial to understanding the directions of labor force dualism and the dynamics of labor politics in the Chinese automobile industry.

CONCLUSION

Contrary to much of the literature on labor and labor movements to date, this chapter demonstrates that labor force dualism has engendered strong labor activism among the "weak" temporary workers. Three main factors can explain this unexpected labor activism. First, the re-composition of the temporary workforce as a group of better-educated, rural and urban youngsters longing for inclusion and equal opportunities has led to their more radical reactions against unequal treatment in the workplace. They are also able to mobilize more effectively through all possible avenues, such as organizing through the concentrated and closely-connected dormitory residences, by using social media, and through formal legal channels. Second, temporary workers have developed intense grievances and a keener sense of injustice against the unequal and arbitrary treatment they receive at work. Their reactions, therefore, tend to be more explosive and morally based. Third, temporary workers have gained growing workplace bargaining power derived from their increasing numbers and strategic positions in the JIT production system. They are thus able to cause stoppages of production and major losses in output by acting suddenly and collectively at the point of production.

On reflection, if we look back at previous experiences of labor unrest by U.S. autoworkers in the early twentieth century and by autoworkers in Western Europe in the 1950s and 1960s, we find that the first generation of migrant workers generally did not openly protest against the harsh conditions of work and life. The arbitrary power of management over issues such as hiring, firing, promotion, and job assignments went unchallenged in automobile factories. But the second generation became the backbone of militant struggles that succeeded in radically transforming relationships within the factory and society (Arrighi and Silver 1984: 196–7; Piore 1979: 156–7; Silver 2003: 51–2; cf. Sabel 1982). As we have seen in this chapter, the new generation of temporary workers in the Chinese auto industry has begun to show their capacity and potential to act collectively and to struggle for change for the better.

To be sure, the relatively high wages offered at the major automobile enterprises, the oversupplied labor market conditions, especially the perceived difficulty in finding formal employment, have inhibited many temporary workers from openly confronting management. Moreover, although the intergroup relationships between formal and temporary workers have tended to be less adverse than the conventional "split labor market" theory would suggest, labor force dualism did create unequal workplaces and divide formal workers from temporary workers. Yet a divided labor force does not necessarily preclude robust and continuing labor movements that can lead to significant change. Indeed, one of the key findings of this chapter is the paradoxical correlation between the divisive labor force dualism and growing activism among the temporary workers.

In retrospect, we see a striking historical parallel of divided workers and strong labor activism throughout the Chinese revolutionary and socialist eras. In her influential works on labor politics in China from the pre-1949 period through the subsequent decades, Elizabeth Perry (1993, 1994a, 1994b, 1997) convincingly demonstrated that labor fragmentation and "the very awareness of substantial differences among workers often encourages strong labor activism" (Perry 1993: 251). For example, during the Hundred Flowers Campaign, labor struggles were launched most fervently by apprentices and temporary workers and those in joint ownership enterprises, with striking workers demanding higher wages, better welfare, permanent worker status, and guaranteed promotions (Perry 1994b). During the Cultural Revolution, labor conflicts were also structured by deep-rooted occupational grievances and inequalities, with apprentices, contract workers, and younger workers being most prominent in making economic demands and joining rebel factions across the country (Perry and Li, 1997). In line with this perspective, the struggles by the new generation of temporary workers in the Chinese automobile industry documented in this book can be understood as the new industrial workforce struggling to break down the existing boundary that excludes them from the regular labor contract system and formal worker status.

Such struggles for equal treatment and betterment at work are taking place amid intensified commodification and flexibilization of labor and a rising tide of labor unrest in China as market reform has deepened since the mid-1990s. Therefore, to fully understand the dynamics and the possible future scenarios of labor relations in the automobile industry, we need go beyond the shop floor to consider the national political process – that is, how the Chinese central state has responded to the pressures of rising labor unrest and the growing legitimacy crisis on the one hand, and the need to continue promoting profitability and accumulation on the other hand. This is the question to which we now turn in the next chapter.

7

The State's response: The making of Labor Contract Law and boundary-drawing strategy

In 2007, three new labor laws were passed by the National People's Congress Standing Committee (NPCSC): the Labor Contract Law (LCL), the Employment Promotion Law, and the Labor Dispute Mediation and Arbitration Law. The most important of these, the LCL, clearly states its pro-labor legislative objective in Article One as "to improve the labor contract system, to specify the rights and obligations of the parties in a labor contract, to protect workers' legitimate rights and interests, and to construct and develop harmonious and stable labor relations" (LCL: Article 1). Among other significant changes, the LCL enhances job security, putting significant restrictions on employers' rights to hire and fire workers without cause. It also makes mandatory the use of written labor contracts and strongly discourages short-term contracts by requiring employers to give non-fixed contracts to workers who have already finished two fixed-term contracts for the same employer. Lastly, it strengthens the role of trade unions and workers' congresses in labor relations.

In particular, directly related to our focus on temporary agency workers in the automobile industry, the LCL devotes one section and eleven articles to regulating labor dispatch. The LCL stipulates that a labor agency is an employer, and shall sign fixed-term labor contracts of no less than two years with agency workers. The labor agency must ensure that agency workers receive at least the minimum wage on a monthly basis, even when they are not placed at a user company. The arrangements between the labor agency and the user company must be governed by a formal contract detailing placements and payments, including arrangements with respect to social insurance premiums for agency workers. Moreover, the LCL stipulates that agency workers shall have the right to equal pay for equal work compared to formal employees of the user company, and they can join the user company's union.[1] The three

---

[1] Information synthesized from *The Labor Contract Law of the People's Republic of China* (Zhonghua Renmin Gongheguo Laodong Hetong Fa) *[in Chinese]* (see Chapter 5, Section 2, Articles 57–67).

new labor laws, and especially the LCL, are considered a major milestone in China's labor legislation since the implementation of the Labor Law in 1995 (Ngok 2008).

What has led to the significant legislative move of the Chinese central government to regulate labor relations in general and labor dispatch in particular? How has the new labor law affected management labor practice and the conditions of temporary workers at the firm level? In this chapter, we will address these questions by examining the driving forces and the law-making process of the LCL with regard to the regulation of labor dispatch and its impact on management labor practice at the firm level.

THE MAKING OF THE LABOR CONTRACT LAW AND ITS "UNINTENDED" CONSEQUENCES

In the reform era, one of the fundamental strategies the CCP has employed to stabilize labor relations and pacify disgruntled workers has been the development of labor laws and a labor dispute resolution system, so as to channel worker protests into the formal legal system and off the street (Cai 2006; Gallagher 2005b; Lee 2002, 2007).Thus important changes in labor relations often have taken place in the arena of labor legislation.

As noted in Chapter 3, the intensified commodification and flexibilization of labor has attacked workers' livelihoods and job security, which has provoked a rising tide of labor unrest in China since the mid-1990s. According to the Chinese government's official figures, "mass incidents" increased rapidly, from 8,709 incidents in 1993 to 87,000 incidents in 2005, among which about one-third were labor-related (Yu 2007).[2] The number of labor disputes also increased dramatically during this period, from 48,121 in 1996 to over 350,182 in 2007 (NBS and MOHRSS 2010). By the turn of the century, widespread and localized labor unrest had begun to raise the specter of social instability and a "legitimacy crisis" for the CCP. This fear has been one of the main driving forces propelling the Chinese central government to introduce new legislation and social policies as part of the pursuit of a "harmonious society," including the passage of three new labor laws in 2007 intended to stabilize labor relations and pacify disgruntled workers.

With respect to labor dispatch in particular, before the enactment of the LCL in 2007, there was no nationwide legislation that pertained to labor dispatch, despite its rampant expansion into almost every sector and enterprises of all ownership types. The ambiguous triangular employment relationship, combined with the lack of regulation in the labor dispatch industry, led to widespread social insurance fraud and labor disputes as both labor agencies and user firms tried to evade their responsibilities for agency workers (Chang

---

[2] The Chinese government stopped publicizing such numbers in 2005, but various sources have pointed to the continued rapid increase in the number of "mass incidents" throughout China.

and Li 2006).[3] Several high-profile labor dispute cases filed by agency workers received extensive attention from officials, scholars and the general public.[4] Between 2005 and 2007, there was extensive media coverage about the plight of agency workers and the negative impact of labor dispatch on regular employment and social harmony.[5] The ACFTU and its local union branches conducted several surveys regarding labor dispatch. The resulting reports found that labor dispatch complicated labor relations, caused an increasing number of labor dispute cases, and made it very difficult to protect agency workers' rights and interests (Tu 2007; Xinhua 2005b; Zhang 2006). The ACFTU called on the relevant legislative and executive departments to regulate labor dispatch (Xinhua 2005b). Under the general political discourse of the Hu-Wen administration to construct a "harmonious society," criticism of labor dispatch as destabilizing employment relations and harming social stability gained prominence in both official and public discourses (Dong 2008; Lian and Chen 2007; Zheng 2008).[6]

A further illustration of this politicized, populist law-making process was the unusual move on the part of the central government to open a public comment period on an early draft of the LCL in 2006. Over 190,000 comments poured in, most from ordinary Chinese workers. But some were from U.S. and European corporations and lobbying organizations that came out squarely against core provisions of the new law. The debate continued throughout the drafting process as corporations fought to weaken the law. In fact, it has continued even after the law was enacted: in the run-up to the implementation of the new law, on January 1, 2008, there was a public outcry in China about steps some corporations had taken to avoid the law's full impact (GLS 2008). During this process, the enactment of the LCL became a highly-publicized political event and the showcase for the Chinese central government's determination to defend Chinese workers' rights and interests, despite the opposition and the threats of multinational and domestic businesses to withdraw their investment. To a large extent, the making of the LCL was a state-led legislative campaign in response to the pressure of rising labor unrest and popular demand for increased labor protection and job security.

---

[3] While there is a lack of nationwide statistics on the number of labor dispute cases related to labor dispatch, my interviews with labor arbitrators in Shanghai and Guangzhou suggested that the number of labor dispute cases brought forth by agency workers had been on the rise between 2002 and 2006, and that many were filed collectively with relatively large numbers of workers involved. The author's interviews with the district LDMAC officials and arbitrators in Guangzhou, September 2006; and in Shanghai, February 2007.

[4] For example, one labor dispute case filed by an agency employee of a KFC chain store in Beijing lasted two years and received wide media coverage and public attention, centered on the legality of agency employment (Chen and Chang 2006, Chen and Dong 2007).

[5] There is a large body of extant literature on the topic. See, in particular, Chang and Li (2006), Lian and Chen (2007), Yu (2007), Zhang (2006), Zhang (2005), Zheng (2008).

[6] The body of literature presenting discussion and debate over the LCL is too large to cite in its entirety. For a quick summary of the battles between corporations and labor over the legislative process, see Global Labor Strategies, 2007.

It was against this backdrop that the LCL devoted an entire section and prescribed tough measures to regulate labor dispatch. The intended objective was twofold: to regulate and limit the scope of labor dispatch; and to provide some legal protections for agency workers, who had not been covered by the 1994 Labor Law. In the three years following the implementation of the LCL in 2008, however, the numbers of agency workers more than tripled, from 17 million to 60 million by the end of 2010. How to explain the seemingly "unintended" impact of the LCL on labor dispatch?

A close look at employers' responses to the LCL concerning the use of agency workers in the auto assembly sector provides some clues. When the LCL took effect, management was hesitant to hire more agency workers given the apparently negative attitude of the law toward labor dispatch. For instance, in January 2008, when a large auto assembly plant sought to use agency workers to staff the entire plant, the proposal was rejected by its Chinese parent company, a large SOE, for fear of coming into conflict with the provisions of the LCL.[7]

In November 2008, China's domestic auto sales slumped in the wake of the global economic crisis. Following the government mandate to keep employment levels steady so as to maintain social stability, the large automobile enterprises cut shifts and work hours and let go temporary workers, but managed to protect formal workers from layoffs. The central government announced stimulus plans for 10 key industries in early 2009, including the auto industry. And the auto industry quickly rebounded and boomed. The major Chinese automakers hired back the laid-off temporary workers and increased the number of agency and student workers, but remained cautious in hiring new formal workers. The reason, according to an HR manager at GER-2, was in part because it had become more difficult to lay off formal workers under the LCL.[8] Meanwhile, the general provisions of the LCL concerning the terms and conditions under which agency workers can be used, and the lack of concrete and enforceable measures, allowed companies to continue using agency workers as before. As a member of the HR managerial staff at GER-1 commented:

The new labor law does not make much difference to our company's hiring practice because we have always followed the labor laws and the government regulations. But the new labor law does put stricter requirements and raise the bar for our company to choose quality labor agencies. Accordingly, our cost of using agency workers has increased. But compared to the cost of hiring formal workers, it is still much cheaper. More importantly, we can still have staff flexibility by using agency workers without worrying about severance compensation and labor contract issues.[9]

---

[7] Interview B1, Beijing, January 2008.
[8] The author's follow-up telephone interview with F15, October 2009.
[9] The author's follow-up phone interview with S13, September 2, 2010.

In other words, the LCL provides agency workers with some legal protections, but it is still much cheaper and more flexible for employers to use agency workers than to hire formal workers, who are more protected under the new law.[10]

To be sure, there have been some improvements in agency workers' conditions under the LCL. For instance, the automobile factories increased agency workers' wages and made sure that the labor agencies they chose actually paid the government-required social insurance premiums for agency workers. They also granted agency workers some benefits that were offered exclusively to formal workers in the past, such as employee car purchase discounts and allowances for holidays and working under high temperatures. But there was still a big gap in social insurance schemes and bonuses between formal and agency workers.[11] Agency workers still lacked job security and advancement opportunities at the automobile factories.

THE STATE BOUNDARY-DRAWING STRATEGY AND ITS UNRESOLVED CONTRADICTIONS

The seemingly unintended consequences the LCL had on labor dispatch, I will argue, were indeed an outcome of the deliberate state strategy to balance the conflicting interests of employers and workers by drawing boundaries within its workforce. This point can be seen clearly from the negotiations over labor dispatch between the "pro-capital" and "pro-labor" forces among law-makers during the revisions of multiple drafts of the LCL. Earlier drafts of the LCL had much stricter regulations on the matter but these were removed in the final version. For instance, the second draft required that a user company must sign labor contracts directly with agency employees once they had worked at the user company for more than one year. This provision was dropped in the final draft due to employers' strong objections. The main argument put forth by employers and some law-makers was that, if this provision was put into effect, it would hurt companies' flexibility and competiveness and do more harm than good on employment. It could also drive employers to stop using agency employees once they had completed a one-year term.[12] As the following quote from a government labor official indicated:

We need to protect our workers, but we also need to allow our enterprises flexibility to make necessary adjustments to the market and production changes. Currently, labor dispatch can function as a flexible valve for necessary adjustment. Too harsh and

---

[10] For instance, Article 14 of the LCL stipulates that formal employees have the right to open-term contracts after two consecutive renewals of their fixed-term labor contracts.

[11] The social insurance schemes of agency workers adhered to the standards set by the labor agencies, which were much lower than the standards of the automobile companies. On average, agency workers received only 25 percent to 50 percent of the social insurance payouts that formal workers received (see Chapter 3).

[12] Interview No. 23, Shanghai, December 2006.

too many restrictions on it will harm enterprises' competitiveness and eventually hurt employment for both formal and agency workers.[13]

Although representatives from the ACFTU insisted on "regulating and inhibiting" labor dispatch to better protect workers, concerns about employment helped the proponents of "regulating and developing" labor dispatch as a "supplementary type of employment" gain the upper hand during the debates.[14] As a result, the final draft dropped this specific provision that could have inhibited the expansion of labor dispatch.

The above evidence suggests that the central state deliberately created boundaries among its working citizens in the drafting of the LCL in order to strike a balance between maintaining legitimacy and promoting profitability. On the one hand, the state attempted to use the LCL to enhance job security and increase protection for formal contract workers, and to provide agency workers with some legal protection to shore up its legitimacy in the eyes of workers. On the other hand, by legalizing labor dispatch while subjecting it to rather general provisions, the state granted employers a "flexible valve" that would allow firms to continue using labor dispatch to lower labor costs and gain flexibility. Although the LCL states that agency workers should have the right to "equal pay for equal work" in comparison to formal employees, the lack of specific, enforceable measures makes it very hard to realize in practice.[15] As a result, it should come as no surprise that employers would opt to entrench labor force dualism and increase the use of temporary agency workers under the LCL.

However, this is not the end of the story. The ongoing struggles over the implementation of the LCL and its subsequent amendments indicate that the boundary-drawing strategy has not resolved the profitability-legitimacy contradiction confronting the Chinese Party-state. In October 2008, the NPCSC carried out an extensive LCL enforcement inspection in six provinces. The inspection found a substantial increase in the number of labor agencies and in the use of agency workers within less than a year since the implementation of the LCL. The NPCSC urged the relevant departments to draft specific regulations to better regulate labor dispatch and safeguard the rights and interests of agency workers. In response, the Ministry of Human Resources and Social Security (MOHRSS) began to draft "Regulations on Labor Dispatching" in 2009 (Xiang 2011a). Again, there was great disagreement among the different interest groups and lawmakers. While the ACFTU insisted on more strictly regulating and restricting labor dispatch, enterprises – and especially large, central SOEs – strongly opposed strict regulation (Geng and Ji 2012). The MOHRSS tended to emphasize the positive effects of labor

---

[13] The author's meeting minutes from attendance at a discussion forum organized by the Ministry of Labor and Social Security on revising the second draft of the LCL, held in Qingdao, September 2006.

[14] Ibid.   [15] See Chapter 6 for discussion on this point.

dispatch in job creation and labor flexibility and was inclined to "regulate and develop" the practice (Xinhua 2008b). Against the backdrop of the 2008 global financial crisis, Beijing's deep concern over the economy and employment might have helped the side that argued for the positive effects of labor dispatch on labor flexibility and overall employment growth. As a result, the attempt to include specific regulations on labor dispatch stalled (Xiang 2011b).

Frustrated by this outcome, in March 2011 and March 2012, the ACFTU submitted two comprehensive reports on the severe problems of labor dispatch to the National People's Congress (NPC) and proposed legislative restrictions on labor dispatch (IHLO 2012a). Meanwhile, the sharp increase in labor dispute cases related to labor dispatch and concerns with social stability drove several local governments and municipalities to impose regulations to restrict labor dispatch and protect agency workers since the LCL had been implemented (IHLO 2012b).[16] For instance, in Jilin Province where FAW is located, the provisions issued by the Jilin MOHRSS in 2011 attempted to provide more job security to agency workers by entitling them to sign non-fixed-term contracts with labor agencies (MOHRSS of Jilin Province 2011). In Shanghai, the Directive issued by Shanghai SASAC in 2011 required those central enterprises based in Shanghai – a group that includes SAIC – to establish specific mechanisms and clear standards for the conversion of agency workers to formal worker status (Shanghai SASAC 2011). The regulation by local government was another reason for management to adopt more inclusive policies toward agency workers, as discussed in Chapter 6.

The push for stricter legislation on labor dispatch from the ACFTU as well as some local governments drew attention from the CCP's top leadership. The NPCSC issued several directives that framed the regulation of labor dispatch as a political issue of "safeguarding the dominant position of the working class and consolidating the foundation of the Party's rule" (Chen 2012). On June 26, 2012, the 27th meeting of the 11th NPCSC began the review of the draft Amendments to the LCL, focused on revising the provisions that pertained to labor dispatch. The four proposed major revisions included: 1) to strictly limit the posts that can use labor dispatch by defining the meanings of "temporary, auxiliary, and substitutive" posts; 2) agency workers' right to equal pay for equal work as formal employees of the user company must be written into the labor contract and enforced; 3) to raise the entry threshold for labor agencies by increasing the required registered capital from half a million to two million *yuan*; and, 4) to add provisions that strengthen the supervisory and administrative responsibilities of the labor departments and stipulate noncompliance penalties (Chen 2012). Clearly, the draft Amendments attempted to tighten loopholes in the LCL and to more strictly regulate labor

---

[16] For instance, in Guangzhou, it was reported that labor dispute cases caused by labor dispatch accounted for 30 percent of all labor dispute cases in 2009 (Xu et al. 2011).

dispatch. In a populist legislative style similar to that used in the making of the LCL, the draft Amendments generated over 550,000 online opinions during the one-month public comment period – a record high in the PRC's legislative history. It reflected the sizeable influence of labor dispatch on workers, employers, and Chinese society. On December 28, 2012, the Amendments were passed almost unanimously, with the proposed stricter regulations taking effect on July 1, 2013 (Lin 2013).

The actual implementation of the Amendments remains to be seen at the time of this writing. It will likely depend on the CCP's ultimate assessment of the weight to be placed on maintaining legitimacy with workers versus the goal of promoting profitability in alignment with capitalists/managers. The ongoing battle over the LCL reflects the unresolved profitability-legitimacy contradiction of the Chinese central state in the development of capitalism.

Notably, the ACFTU played a prominent role in pushing through the passage of the LCL, as well as in its subsequent implementation and amendments. The active role of the ACFTU in the labor legislation process first had to do with the official union's attempt to strengthen its own bureaucratic position within the government (Gallagher and Dong 2011). As political scientist Chen Feng explained, the power of the ACFTU "comes from the mandate granted by the state to manage industrial conflict. The state views the stabilization of labor relations as crucial for its political legitimacy. State mandates have increased the authority and hence the salience of the union as a key government organ in labor affairs" (2009: 665). But the ACFTU's governmental status also prevents it from operating through mobilizing the rank and file or from exerting its influence by empowering its grassroots branches (2009: 662). Nevertheless, by standing up for pro-labor legislation, the ACFTU has begun making some changes in order to retain its relevance in the eyes of workers. This has further implications for Chinese trade union reforms, to which I will return in the concluding chapter.

CONCLUSION

This chapter has shown how the widespread labor disputes and discontent caused by labor dispatch have driven the central government to regulate the practice and to move to stabilize labor relations through the LCL. Although the state boundary-drawing strategy in the law-making process tended to institutionalize an unequal, dualist labor system, it has also sparked protests for inclusion and equal treatment by the excluded workers. In retrospect, a parallel example comes to mind. During the Mao era, the discriminatory treatment of rural contract workers led to protests and criticisms that eventually pressured the State Council to grant permanent worker status to the 13 million rural contract workers working in urban SOEs in 1971 (White 1976). In this regard, Chinese labor politics is not a settled fact. Rather, it is better understood as a state-centered, *dynamic* process, carried out through contestation, negotiation, and compromise among state policy elites, capitalists/employers, and workers. Struggles for inclusion by excluded workers can periodically push the state to redraw boundaries and expand protections and rights to some of the excluded through changes in labor laws and policies.

So what are some of the implications of the new labor laws for the long-term dynamics of labor relations in China? For one thing, the new labor laws have empowered ordinary Chinese workers to become more proactive in taking their grievances before the courts. According to the Chinese official statistics, in 2008, 1.2 million workers filed over 693,000 labor dispute cases with Chinese authorities, a 98 percent increase from 2007.[17] The doubling of labor dispute cases had partly to do with the sharp increase in factory closures and wage defaults in the wake of the 2008 global economic downturn. But it also reflected workers' growing awareness of their rights and confidence in China's legal systems of public redress (CLB 2009a). China's new labor laws, as recent events indicate, have served as the catalyst for new labor activism in China – especially when employers have attempted to evade the law and when the arbitration system has become too burdened with cases to be able to resolve workers' grievances quickly, thereby encouraging them to turn to direct action.

An analogy between the 2007 LCL in China and the 1935 National Labor Relations Act (the Wagner Act) in the U.S. is instructive. In both cases, government was responding to the threat of social instability posed by mounting labor unrest, on the one hand, and the threat of economic instability posed by a more or less open "underconsumption crisis," on the other hand. In both cases, the new legislation sought to specify and expand workers' rights while channeling unrest into formal legal (routine) mechanisms. We know that the National Labor Relations Act in the United States served as a catalyst for a major nationwide wave of strikes in 1936–7; and that the strike wave fundamentally transformed the industrial relations environment in the U.S., as workers felt empowered to stand up for their rights in the face of employer intransigence. Moreover, the 1930s–1940s strike waves in the U.S. culminated in a labor-capital-state "social contract," in which employers – and especially those in mass production manufacturing – agreed to recognize unions and to steadily increase wages and benefits in step with labor productivity increases. In exchange, workers (and their unions) were to channel grievances through established formal procedures and were to accept management's right to make decisions about the organization and location of production. The state, in turn, was to promote a macroeconomic environment suitable to this exchange, including keeping unemployment levels low (Silver and Zhang 2009: 182).

---

[17] An additional 237,000 cases were settled through mediation outside of the courts (MOHRSS 2009).

Will the new labor laws and rising labor unrest in China eventually lead to a new social contract between the state, labor, and capital, analogous to the post-World War II New Deal in the U.S.? What are the possible scenarios of labor relations in the Chinese automobile industry in the coming decade? What are the broader implications of this study on Chinese autoworkers for understanding the strategy, potential, and dynamics of labor movements within and outside China? These are the questions to which we now turn in the next and concluding chapter.

8

Conclusion

This book has sought to explore the current conditions, subjectivity and collective actions of Chinese autoworkers, and how *shop-floor, national* and *global* processes have interacted in complex ways to produce the specific labor relations and dynamics of labor unrest in the Chinese automobile industry.

Over the course of this study, I have come to the conclusion that massive foreign investment and the increased scale and concentration of automobile production in China in the past two decades have created and strengthened a new generation of autoworkers with growing workplace bargaining power and grievances. In Chapters 2–6, I have shown that the generalized Taylorist/ Fordist mass assembly production, combined with the "buffer-less" lean production system, has indeed increased the vulnerability of capital to disruptions in the flow of production, thereby boosting the workplace bargaining power of Chinese autoworkers. At the same time, intense competition and profitability pressures have driven the major automakers in China – both SOEs and JVs – to prioritize profitability and move toward a leaner and meaner factory regime with aggressive cost-cutting measures. As a result, despite their relatively high wages, the new generation of autoworkers expresses strong grievances rooted, among other places, in the increased intensity and the grueling nature of their work, their reduced job security, stagnant wages, the arbitrary exercise of managerial authority, the lack of advancement opportunities, and their inferior status as blue-collar workers in a hierarchical factory setting.

Furthermore, Chapters 5 and 6 have shown that both formal and temporary workers have a growing consciousness of and have been able to exploit their strong workplace bargaining power to push for higher pay and better working conditions. In particular, Chapter 6 documented the willingness and capacity of the new generation of temporary workers, who are increasingly urban and better-educated than the previous generation of temporary workers, to protest and to demand equal treatment at work. Resonant with previous cases of autoworkers' movements, strong grievances combined with strong workplace bargaining power have given rise to labor activism among the current generation of autoworkers in China.

My empirical evidence also suggests that Chinese autoworkers' struggles have so far remained localized, short-lived, and limited in their goals. Autoworkers' relatively high wages, the perceived oversupply of assembly line workers in the labor market, and the difficulty in finding better alternative jobs, combined with the lack of independent unions and collective bargaining, have inhibited many autoworkers from openly confronting management. In particular, labor force dualism creates an unequal workplace experience and detaches formal workers from supporting temporary workers' struggles.

Nonetheless, workers' localized and apolitical collective actions have won specific management concessions, including increased wages and improved working conditions for both formal and temporary workers. Furthermore, by situating autoworkers' resistance in the broader national context of rising labor unrest, I have shown in Chapter 7 how concerns with maintaining social stability and political legitimacy have driven the central government to pass pro-labor laws in order to stabilize labor relations and pacify disgruntled workers.

In fact, as I have attempted to illustrate throughout this book, national context and historical legacies matter, and China's conditions are different from previous cases of autoworkers' uprisings from Detroit to Ulsan. For one thing, the Chinese central state still controls the commanding heights in strategic industries and key enterprises, including the automobile industry and the major auto assemblers. The central state has played a decisive role in fostering a heretofore cautious restructuring of the automobile industry in the reform era. It also has taken a more interventionist approach in regulating labor relations at large SOEs and JVs through the cadre-managerial personnel system. Moreover, China's revolutionary and socialist legacies still have an impact on state labor policies and factory shop floors, including the conciliatory strategies and mediating role of shop-floor managers, enterprise unions, and Party factory committees. All of these factors have mitigated Chinese autoworkers' militancy to a certain extent. But the above factors cannot explain – and indeed, make it even more puzzling – why there has been constant, bottom-up labor activism by the rank-and-file workers despite all the "hegemony-building" efforts by the state and management. How, then, can we explain the twists?

My explanation, as well as the central argument of this book, lies in the state-centered, dynamic relations between the state, labor, and capital in post-socialist China. Such relations are underpinned by the inherent contradiction between increasing profitability and maintaining legitimacy, and the efforts of both firms and the state to strike a balance by drawing boundaries within the workforce. This contradiction is exemplified in the paradox of labor force dualism at the factory level.

I have shown how the pressures of simultaneously increasing profitability and maintaining legitimacy with labor have driven large SOEs and JVs to strive for a relatively stable solution through labor force dualism that draws boundaries between formal and temporary workers. To the extent that assembly plants are able to provide job security and relatively high wages to a core labor force, they push down job insecurity and cost-cutting measures either to parts suppliers or by constructing a dual labor force within the assembly plants. It is thus not a coincidence that the main source of militancy has so far resided among parts workers in the subcontracting system and among temporary workers in the assembly plants. But under the highly integrated JIT production system, the strikes at parts suppliers and by temporary workers can effectively shut down the assembly plants and the entire production chain. The paradox of labor force dualism documented in this study reveals this ongoing tension at the factory level.

In a similar vein, at the national level, we have seen how the Party-state has attempted to strike a balance between profitability and legitimacy by recurrently drawing boundaries within its working population. The strategy often has backfired, however, by driving the excluded workers to protest and to demand inclusion and equal treatment. Therefore, like other types of capital "fixes,"[1] the attempt to fix the problem by drawing boundaries within the working class only temporarily shifts the terrain on which the contradiction unfolds. It does not resolve the fundamental contradiction of capitalism. But it does change the realm and focus of struggles, and the key question in terms of the outcome largely depends on whether regular workers (and their unions) and temporary workers can make common cause.[2]

Indeed, to the extent that "boundary-drawing" strategies are "immanent" to the "flexible accumulation" of post-Fordism (Harvey 1989; Vallas 1999: 94), and are essential to defer or temporarily shift the inherent contradictions of capitalism,[3] we have witnessed the spread of labor dualism and the widening

---

[1] Beverly Silver has argued that the expansion of capitalist production tends to strengthen labor and brings capital (and states) recurrently face to face with strong labor movements. Capital responds with various "fixes": "spatial fix" (Harvey 1989) by geographically relocating production in search of cheaper or more docile labor; "technological fixes" through technological/organizational innovation in the production process; "product fix" by turning to a new product or industry where profits are initially high; and "financial fix" in which excess capital turns to financial outlets. But all the fixes are only temporary. For detailed discussions on various types of capital fixes, see Silver (2003): chapters 2–4.

[2] For example, in South Korea, major automakers such as Hyundai have employed a very similar kind of labor force dualism, in which one quarter of its workforce is temporary and receives pay equivalent to 65 percent of that of permanent workers for doing the same job. Until recently, the powerful Hyundai union had taken an exclusionary policy toward temporary workers. It even supported the company's efforts to institutionalize dualism by keeping temporary workers from becoming permanent workers in order to protect its own members' interests as permanent workers. I thank Byoung-Hoon Lee for his useful comparative comments on this point.

[3] On interconnected boundary-drawing strategies pursued by capital, states, and workers, see Silver (2003: 20–25). See also Wallerstein (1995, 2004) for discussions on the importance of boundary-drawing strategies based on criteria such as race, gender, and ethnicity to the operation of historical capitalism.

and deepening of inequality between insiders and outsiders with explicit state policy support.[4] Today, workers everywhere are confronted with growing job insecurity and inequality between a shrinking segment of core/regular workers and an ever-expanding population of peripheral/non-regular workers.[5] A central question for the twenty-first-century labor movements will be the question of how to find common ground and build solidarity among workers across the boundaries in order to struggle for a more just, equitable, and inclusive world. This will require concerted struggles both in the workplace and within society, by targeting the state in the realm of legal, political, and social rights.

Contrary to the dominant view in the relevant literature that asserts the structural weakness of Chinese workers and discounts their localized struggles, this study shows that workers in China do have bargaining power and the will to struggle for change. The Party-state has had to respond to widespread, albeit localized labor unrest, out of its own fundamental interests in maintaining stability and legitimacy. Despite, and indeed in large part because of the lack of electoral legitimacy, the authoritarian regime has to be more responsive to popular pressure for fear of "ungovernability." Scholars have noted that by permitting "routine and officially circumscribed" protests and contentious bargaining between the government and ordinary people, the CCP has been able to stay informed and responsive to grassroots grievances and demands, which arguably contributes to the resilience of the regime (Chen 2012; Lorentzen 2008; Perry 2007: 21). I argue that the CCP's top priority in maintaining stability and its continuing public commitment to the legitimate rights and interests of workers undergird Chinese workers' legitimacy leverage. Ironically, the feeble role of the ACFTU in representing the interests of workers and in bargaining with employers often forces the central and local governments to directly intervene in workplace labor-capital conflicts, and more often than not, to act to settle some worker grievances quickly to restore social stability. As the China Labor Bulletin observed:

Chinese workers, ...emboldened by the passage of the Labor Contract Law and their own improved ability to organize, staged strikes and protests across the country demanding government intervention. And, more often than not, they were successful. Striking taxi drivers forced local governments in dozens of cities to curtail the excessive fees charged by cab companies, and in China's manufacturing heartland, Dongguan, tens of thousands of laid-off factory workers secured payments for wages in arrears after staging demonstrations in front of the city government building (2009b:3).

---

[4] For instance, Emmenegger et al. (2012) compared the recent trends of dualization in the labor market and welfare in developed countries, and found that dualization and inequality are consequences of deliberate state policies and conscious political choices made in favor of some social groups while at the expense of others. On a similar theme, see also Palier and Thelen (2010) and Song (2012).

[5] One telling example is the widespread use of the two-tier system in almost every sector, including higher education, where faculty members are divided between tenured/tenure-track faculty and non-tenure track faculty, adjuncts and part-time lecturers.

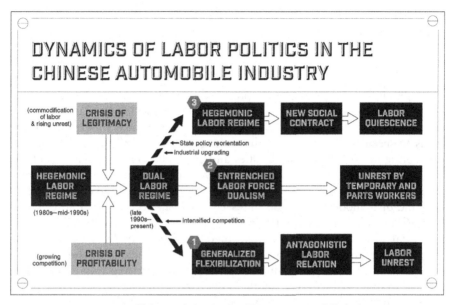

FIGURE 8.1. Dynamics of labor politics in the Chinese automobile industry

In other words, Chinese workers are indeed "bargaining without union" – they are making use of their legitimacy leverage over the state to wring concessions from their employers. To be sure, while my study emphasizes the significance of Chinese autoworkers' grassroots struggles and the use of legitimacy leverage to win employers' concessions, I am not disputing the importance of organized labor and the efforts to build a genuine labor union to represent and struggle for workers' rights and interests. Nor am I denying that a repressive authoritarian political system remains a formidable barrier for Chinese workers' collective pursuit of a better workplace. The important point highlighted in this study is that grassroots labor unrest and pressure from below are the genuine forces that drive meaningful change in the workplace and reforms from above. Chinese workers themselves have proven the basic idea that workers do indeed have power, and that they can use their power to improve their working and living conditions through collective action. It is in this regard that I argue that we should not underestimate the impact of widespread, localized, and apolitical labor protests in China.

Following this state-centered, dynamic approach, I argue that the long-term dynamics of labor politics in the Chinese automobile industry largely depend on the directions and outcomes of labor force dualism, as summed up in Figure 8.1. It depicts the transition from a hegemonic labor regime in the early reform era (1980s–mid-1990s) to a dual labor regime characterized by widespread labor force dualism since the late 1990s. The diagram also shows the inherent instability of labor force dualism as a solution to the profitability-legitimacy contradiction, and suggests three possible scenarios of how the contradiction may play out. So which scenario(s) is more likely to come to pass in the near future, informed now by our empirical study?

POSSIBLE FUTURE SCENARIOS

Throughout this book I have attempted to illuminate how *shop-floor, national* and *global* processes interact to produce the specific labor relations in the Chinese automobile industry. In my conclusion, I seek to synthesize these three levels to speculate on possible future scenarios. First, our shop-floor observations bring into relief the peculiarities and contradictions of labor force dualism, which shed light on its likely future evolution as a mode of labor control from the perspective of management. On the one hand, unlike the Japanese lean-and-dual model, which promises employment security to a core workforce, Chapters 3 and 5 have shown that the job security of the "core" segment of formal workers varies widely, and there has been a decline of job security among the younger generation of formal workers under the labor contract system. As such, labor force dualism is limited in soliciting commitment and consent from formal workers. On the other hand, as detailed in Chapters 3 and 6, the re-composition of temporary workers has blurred the boundary between formal and temporary workers based on their urban-rural *hukou* status and delegitimized labor force dualism. Moreover, the socialist egalitarian legacies are still alive on the shop floor and tend to generate more indignation at unequal treatment among the temporary workers. These factors, coupled with their growing workplace bargaining power, have led to rising activism among temporary workers. Thus, labor force dualism is limited as a management labor control strategy.

The shop-floor observations suggest that the current mode of labor force dualism as documented in this book is indeed a transitional *modus vivendi* for large SOEs that are moving away from the old *danwei* system of permanent employment to a more flexible labor system. It can be viewed as a quasi "lean-and-dual" model. Can we expect the current dualism to further evolve into the "mature" lean-and-dual model of Japanese automakers, as Scenario (II) in Figure 8.1 predicts? That is, will management at major assemblers entrench dualism by promising real job security to the core formal workforce? My latest research suggests that some of the major automakers in China are moving in this direction. On the one hand, the use of temporary workers on assembly lines has become more limited to certain operative and auxiliary posts, to provide numerical flexibility. Some automakers – for instance, GER-1, GER-2, and USA-1 – have also begun subcontracting certain production segments as a whole to their first-tier parts suppliers, who are responsible for bringing in and controlling their own workforce in the assembly plants. This can be viewed as part of management's response to the problems of labor control over temporary workers. It also allows assemblers to avoid dealing with the stricter regulations introduced in the Amendments to the LCL that bear on labor dispatch. On the other hand, large assemblers, in compliance with the LCL, have begun offering their formal workers three- to five-year labor contracts with the prospect for open-term contracts – that is, permanent employment – after two consecutive renewals. In this case, formal and temporary workers could be further divided, and temporary workers at upper-tier assemblers could be weakened. Labor unrest is more likely to occur among workers at lower-tier auto parts plants in the subcontracting system.

The division between assembly and parts workers, however, does not preclude robust and effective labor unrest. For one thing, recent strikes by auto parts workers in China and India demonstrate that parts workers have gained significant workplace bargaining power when enmeshed in the JIT production system and the global sourcing of auto parts production.[6] Moreover, when around 90,000 autoworkers, including both parts and assembly workers, in the Gurgaon-Manesar industrial belt in the state of Haryana – India's auto industry hub – went on strike to protest the killing of an auto parts worker during a previous parts worker strike, production at many auto corporations in India experienced serious interruptions. It was reported that the whole country's auto sector was under threat by labor unrest (Wonacott and Pokharel 2009). In China, similarly, the integrated JIT production system and the concentrated work and living spaces of assembly and parts workers at those huge automobile production bases, such as "FAW auto city" in Changchun, and "Dongfeng motor town" in Shiyan,[7] indicate the potential for cooperation and alliance between assembly and parts workers who are closely connected through local communities.

Yet from management's perspective it is also possible that intensified competition and increased profitability pressures could drive some Chinese automakers currently utilizing labor force dualism to further reduce the privileges and protections for formal workers, and to move toward more generalized flexibilization – that is, the lean-and-mean model described in Chapter 2, which does not promise job security for the majority of semi-skilled line operators. In this circumstance, we may expect formal workers to share similar grievances and to stand in solidarity with temporary workers. Or, there might be increased antagonism between formal and temporary workers if management moves to replace formal workers with temporary workers, as was the case at a Korean automobile company (see Chapter 6).

A full assessment of the possible future scenarios, however, requires us to go beyond the factory level and to consider national political dynamics.

---

[6] Similar to the Honda parts worker strike in China, the strike at one auto parts plant in India that manufactures a single transmission bracket had the cascading effect of shutting down three assembly plants operated by GM and Ford in the U.S. and Canada in 2009 (Nair and Green 2009).

[7] In recent years, Dongfeng Motor has relocated its headquarters and main operations from Shiyan to Wuhan, although Shiyan remains one of Dongfeng's major production bases, with about 170,000 people in Shiyan employed by Dongfeng Motor and its parts suppliers.

As discussed in Chapter 7, through new legislation, the central government has attempted to stabilize labor relations and provide more protection and rights to Chinese workers, including the fast-expanding segment of agency workers. There is also evidence that the new labor laws are being taken seriously by the central government, and as a consequence, also by large state-owned and state-controlled enterprises. Under the current political climate, it is less likely that the major automakers in China will move further toward generalized flexibilization, as Scenario (I) in Figure 8.1 predicts.

Can we, then, expect some kind of social contract between the state, labor, and capital to emerge in China, as Scenario (III) predicts? To assess this possibility, it is important to first return to the dynamics of the global automobile industry. In the United States, autoworkers were able to translate their strong workplace bargaining power into several decades of rising wages and expanding benefits based on the high profits accruing to U.S. automakers in the "innovation phase" of the automobile product cycle in the mid-twentieth century. By contrast, Chinese autoworkers at the late stage of the product cycle in the early twenty-first century, despite possessing a similar level of workplace bargaining power, have so far experienced stagnant wages. By placing the ongoing dynamics in the context of the product cycle in global automobile production, we can understand better the tensions involved with labor force dualism. In the other words, latecomers, including China, face a more acute contradiction between profitability and legitimacy when competition is high and profit margins become thinner. That means they may have less room for implementing an expensive social contract – like the U.S. "New Deal" enacted in the wake of the 1930s auto strike waves – in the competitive environment of the early twenty-first century.

Yet it is not at all clear that this is the best way to understand contemporary Chinese dynamics. For one thing, according to a recent report by McKinsey, Chinese automakers still enjoy a 35-percent cost advantage over automakers in developed markets in spite of rising manufacturing costs in China in recent years (Barbosa et al. 2010: 2). More importantly, as discussed in Chapter 2, unlike most other late-developers, China's huge size enables the central state more market leverage and autonomy over global capital (especially the long-term, market-seeking breed of capital) in negotiating terms and conditions for FDI to access China's domestic markets. This suggests China may be able to negotiate a better position in the international division of labor so as to jump up in the global value-added hierarchy.

There has also been ample evidence that the Chinese government is making a conscious effort to make such a jump to capture some of the windfall profits that accrue to innovation. This effort can be seen from the massive investments by the central government in the expansion of tertiary education and in R&D in technology and industrial innovation.[8] For example, the

---

[8] As of 2010, China had 31 million students enrolled in higher education; India had 20.7 million; the US had 20.3 million; and, the European Union had 20 million (Bradsher 2013; U.S. Department of Education, National Center for Education Statistics 2012).

central government's 4-trillion *yuan* stimulus package has provided ample funds to the automotive industry, one of 10 major industries identified under the revitalization scheme, to promote industry consolidation and upgrading, technological innovations, and the development of China's own brand cars and exports of China-made vehicles.

Yet even if China was able to jump up in the global value-added hierarchy, a simple copying of the wasteful U.S. mass-consumption model would be unsustainable and undesirable on ecological and other grounds. As China has become the world's largest vehicle manufacturer and auto market, the directions for further development of China's auto industry will no doubt have significant and long-term impacts on energy consumption and the environment in China as well as in the rest of the world. Although the number of vehicles per capita in China is still very low by international standards – 85 cars per 1,000 persons in China as of 2012[9] – rapid growth in private car ownership has already caused serious problems such as traffic congestion and air pollution in many Chinese cities. Beijing has begun addressing these concerns in recent years. For example, the 2009 *Automotive Industry Revitalization Plan* included initiatives that aim to increase energy efficiency and reduce greenhouse gas emissions through the following measures: cutting the sales tax for 1.6-liter or smaller cars by half, reducing energy intensity, increasing the share of renewable energy used, implementing tough auto emissions standards, increasing investments for clean energy.

More to the point, as the world's largest and fastest-growing auto market, and a country with an urgent need for alternative energy solutions, the Chinese central government has in recent years vigorously promoted the development of new-energy and energy-saving vehicles and technologies. As a result, industrial experts generally expect that electric vehicles and alternative propulsion technology are the fields where China may have a chance to take the lead. As one industrial expert analyzed:

What makes the development of alternative propulsion technology particularly challenging is...the need for invention of the infrastructure for delivering renewable sources of electricity and installation of battery charging/replacement stations... It takes a combination of business and government working together to make such a transformational change possible – and nowhere in the world is there a closer link between business and government than in China. (Russo 2009)

We might add to this that the Chinese central government has been and is still sitting firmly in the driver's seat. But without a paradigm shift and reorientation toward more balanced development focusing on peoples' livelihoods, social equity, and ecological sustainability that goes beyond state developmentalism,

---

[9] According to the Ministry of Public Security, there were 114 million automobiles registered in China by the end of June 2012 (Xinhua 2012). This means there were about 85 cars per 1,000 persons in China in 2012, ranking China 111th among 191 countries. For the full country rankings, see (http://en.wikipedia.org/wiki/List_of_countries_by_vehicles_per_capita).

the prospects for China to escape the pitfalls of the energy-intensive, mass-consumption model remain dim. In fact, according to a high-profile social progress report by scholars at Tsinghua University, the formation of "powerful vested interests" during the reform process has stalled further political and economic reforms that are much needed for such a reorientation (Zhuang 2012).[10] Whether the CCP's new leadership is able to break through the status quo and redirect China's development toward a more equitable and sustainable direction is still an open question. What is clear, however, is that the Chinese subaltern strata are not passive, and widespread grassroots protests and pressures from below have been and will continue to be an important force in pushing for change and shaping the eventual outcome of China's development trajectory in marked ways.

BROADER IMPLICATIONS

What, then, can we take away about the broader implications of this case study of Chinese autoworkers for labor and labor movements within and outside China?

One set of important implications derived from this study has to do with the role, potential, and strategies of labor and labor movements, and more generally, the exercise of power from below to push for change for the better. We have seen in this study that the widespread, localized, and apolitical labor unrest in China can force the central government to amend its labor legislation in a way that expands protections and rights for workers. We also observe similar dynamics in other social protests by "the weak" – those without what we normally define as "power" – to push for transformation from below in China as well as across the world. For instance, Elizabeth Perry noted how Chinese protesters have over time wrung some significant concessions from the state, such as the historic abolition of the agricultural tax in 2006, and the property rights law in 2007 (2010: 13). The road blockades by unemployed workers in the piquetero movement in Argentina forced the government to initiate the first unemployment subsidies in the history of Latin America. This helped to spur a far broader insurgency that toppled a succession of presidents (Auyero 2005, Sitrin 2006: 8–16, as cited in Piven 2008: 1–14). Indeed, the key theoretical insight of Piven and Cloward (1977) was precisely that many of the gains made by "poor peoples' movements" do not come from the establishment of formal organizations oriented toward the capture of state power, but are

---

[10] According to this report, the "powerful vested interests" consist of government officials, state monopolies, and the property and energy industries, which are closely linked to the government. It is worth noting that the chief author of this report is Sun Liping, a renowned sociology professor at Tsinghua University who served as the Ph.D. advisor for the current Chinese President, Xi Jinping. Sun is known as an outspoken critic of social inequality in China. For more details on the report, and on Sun Liping, see "China Media Project" (http://cmp.hku.hk/2013/03/27/32147/).

a result of concessions wrung from the powerful in response to widespread, intense, spontaneous disruptions from below in response to the threat of "ungovernability" (Silver and Zhang 2009).

But in order to exercise this disruptive power from below effectively, "people must also recognize that they do have some power, that elites also depend on the masses. People have to organize, to contrive ways of acting in concert, at least insofar as concerted action is necessary to make their power effective" (Piven 2008: 8). It is important to remember that the "idea of power" itself has been an important source of workers' power (Piven and Cloward 2000: 413–4). A good illustration of this point is the empowering effects of the new labor laws on ordinary Chinese workers, facilitating their ability to stand up and defend their labor rights through the formal legal system and direct actions. By contrast, the popular perception of American autoworkers as having lost their bargaining power and therefore having to accept whatever concessions are needed to keep the US auto industry competitive, "has dramatically deflated popular political morale and the willingness to struggle for change. Such shifts in workers' beliefs partly mirror shifts in structural and associational bargaining power but, no doubt, also play a role of their own in dynamics of labor movements" (Silver 2003: 16). The UAW, for example, has decided to make "strategic concessions" with Detroit's Big Three, sacrificing new hires – typically lower-paid, second-tier workers – in order to protect the benefits of first-tier workers and in hopes of getting more jobs (Shapiro 2011; Welch 2011). This is one of the main reasons behind the "smooth" spread of the two-tier system without having encountered much resistance in the U.S. auto industry. However, studies have shown that restructuring in the auto industry has multiple determinants, such as the automakers' desire to attain access to a large or growing market with a skilled, healthy workforce; the demands of the assembler-supplier relationship; government policies; and financial pressures (Aschoff 2010). Therefore, it is far from clear whether the concessions that the UAW has made on behalf of American autoworkers are the only or best choice for workers.[11] Indeed, as labor historian Nelson Lichtenstein (2002) incisively argued, the real failure of American trade unionism in the neoliberal era was one of ideas and political will. Thus, there is an urgent need to confront neoliberal ideology and raise workers' recognition of their own bargaining power and political will to strive for a just and democratic world, both at work and in society at large. To this end, my conceptualization of legitimacy leverage as an important source of workers' bargaining power in contemporary China is a step toward a systematic understanding of the operation of ideological power in constituting and reconstructing workers' bargaining power and conditions for counter-movements.

---

[11] Labor researcher and activist Kim Moody (1997) has noted that many unions in the North (e.g., the U.S., Europe and Japan) have been coopted by management and, as a consequence, have lost much of their effectiveness and the political will to mobilize and represent the rank-and-file members.

Another related question is where Chinese workers' localized and apolitical labor unrest will lead, and whether it can push for the establishment of independent unions and collective bargaining. This study has led me to a dynamic view that workers' grassroots protests will continue to push for higher wages, better working conditions, and more union organizing and pro-labor reforms from the official union, the ACFTU. But the labor movement in China will not follow the schema of the "master narrative" from working class formation to trade union organization to political party to state power, which is still surprisingly alive in many discussions about labor unrest in China today.[12] First of all, faced with mounting labor unrest and concerned with maintaining social and political stability, the ruling Communist Party has explicitly urged the ACFTU to "further protect workers' legitimate rights and interests," to "improve labor protection mechanisms," to "achieve decent work for the laboring masses," and to promote "harmonious labor relations and social harmony."[13] Recent empirical studies have suggested that the ACFTU, especially its branches at the local municipality and district levels, has been taking a more active role in organizing workers and negotiating with employers to improve conditions for workers (Chan 2006; Chen 2009, 2010; Han 2013; Liu 2010). While the CCP is unlikely to allow any independent unions to exist outside of its control, the ACFTU is likely to become more active in organizing workers and responding to their grievances and demands, under the threat that it could become totally irrelevant to workers and state bureaucrats if it cannot deliver any meaningful gains for workers and thereby mediate labor-capital conflicts and preempt strikes.

In retrospect, throughout the twentieth century, "bottom-up pressures from workers and concerns about social unrest from ruling groups have led to new labor legislation and policies designed to stabilize labor markets and industrial relations. Better working conditions, decent wage for decent work, access to more benefits, and long-term employment meant rising living standards for ordinary working people as both laborers and consumers. In this regard, the dynamics currently at work in China parallel those in many other developed countries in the early to mid decades of the 20th century" (GLS 2008: 6).

At the same time, however, it is also clear that no mechanical application of general theory will suffice. As I have attempted to illuminate throughout this study, national context and historical legacies matter. We should not assume that the organizing strategies, patterns, rhetoric, and dynamics at work for the

---

[12] A common argument in this master narrative, and one I have argued against in Chapter 1, is that labor unrest in China is not consequential or significant because worker activism is still "cellular" and apolitical, and because there are no independent unions in China.

[13] The Party's calls for the ACFTU to play a more active role can be found in many of former President Hu Jintao's speeches, for example, Xinhua (2007, 2008a, 2010). Apparently, the Chinese central government would prefer to resolve workplace conflicts and disputes through normalized dialogue and negotiation with the ACFTU playing an active role, rather than through workers' wildcat strikes and street protests.

labor movement and the general improvement of workers' welfare in China are the same as the conventional wisdoms generated from the experiences of core countries. For one thing, the revolutionary and socialist legacies of the CCP and its continuing official adherence to such legacies have played and will continue to play an important role in shaping the mobilizing strategies, patterns, languages, and outcomes of labor protests in today's China. Another important feature of Chinese labor politics highlighted in this study is that instead of viewing divided labor as passive and weak in an absolute way, it is more advisable to understand the divisive nature of Chinese labor politics as a dynamic and contradictory boundary-drawing process pursued by state policy elites, capitalists/employers, and workers through contestation, negotiation, and compromise. Rather than solely emphasizing the weaknesses and limitations of Chinese workers' localized, cellular, and apolitical struggles, a more constructive approach is to develop a set of analytical tools that are historically and geographically grounded, and that can help us identify the potential for transformation from below.

A fuller answer of what roles Chinese autoworkers are likely to play awaits further analysis along these and related lines. And it also awaits the coming words and deeds of Chinese autoworkers themselves.

Methodological appendix

This industrial ethnography of Chinese autoworkers is based primarily on my twenty months of qualitative research, including shop-floor observations, interviews, and archival research conducted in seven large automobile assembly factories in six cities in China. My field research took place during multiple field trips over the course of eight years between 2004 and 2011: June–August 2004; January, July, and August 2005; August 2006–June 2007; January 2008; and July–August 2011.

As noted in Chapter 1, in addition to shop-floor observations inside two auto factories,[1] I conducted a total of 278 in-depth interviews with workers, managers, and factory Party and union cadres at the seven auto assemblers. Information on the precise breakdown of my interviewees by enterprise and category is shown in Table A.1 and in the Interviewee Index.

In order to make sure that my interviewee sample was as representative as possible, I divided workers into different categories by contract type (formal or temporary), age and seniority (see Table A.2), skill level, and area of production. I then interviewed workers from each category.[2] I also divided managers into two categories and interviewed individuals from both: shop-floor managers who have regular, direct contact and interactions with workers, such as supervisors/foremen, shift leaders, and shop directors; and firm-level managers who do not have frequent, direct contact and interactions with workers, such as Human Resource managers and production managers. Factory Party committee and union leaders were listed separately from managers.

The interviews were conducted in a semi-structured manner, and on average, each interview lasted about 2–3 hours. The interviews with workers included questions about their job histories, recruitment and training experiences, working conditions, daily tasks performed, wages and labor contract terms,

---

[1] See also Chapter 1 for a discussion on how I gained access to the seven case-study automobile factories.

[2] Team leaders are defined by management as workers and are included in the worker sample (see Chapters 4 and 5). For information on workers' skill levels, see Chapter 3; on distribution by production areas, see the Interviewee Index.

TABLE A.I. *Numbers of interviewees, by enterprise and category*

Enterprise Name	Formal Worker	Temp. Worker	Manager	Party & Union Cadres	Total
SOE-2	15	17	6	5	43
GER-1	14	19	6	5	44
GER-2	16	18	7	4	45
USA-1	20	3	8	4	35
SOE-1	15	20	8	4	47
USA-2	17	3	6	4	30
JAP-1	21	n/a	5	4	30
Other	2	n/a	2	0	4
TOTAL	120	80	48	30	278

TABLE A.2. *Age and seniority of formal workers interviewed*

Age	Number	%	Seniority	Number	%
<25	39	32.5	<2 years	34	28.3
25–34	57	47.5	2–5 years	57	47.5
35–44	15	12.5	6–10 years	18	15.0
>45	9	7.5	>10 years	11	9.2
TOTALS	120	100	TOTAL	120	100

relations with managers and fellow workers, perceptions of and attitudes toward the factory Party committee and unions, perceived labor market conditions such as job security, activities they undertake in their spare time, and their hopes and aspirations. The interviews with managers focused on company profiles, corporate culture, employment and HRM policies, production specifics – for instance, line speed, level of automation, etc. – work rules, skills and quality of workforce, managerial responsibilities, personal experience of managing and dealing with workers, and opinions on labor relations in China today. The interviews with factory Party and union officials focused on their roles and relations with workers and management, the changes and challenges they were confronting, and the strategies and actions they were or had been taking.

Sitting down with my interviewees and listening to them describe their own experiences and opinions on their work, lives, and relations with their superiors and workmates allowed me to better understand how workers perceive and interpret their everyday workplace experiences. The initial interviews with workers – 29 out of the 200 interviewed workers – were arranged through managers and conducted within the factories. It was not a surprise that management would introduce me to "model workers," or to those team leaders who were most likely to present the "positive" side of management and companies. In order to minimize the bias in my interview sample, I managed to pursue research avenues independently and arranged most worker interviews through my personal connections and a snowballing strategy without interference from management. Most of my interviews with workers were conducted outside the factory at local teahouses, restaurants, or in workers' homes and dormitories. Since the interviewees generally preferred not to be tape recorded during the interviews, I took extensive notes and tidied them up immediately after the interviews, to keep the notes as accurate and complete as possible.

In order to examine the state's role in the automobile industry and labor relations, I interviewed a total of 41 local government and trade union officials, labor dispute arbitrators, labor scholars, and automotive industry experts in five cities – Beijing, Shanghai, Guangzhou, Qingdao, and Yantai.

In addition to the first-hand material collected from interviews and observations, I also collected archival and documentary data including: (1) published quantitative data from national and local statistical yearbooks and government and company documents; (2) published and unpublished company documents, including annual employees' satisfaction survey reports, meeting memorandums, and internal circulations; and, (3) articles and reports from Chinese newspapers, journals, online forums and blogs. The multiple data sources provide a solid empirical foundation for the narratives and analysis I present in this book.

Over the course of this study, I owe a great debt to the interviewees who gave their time, energy, and support to my research. I promised my interviewees that their identities would not be revealed under any circumstances. Thus the interviews are coded to preserve confidentiality. Below I list the coded interviewees' index. For each interviewee, I provide a brief description of his or her work position, contract type, and interview location and time. Certain interviews were conducted as group interviews with several interviewees present. In such cases, each interviewee is marked with an (*).

INTERVIEWEE INDEX

SOE-2

Q1 Administration Department manager, Qingdao, June 2004.
Q2 HR Department manager, Qingdao, June 2004.
Q3 Secretary of factory Party committee, Qingdao, June 2004.
Q4 Formal worker (assembler), Qingdao June 2004.
Q5 Temporary peasant worker (assembler), Qingdao, June 2004.
Q6* Student worker (assembler), Qingdao, June 2004.
Q7* Student worker (assembler), Qingdao, June 2004.
Q8* Student worker (assembler), Qingdao, June 2004.
Q9* Student worker (assembler), Qingdao, June 2004.
Q10 Formal worker (team leader), Qingdao, June 2004.
Q11 Formal worker (assembler), Qingdao, June 2004.
Q12 Temporary peasant worker (team leader), Qingdao, June 2004.
Q13 Formal worker (quality inspection), Qingdao, June 2004.

Q14 Formal worker (material control), Qingdao, September 2006.
Q15 Formal worker (mechanic), Qingdao, September 2006.
Q16 HR managerial staff, Qingdao, September 2006.
Q17 Factory Party committee staff, Qingdao, September 2006.
Q18 Assembly shop manager, Qingdao, September 2006.
Q19 Section Chief/Foreman (assembly shop), Qingdao, September 2006.
Q20 Formal worker (team leader), Qingdao, September 2006.
Q21 Formal worker (electronic mechanic), Qingdao, September 2006.
Q22 Formal worker (welder), Qingdao, September 2006.
Q23 Formal worker (painter), Qingdao, September 2006.
Q24 Formal worker (painter), Qingdao, September 2006.
Q25 Factory Union Chairman, Qingdao, October 2006.
Q26 Student worker, Qingdao (assembler), October 2006.
Q27 Formal worker (assembler), Qingdao, October 2006
Q28 Production manager, Qingdao, October 2006.
Q29* Student worker (assembler), Qingdao, October 2006.
Q30* Student worker (assembler), Qingdao, October 2006.
Q31* Student worker (assembler), Qingdao, October 2006.
Q32* Student worker (assembler), Qingdao, October 2006.
Q33 Formal worker (maintenance), Qingdao, October 2006.
Q34 Formal worker (team leader), Qingdao, October 2006
Q35 Factory Union staff, Qingdao, February 2007.
Q36 Secretary of Factory Youth League Committee, February 2007.
Q37 Temporary agency worker (welder), Qingdao, February 2007.
Q38 Temporary agency worker (welder), Qingdao, February 2007.
Q39 Temporary agency worker (welder), Qingdao, February 2007.
Q40* Student worker (assembler), Qingdao, February 2007.
Q41* Student worker (assembler), Qingdao, February 2007.
Q42 Student worker (assembler), Qingdao, February 2007.
Q43 Formal worker (press machine technician), Qingdao, February 2007.

GER-I

S1 Secretary of factory Party committee, Shanghai, July 2004.
S2 Deputy General Manager, Shanghai, July 2004.
S3 Formal worker (team leader), Shanghai, July 2004.
S4 Formal worker (assembler), Shanghai, July 2004.
S5 Formal worker (electronic technician), Shanghai, July 2004.
S6 Factory Union Chairman, Shanghai, July 2004.
S7 Temporary agency worker (assembler), Shanghai, July 2004.
S8 Temporary agency worker (assembler), Shanghai, July 2004.
S9 Temporary agency worker (assembler), Shanghai, July 2004.
S10 Assembly shop manager, Shanghai, July 2004.
S11 Formal worker (assembler), Shanghai, July 2004.
S12 Production Engineering manager, Shanghai, July 2004.

S13 HR Department managerial staff, Shanghai, November 2006.
S14 Temporary agency worker (assembler), Shanghai, November 2006.
S15 Temporary agency worker (assembler), Shanghai, November 2006.
S16 Factory Party committee staff, Shanghai, November 2006.
S17 HR manager, Shanghai, November 2006.
S18 Formal worker (painter), Shanghai, November 2006.
S19 Formal worker (team leader), Shanghai, November 2006.
S20 Temporary agency worker (assembler), Shanghai, November 2006.
S21 Temporary agency worker (assembler), Shanghai, November 2006.
S22 Temporary agency worker (assembler), Shanghai, November 2006.
S23 Formal worker (maintenance), Shanghai, November 2006.
S24 Formal worker (painter), Shanghai, November 2006.
S25 Temporary agency worker (assembler), Shanghai, November 2006.
S26 Temporary agency worker (welder), Shanghai, November 2006.
S27 Temporary agency worker (welder), Shanghai, November 2006.
S28 Formal worker (car body polisher), Shanghai, November 2006.
S29 Temporary agency worker (welder), Shanghai, November 2006.
S30 Formal worker (team leader), Shanghai, November 2006.
S31 Temporary agency worker (assembler), Shanghai, December 2006.
S32 Formal worker (quality control), Shanghai, December 2006.
S33* Temporary agency worker (assembler), Shanghai, December 2006.
S34* Temporary agency worker (assembler), Shanghai, December 2006.
S35 Formal worker (tool room), Shanghai, December 2006.
S36 Temporary agency worker (painter), Shanghai, December 2006.
S37 Temporary agency worker (assembler), Shanghai, December 2006.
S38 Secretary of factory Party committee, Shanghai, July 2011.
S39 Factory Union staff, Shanghai, July 2011.
S40 Section Chief/Foreman (assembly shop), Shanghai, July 2011.
S41 Formal worker (final car inspection), Shanghai, July 2011.
S42 Formal worker (team leader, former temporary agency worker), Shanghai, July 2011.
S43 Temporary agency worker (assembler), Shanghai, July 2011.
S44 Temporary agency worker (assembler), Shanghai, July 2011.

GER-2

F1 Production manager, Changchun, August 2004.
F2 Deputy Secretary of factory Party committee, Changchun, August 2004.
F3 Formal worker (team leader), Changchun, August 2004.
F4 Formal worker (assembler), Changchun, August 2004.
F5 Factory Union staff, Changchun, August 2004.
F6 Temporary peasant worker (welder), Changchun, August 2004.
F7 Formal worker (welder), Changchun, August 2004.
F8 Temporary agency worker (welder), Changchun, August 2004.
F9 Formal workers (electronic mechanic), Changchun, August 2004.

F10 Formal worker (team leader), Changchun, October 2006.
F11 Vice Chairman of factory union, Changchun, October 2006.
F12 Formal worker (maintenance), Changchun, October 2006.
F13 Formal worker (mental polisher/repair), Changchun. October, 2006.
F14 Temporary agency worker (welder), Changchun, October 2006.
F15 HR manager, Changchun, October 2006.
F16 Production engineering managerial staff (retired), Changchun, October 2006.
F17 Formal worker (team leader), Changchun, October 2006.
F18 Formal worker (welder), Changchun, October, 2006.
F19 Temporary agency worker (welder), Changchun, October 2006.
F20 Production manager, Changchun, October 2006.
F21 Temporary peasant worker (assembler), Changchun, October 2006.
F22 Temporary peasant worker (assembler), Changchun, October 2006.
F23 Formal worker (assembler), Changchun, October 2006.
F24 Section Chief/Foreman (body shop), Changchun, October 2006.
F25* Temporary agency worker (welder) Changchun, October 2006.
F26* Temporary agency worker (welder), Changchun, October 2006.
F27 Formal worker (mental finisher), Changchun, October 2006.
F28 Formal worker (painter), Changchun, October 2006.
F29 Formal worker (team leader), Changchun, October 2006.
F30 Formal worker (assembler), Changchun, October 2006.
F31* Student worker (assembler), Changchun, October 2006.
F32* Student worker (assembler), Changchun, October 2006.
F33 Temporary agency worker (assembler), Changchun, October 2006.
F34 Formal worker (welder), Changchun, October 2006.
F35 Assistant Foreman (body shop), October 2006.
F36 Temporary agency worker (welder) Changchun, October 2006.
F37 Temporary agency worker (welder) Changchun, October 2006.
F38 Former temporary agency worker (metal finisher), Guangzhou, June 2007.
F39 Production manager, Changchun, July 2011.
F40 Factory Party committee staff, Changchun, July 2011
F41 Temporary agency worker (team leader), Changchun, July 2011.
F42 Formal worker (welder, former temporary agency worker), Changchun, July 2011.
F43 Student worker (welder), Changchun, July 2011.
F44 Student worker (assembler), Changchun, July 2011.
F45 Student worker (assembler), Changchun, July 2011.

USA-1

M1 HR managerial staff, Shanghai, January 2005.
M2 Team leader (general assembly shop), Shanghai, January 2005.
M3 Assembler, Shanghai, January 2005.
M4 Assembler, Shanghai, January 2005.

M5   Maintenance technician, Shanghai, January 2005.
M6   Assembler, Shanghai, January 2005.
M7   Assembler, Shanghai, January 2005.
M8   Electronic Mechanic, Shanghai, January 2005.
M9   Painter, Shanghai, November 2006.
M10 Painter, Shanghai, November 2006.
M11 Assembler, Shanghai, November 2006.
M12 Assembler, Shanghai, November 2006.
M13 HR managerial staff, Shanghai, November 2006.
M14 Shop manager (general assembly shop), Shanghai, November 2006.
M15 Supervisor/Foreman (general assembly shop), Shanghai, December 2006.
M16 Factory union staff, Shanghai, December 2006.
M17 Factory union Chairman, Shanghai, December 2006.
M18 Factory Party committee staff, Shanghai, December 2006.
M19 Production safety manager, Shanghai, December 2006.
M20 Deputy Secretary of factory Party Community, Shanghai, December 2006.
M21 Welder, Shanghai, December 2006.
M22 Welder, Shanghai, December 2006.
M23 Final car inspector, Shanghai, December 2006.
M24 Quality control technician, Shanghai, December 2006.
M25 Facilities project engineer, Shanghai, January 2008.
M26 Team leader (body shop), Shanghai, January 2008.
M27 Metal finisher, Shanghai, January 2008.
M28 Car body modeler, Shanghai, January 2008.
M29 Welder, Shanghai, January 2008.
M30 Production engineering manager, Shanghai, August 2011.
M31 HR manager, Shanghai, August 2011.
M32 Maintenance technician, Shanghai, August 2011.
M33 Temporary agency worker (CNC operator), Shanghai, August 2011
M34 Temporary agency worker (painter), Shanghai, August 2011
M35 Temporary agency worker (painter), Shanghai, August 2011

SOE-1

C1   Former R&D engineer, Shanghai, July 2005.
C2   Former HR managerial staff, Shanghai, July 2005
C3   Production managerial staff, Wuhu, August 2005.
C4   Formal worker (assembler), Wuhu, August 2005.
C5   Temporary agency worker (assembler), Wuhu, August 2005.
C6   Student worker (assembler), Wuhu, August 2005.
C7   Student worker (welder), Wuhu, August 2005.
C8   Student worker (welder), Wuhu, August 2005.
C9   Formal worker (welder), Wuhu, August 2005.
C10 Production managerial staff, Wuhu, March 2007.
C11 Formal worker (assembler), Wuhu, March 2007.

C12 Formal worker (team leader), Wuhu, March 2007.
C13 Formal worker (assembler), Wuhu, March 2007.
C14 Temporary agency worker (assembler), Wuhu, March 2007.
C15 Student worker (assembler), Wuhu, March 2007.
C16 Formal worker (assembler), Wuhu, March 2007.
C17 Temporary agency worker (assembler), Wuhu, March 2007.
C18 Temporary agency worker (assembler), Wuhu, March 2007.
C19 Factory Party committee staff, Wuhu, March 2007.
C20 Shop manager (general assembly shop), Wuhu, March 2007.
C21 Formal worker (team leader), Wuhu, March 2007.
C22 Student worker (assembler), Wuhu, March 2007.
C23 Student worker (assembler), Wuhu, March 2007.
C24 Student worker (assembler), Wuhu, March 2007.
C25 Temporary agency worker (assembler), Wuhu, March 2007.
C26 Temporary agency worker (assembler), Wuhu, March 2007.
C27 Formal worker (painter), Wuhu, March 2007.
C28 Formal worker (painter), Wuhu, March 2007.
C29 Formal worker (team leader), Wuhu, March 2007.
C30 Formal worker (quality control), Wuhu, March 2007.
C31 Formal worker (electronic mechanic technician), Wuhu, March 2007.
C32 Factory union staff, Wuhu, April 2007.
C33 HR managerial staff, Wuhu, April 2007.
C34 Factory Party committee staff, Wuhu, April 2007.
C35 Supervisor/Foreman (body shop), Wuhu, April 2007.
C36 Formal worker (maintenance/repair worker), Wuhu, April 2007.
C37 Formal worker (welder), Wuhu, April 2007.
C38* Student worker (welder), Wuhu, April 2007.
C39* Student worker (welder), Wuhu, April 2007.
C40 Temporary agency worker (welder), Wuhu, April 2007.
C41 Deputy Director, Passenger Car Division, Wuhu, August 2011.
C42 Newsletter editor and Youth League Committee staff, Wuhu, August 2011.
C43 Formal worker (team leader), Wuhu, August 2011.
C44 Student worker (assembler), Wuhu, August 2011.
C45 Student worker (assembler), Wuhu, August 2011.
C46 Temporary agency worker (warehouse worker), Wuhu, August 2011.
C47 Temporary agency worker (warehouse worker), Wuhu, August 2011.

USA-2

D1 Formal worker (former team leader), Yantai, September 2006.
D2 Formal worker (team leader), Yantai, September 2006.
D3 Formal worker (assembler), Yantai, September 2006.
D4 Formal worker (assembler), Yantai, September 2006.
D5 Production managerial staff, Yantai, September 2006.
D6 Supervisor/Foreman (assembly shop), Yantai, September 2006.

D7   Formal worker (electronic mechanic), Yantai, September 2006.
D8   Formal worker (assembler), Yantai, September 2006.
D9   R & D engineer, Yantai, April 2007.
D10 HR managerial staff, Yantai, April 2007.
D11 Factory Union staff, Yantai, April 2007.
D12 Factory Party committee staff, Yantai, April 2007.
D13 Formal worker (welder), Yantai, April 2007.
D14 Formal worker (welder), Yantai, April 2007.
D15 Formal worker (Maintenance technician), Yantai, April 2007.
D16 Formal worker (painter), Yantai, April 2007.
D17 Formal worker (painter), Yantai, April 2007.
D18 Factory union staff, Yantai, April 2007.
D19 Shop manager (Assembly shop), Yantai, April 2007.
D20 Formal worker (team leader), Yantai, April 2007.
D21 Formal worker (assembler), Yantai, May 2007.
D22 Formal worker (assembler), Yantai, May 2007.
D23 Formal worker (mechanic), Yantai, May 2007.
D24 Factory union Chairman, August 2011.
D25 HR manager, Yantai, August 2011
D26 Formal worker (team leader), Yantai, August 2011
D27 Formal worker (assembler), Yantai, August 2011.
D28 Temporary agency worker (assembler), Yantai, August 2011.
D29 Student worker (assembler), Yantai, August 2011
D30 Student worker (assembler), Yantai, August 2011.

JPN-I

H1   HR manager, Guangzhou, September 2006.
H2   Production managerial staff, Guangzhou, May 2007.
H3   Assembler, Guangzhou, May 2007.
H4   Assembler, Guangzhou, May 2007.
H5   Assembler, Guangzhou, May 2007.
H6   Team leader, Guangzhou, May 2007.
H7   Factory union staff, Guangzhou, May 2007.
H8   Factory Party Committee staff, Guangzhou, May 2007.
H9   Shift leader (foreman), Guangzhou, May 2007.
H10 Painter, Guangzhou, May 2007.
H11 Painter, Guangzhou, May 2007.
H12 Team leader, Guangzhou, May 2007.
H13 Welder, Guangzhou, May 2007.
H14 Welder, Guangzhou, May 2007.
H15 Welder, Guangzhou, May 2007.
H16 HR managerial staff, Guangzhou, June 2007.
H17 Secretary of Factory Youth League Committee, Guangzhou, June 2007.
H18 Shop manager (assembly shop), Guangzhou, June 2007.

H19 Team leader, Guangzhou, June 2007.
H20 Assembler, Guangzhou, June 2007.
H21 Assembler, Guangzhou, June 2007.
H22 Assembler, Guangzhou, June 2007.
H23 Electronic mechanic engineer, Guangzhou, June 2007.
H24 Final car inspector, Guangzhou, June 2007.
H25 Test driver, Guangzhou, June 2007.
H26 Vice Chairman of Factory union, Guangzhou, July 2011.
H27 Maintenance technician, Guangzhou, July 2011.
H28 Quality control, Guangzhou, July 2011.
H29 Painter, Guangzhou, July 2011.
H30 Car body modeler, Guangzhou, July 2011.

OTHER

B1 Shop manager at a Sino-Korean automaker, Beijing, January 2008.
B2 HR managerial staff at a Sino-Korean automaker, Beijing, January 2008.
T1 Team leader at a Sino-Japanese automaker, Tianjin, August 2005.
T2 Assembler at a Sino-Japanese automaker, Tianjin, January 2008.

LOCAL OFFICIALS, LABOR DISPUTE ARBITRATORS,
AND SCHOLARS
NO.

1 Qingdao Municipal Labor and Social Security Bureau (LSSB) Deputy Director, Qingdao, June 2004.
2 Qingdao Licang district LSSB Director, Qingdao, June 2004.
3 Qingdao Shinan district Labor Dispute Arbitration Committee (LDAC) arbitrator, Qingdao, June 2004.
4 Qingdao Shinan district LDAC arbitrator, Qingdao, June 2004.
5 Shanghai Qingpu district LSSB official, Shanghai, July 2004.
6 Shanghai Huangpu district LSSB official, Shanghai, July 2004.
7 Shanghai Pudong New District LSSB official, Shanghai, July 2004.
8 Shanghai Pudong New District LDAC Depute Director, Shanghai, July 2004.
9 Shanghai municipal Federal Trade Union official, Shanghai, July 2004.
10 Project Cost Management Engineer, Pan-Asia Technical Automotive Center, Shanghai, January 2005.
11 SAIC HR managerial staff, Shanghai, January 2005.
12 Professor, Sociology, Fudan University, Shanghai, January 2005.
13 Arbitrator, Guangzhou LDAC, Guangzhou, September, 2006.
14 Arbitrator, Guangzhou LDAC, Guangzhou, September, 2006.
15 Secretary General, Guangzhou Federation of Trade Union, International Liaison Department, Guangzhou, September 2006.
16 Professor, School of Government, Sun Yat-Sen University, Guangzhou, September 2006.

17 Labor law professor, East China University of Political Science and Law, Qingdao, September 2006.
18 Labor law professor, Zhongnan University of Economics and Law, Qingdao, September 2006.
19 Senior official, MOHRSS, Labor & Wage Division, Qingdao, September 2006.
20 President, Qingdao Labor Dispute Arbitration Court, Qingdao, September 2006.
21 Deputy Director, MOHRSS, Institute for Labor Studies, Qingdao, September 2006.
22 Deputy Director, FAW R & D Institute Changchun, October 2006.
23 Director, Pudong Institute for the US Economy, Pudong Academy of Development, Shanghai, December 2006.
24 Assistant Director, Institute of World Economy, Shanghai Academy of Social Science (SASS), Shanghai, December 2006.
25 Professor, Sociology, Tsinghua University, Beijing, December 2006.
26 Professor, Sociology, Beijing University, Beijing, December 2006.
27 Professor, Institute of Sociology, China Academy of Social Science (CASS), Beijing, December 2006.
28 Professor, China Institute of Industrial Relations, Beijing, December 2006.
29 Arbitrator, Pudong New District LDAC, Shanghai, February 2007.
30 Member of SAIC Strategy Committee and Senior Engineer, Shanghai, February 2007.
31 Researcher, SASS, Shanghai, March 2007.
32 Official, Yantai LSSB, Yantai, April 2007.
33 Director, Yantai Economic and Technological Development Zone, the Office of Labor and Employment, Yantai, April 2007.
34 Official, Party Committee of Wuhu Economic & Technological Development Area (WEDA), Wuhu, April 2007.
35 Official, WEDA LSSB, Wuhu, April 2007.
36 President, Guangzhou Institute of Technology, Guangzhou, May 2007.
37 HR managerial staff, Shanghai Foreign Service Co., Ltd., Shanghai, January 2008.
38 HR managerial staff, China International Intellectech Shanghai Corporation, Shanghai, January 2008.
39 Deputy Director of the Policy Research Department of ACFTU, Beijing, July 2011.
40 Professor, Sociology, Sun Yat-Sen University, Guangzhou, July 2011.
41 Professor, College of Automotive Engineering, Tongji University, Shanghai, August 2011.

Bibliography

Amin, Samir. 2005. "China, Market Socialism, and U.S. Hegemony." *Review (Fernand Braudel Center)* 28 (3): 259–79.

Anderson, G. E. 2012. *Designated Drivers: How China Plans to Dominate the Global Auto Industry*. Singapore: Johns Wiley & Sons Singapore Pte. Ltd.

Andors, Stephen. 1977. *China's Industrial Revolution: Politics, Planning, and Management, 1949 to the Present*. New York, NY: Pantheon Books.

Aronowitz, Stanley. [1973] 1991. *False Promises: The Shaping of American Working Class Consciousness*. Durham, NC: Duke University Press.

Arrighi, Giovanni. 1990a. "The Development Illusion: A Reconceptualization of the Semiperiphery," pp.11–42. In *Semiperipheral States in the World-Economy*, edited by W. G. Martin. New York: Greenwood Press.

  1990b. "Marxist-Century, American-Century: The Making and Remaking of the World Labor Movement." *New Left Review* 179: 29–63.

  2007. *Adam Smith in Beijing: Lineages of the Twenty-First Century*. London: Verso.

Arrighi, Giovanni and Beverly Silver. 1984. "Labor movement and capital migration: The United States and Western Europe in World-Historical Perspective," pp.183–216. In *Labor in the Capitalist World-Economy*, edited by C. Bergquist. Beverly Hills, CA: Sage.

Aschoff, Nicole. 2010. "Globalization and Capital Mobility in the Automobile Industry." PhD dissertation, Department of Sociology, Johns Hopkins University, Baltimore, MD.

Asher, Robert, Ronald Edsforth (with the assistance of Stephen Merlino). (Eds.) 1995. *Autowork*. Albany, NY: State University of New York Press.

Atkinson, John. 1987. "Flexibility or Fragmentation? The United Kingdom Labour Market in the Eighties." *Labour and Society* 12 (1): 87–105.

Auyero, Javier. 2005. "Protest and Politics in Contemporary Argentina," pp. 250–68. In *Argentine Democracy: The Politics of Institutional Weakness*, edited by S. Levitsky and M. Murillo. University Park, PA: Pennsylvania State University Press.

Babson, Steve. (Ed.) 2009. *Lean Work: Empowerment and Exploitation in the Global Auto Industry*. Detroit, MI: Wayne State University Press.

Bair, Jennifer, ed. 2009. *Frontiers of Commodity Chain Research*. Stanford, CA: Stanford University Press.

Banister, Judith. 2005. "Manufacturing Earnings and Compensation in China." *Monthly Labor Review* (June): 11–29. Retrieved April 11, 2014 (www.bls.gov/opub/mlr/2005/07/art2full.pdf).

Barbosa, Filipe, Damian Hattingh, and Michael Kloss. 2010. "Applying Global Trends: A Look at China's Auto Industry." *McKinsey Quarterly*, July: 1–7.

Barboza, David. 2010. "Strike Status at Honda in China Is Uncertain." *New York Times*. June 1. Retrieved June 5, 2010 (www.nytimes.com/2010/06/02/business/global/02strike.html?src=busln).

Beeson, Mark. 2009. "Developmental States in East Asia: A Comparison of the Japanese and Chinese Experiences." *Asian Perspective*, 33 (2): 5–39.

Bergquist, Charles. 1986. *Labor in Latin America: Comparative Essays on Chile, Argentina, Venezuela, and Colombia*. Stanford, CA: Stanford University Press.

Beynon, Huw. 1973. *Working for Ford*. London: Allen Lane.

Blecher, Marc. 1983. "Peasant Labour for Urban Industry: Temporary Contract Labour, Urban-Rural Balance and Class Relations in a Chinese County." *World Development*, 11 (8): 731–45.

   2002. "Hegemony and Workers' Politics in China". *The China Quarterly* 170: 283–303.

Bloomberg, 2010. "Honda Halts Auto Production in China Amid Parts-Factory Strike." May 27. Retrieved June 1, 2010 (www.businessweek.com/news/2010-05-27/honda-halts-auto-production-in-china-amid-parts-factory-strike.html).

Bonacich, Edna. 1972. "A Theory of Ethnic Antagonism: The Split Labor Market." *American Sociological Review* 37 (5): 547–59.

   1976. "Advanced Capitalism and Black/White Race Relations in the United States: A Split Labor Market Interpretation." *American Sociological Review* 41 (1): 34–51.

Bradsher, Keith. 2010a. "Strike Forces Honda to Shut Plants in China." *The New York Times*. May 27. Retrieved June 1, 2010 (www.nytimes.com/2010/05/28/business/global/28honda.html).

   2010b. "A Labor Movement Stirs in China." *The New York Times*, June 10. Retrieved June 11, 2010 (www.nytimes.com/2010/06/11/business/global/11strike.html?src=mv).

   2013. "Asia's Challenge to Europe." *The New York Times*, October 14. Retrieved October 15, 2013 (www.nytimes.com/2013/10/15/world/asia/asias-challenge-to-europe.html?ref=global-home&pagewanted=all&_r=0).

Bradsher, Keith and David Barboza. 2010. "Strike in China Highlights Gap in Workers' Pay." *The New York Times*. May 28. Retrieved June 1, 2010 (www.nytimes.com/2010/05/29/business/global/29honda.html?pagewanted=1&ref=business).

Braverman, Harry. 1974. *Labor and Monopoly Capital: The Degradation of Work in the Twentieth Century*. New York, NY: Monthly Review Press.

Buckley, Peter, Jeremy Clegg, Ping Zheng, et al. 2007. "The Impact of Foreign Direct Investment on the Productivity of China's Automotive Industry." *Management International Review* 47 (5): 707–24.

Bunce, Valerie. 1999. *Subversive Institutions: The Design and the Destruction of Socialism and the State*. New York, NY: Cambridge University Press.

Burawoy, Michael. 1976. "The Functions and Reproduction of Migrant Labor: Comparative Material From Southern Africa and the United States." *American Journal of Sociology* 81, No. 5: 1050–87.

   1979. *Manufacturing Consent: Changes in the Labor Process under Monopoly Capitalism*. Chicago, IL: Chicago University Press.

   1983. "Between the Labor Process and the State: The Changing Face of Factory Regimes Under Advanced Capitalism." *American Sociological Review* 48 (5): 587–605.

   1985. *The Politics of Production: Factory Regimes under Capitalism and Socialism*. London: Verso.

Burawoy, Michael and Janos Lukacs. 1992. *The Radiant Past: Ideology and Reality in Hungary's Road to Capitalism.* Chicago, IL: University of Chicago Press.
Burawoy, Michael and Erik Olin Wright. 1990. "Coercion and Consent in Contested Exchange." *Politics & Society* 18 (2): 251–66.
Burgess, John and Julia Connell. (Eds.) 2004. *International Perspectives in Temporary Agency Work.* London: Routledge.
Cai, Yongshun. 2006. *State and Laid-Off Workers in Reform China: The Silence and Collective Action of the Retrenched.* London: Routledge.
Carter, Lance. 2010. "Auto Industry Strikes in China." *Insurgent Notes* No. 2, October 30. Retrieved November 15, 2010 (http://libcom.org/library/auto-industry-strikes-china-lance-carter).
Castells, Manuel. 1992. "Four Asian Tigers with a dragon head: A comparative analysis of the state, economy, and society in the Asian Pacific Rim," pp.33–70. In *States and Development in the Asian Pacific Rim,* edited by R. Appelbaum and J. Henderson. London: Sage Publications, Inc.
Chan, Anita. 2001. *China's Workers under Assault: The Exploitation of Labor in a Globalizing Economy.* Armonk, NY: M.E. Sharpe.
 2006. "Organizing Wal-Mart: The Chinese Trade Union at a Crossroads." *Japan Focus,* September 8.
Chan, Anita and Xiaoyang Zhu. 2003. "Disciplinary Labor Regimes in Chinese Factories." *Critical Asian Studies* 35 (4): 559–84.
Chan, Chris King-Chi. 2010. *The Challenge of Labour in China: Strikes and the Changing Labour Regime in Global Factories.* London: Routledge.
Chang, Kai and Kungang Li. 2006. "bixu yange guizhi laodongzhe paiqian" (Labor Dispatch Must be Strictly Regulated and Restrained). *China Labor* March: 9–12.
Chen, Chen and Jun Dong. 2007. "kendeji laowu paiqian'an yinfa de faxue sikao" (*Legal Reflection from the KFC Labor Dispatch Case*). *Labor Law Network.* April 4. Retrieved March 7, 2008 (www.shlaodong.com/lswz/20070404/152622.htm).
Chen, Feng. 2003. "Between the State and Labour: The Conflict of Chinese Trade Unions' Double Identity in Market Reform." *The China Quarterly* 176: 1006–28.
 2009. "Union Power in China: Source, Operation, and Constraints." *Modern China* 35 (6): 662–89.
 2010. "Trade Unions and the Quadripartite Interactions in Strike Settlement in China." *The China Quarterly* 201: 104–124.
Chen, Lin and Liang Chang. 2006. "Laodong paiqianzhong de falv wenti" (Some Legal Issues in Labor Dispatch) *Beijing Daily,* July 27. Retrieved March 7, 2008 (www.beijingdaily.com.cn/).
Chen, Liping. 2012. "Laodong Hetong Fa Xiuzheng An Chushen: Paiqian Laodongzhe Yu Yonggong Danwei Laodongzhe Tong Gong Tong Chou" (First Review of the Draft Amendments to the Labor Contract Law: Agency Workers Entitled to Equal Pay for Equal Work). *Legal Daily,* June 27. Retrieved June 28, 2012 (http://news.xinmin.cn/domestic/gnkb/2012/06/27/15301851.html).
Chen, Xi. 2012. *Social Protest and Contentious Authoritarianism in China.* New York, NY: Cambridge University Press.
Cheng, Yuanhui and Yachan Li. 2010. "Bentian zhongwai yuangong gongzi xiang cha 50 bei, shubai gongren bagong" (Wage Differences among Honda Employees Reach 50 times, Several Hundred Workers Went on Strike). *Daily Economic News,* May 21. Retrieved May 27, 2010 (http://business.sohu.com/20100521/n272253154.shtml).

Chin, Gregory T. 2003. *Building Capitalism with China's Characteristics: The Political Economy of Model Joint Ventures in the Automotive Industry*. PhD Dissertation, Department of Political Science, York University, North York, Ontario, Canada.

———. 2010. *China's Automotive Modernization: The Party-State and Multinational Corporations*. New York, NY: Palgrave Macmillan.

China Association of Automobile Manufacturers (CAAM). 2005. "Qiche zhizaoye zhiye jishu jiaoyu diaoyan baogao" ("Survey Report on Vocational Technical Education in Automobile Manufacturing Sector"), unpublished report.

———. 2013. "2012 nian qiche gongye jingji yunxing qingkuang" ("Conditions of economic operation in the automobile industry in 2012"). January 14. Retrieved July 28, 2013 (www.autoinfo.gov.cn/autoinfo_cn/xwzx/rdts/webinfo/2013/01/14/1353302 433103337.htm).

———. 2014. "Qiche gongye Xiehui: 2013 nian guochan qiche chanxiao tupo liangqianwan liang" (CAAM: 2013 domestic car sales exceeded twenty million). January 9. Retrieved January 10, 2014 (www.gov.cn/jrzg/2014–01/09/content_2563281.htm).

China Automotive Technology Research Center (CATRC), 1992–2012. *China Automotive Industry Yearbook (Zhongguo qiche gongye nianjian)*. Tianjin, China: China Automotive Industry Yearbook Press.

China.com.cn. 2010. "ACFTU: Labor dispatch should only be used at substitutive, short-term and temporary posts" March 9. Retrieved March 18, 2010. (www. china.com.cn/gonghui/2010-03/09/content_19566933.htm)

China Economic Information Network (CEIN). 2008–2012. "*China Industry Annual Report Series: Automobile*." Beijing: CEIN (www.cei.gov.cn/).

China Economic Weekly (Zhongguo Jingji Zhoukan). 2007. "Baohu laodong zhe – xin laodong hetong fa de jiedu he shiyi" ("Protecting Workers: The Interpretation and Clarification of the new Labor Contract Law"). November 19. Retrieved January 24, 2014 (http://finance.people.com.cn/GB/1045/6544536.html.).

ChinaHR.com. 2007. "Zhonghua yingcaiwang diaocha: qiche hangye shouru gao rencai qiao" ("ChinaHR.com survey: the auto industry has high earnings and high demand for talent"). April 16. Retrieved August 7, 2008 (http://content.chinahr. com/Article(49355)ArticleInfo.view).

China Labour Bulletin (CLB). 2009a. "Protecting Workers' Rights or Serving the Party: The Way Forward for China's Trade Unions." March. Retrieved June 16, 2012 (www.clb.org.hk/en/files/share/File/research_reports/acftu_report.pdf).

———. 2009b. "Chinese Government says Labor Disputes Doubled in 2008." May 11. Retrieved November 2, 2009 (www.china-labour.org.hk/en/node/100461).

———. 2011. "Unity is Strength: The Workers' Movement in China 2009–2011." October. Retrieved January 21, 2012 (www.clb.org.hk/en/files/share/File/research_reports/ unity_is_strength_web.pdf).

China Talent Group (CTG). 2010. *CTG China Employment Index Report*. Beijing: China Talent Group.

Chinoy, Ely. 1955 (1992). *Automobile Workers and the American Dream*. (2nd ed.) Boston, MA: Beacon Press.

Chossudovsky, Michel. 1986. *Towards Capitalist Restoration?: Chinese Socialism after Mao*. London: Palgrave Macmillan.

Clawson, Dan. 2003. *The Next Upsurge: Labor and the New Social Movements*. Ithaca, NY: ILR Press.

Clifford, Paul, August Joas, and Frank Leung. 2009. "A New Vroom in Beijing: How consumer behavior is changing China's auto market." *Mercer Management Journal* 19: 49–56.

Collinson, David. 1992. *Managing the Shopfloor: Subjectivity, Masculinity, and Workplace Culture.* Berlin: Walter de Gruyter.

Connell, Raewyn. 1983. *Which Way Is Up? Essays on Sex, Class and Culture.* Sydney: George Allen and Unwin.

Connelly, Catherine and Daniel Gallagher. 2004. "Emerging Trends in Contingent Work Research." *Journal of Management* 30 (6): 959–83.

Cook, Linda.1993. *The Soviet Social Contract and Why It Failed: Welfare Policy and Workers' Politics from Brezhnev to Yeltsin.* Cambridge, MA: Harvard University Press.

Cui, Zhiyuan. 1996. "An'gang Constitution and Post-Fordism. ("Angang Xianfa yu Hou Fute Zhuyi"). *Du Shu* 3: 11–21.

Degiuli, Francesca and Christopher Kollmeyer. 2007. "Bringing Gramsci Back In: Labor Control in Italy's new Temporary Help Industry." *Work, Employment and Society* 21 (3): 497–515.

Deyo, Frederic. 1989. *Beneath the Miracle: Labor Subordination in the New Asian Industrialism.* Berkeley, CA: University of California Press.

Dicken, Peter. 2011. *Global Shift: Mapping the Changing Contours of the World Economy.* (6th ed.) New York, NY: Guilford Press.

Doeringer, Peter and Michael Piore. 1971. *Internal Labor Markets and Manpower Analysis.* Lexington, MA: D. C. Heath & Co.

Dong, Baohua. 2008. "From the Labor Law to the Labor Contract Law." Paper presented at *Breaking Down Chinese Walls: The Changing Faces of Labor and Employment in China."* Cornell University, Ithaca, NY, September 26–28.

Dore, Ronald. 1973. *British Factory–Japanese Factory: The Origins of National Diversity in Industrial Relations.* Berkeley, CA: University of California Press.

Drucker, Peter. 1946. *Concept of the Corporation.* New York, NY: The John Day Company.

Dunning, John. 1981. *International Production and the Multinational Enterprise.* London: George Allen & Unwin.

Durand, Jean-Pierre and Nicolas Hatzfeld. 2003. *Living Labour: Life on the Line at Peugeot France.* Translated by Dafydd Roberts. New York, NY: Palgrave Macmillan.

Durand, Jean-Pierre, Paul Stewart, and Juan Jose Castillo (Eds.). 1999. *Teamwork in the Automobile Industry: Radical Change or Passing Fashion?* London: Macmillan Press.

Dyer, Geoff. 2005. "Carmakers Feel Pain in Chinese Market." *Financial Times*, April 23.

Edwards, Paul. 1986. *Conflict at Work: A Materialist Analysis of Workplace Relations.* New York, NY: Blackwell.

Edwards, Richard. 1975. "The Social Relations of Production in the Firm and Labor Market Structure." *Politics & Society* 5 (1): 83–108.

   1979. *Contested Terrain: The Transformation of the Workplace in the Twentieth Century.* New York, NY: Basic Books.

Eisenstein, Paul. 2011. "UAW May Skip Strike Deadline in Talks with Detroit Big Three." *The Detroit Bureau*, April 26. Retrieved June 8, 2012 (www.thedetroitbureau.com/2011/04/uaw-may-skip-strike-deadline-in-talks-with-detroit-big-three/).

Emmenegger, Patrick, Silja Häusermann, Bruno Palier, and Martin Seeleib-Kaiser. (Eds.). 2012. *The Age of Dualization: The Changing Face of Inequality in Deindustrializing Societies*. New York, NY: Oxford University Press.

Evans, Peter. 1979. *Dependent Development: The Alliance of Multinational, State, and Local Capital in Brazil*. Princeton, NJ: Princeton University Press.

Eyferth, Jacob, ed. 2006. *How China Works: Perspectives on the Twentieth-Century Industrial Workplace*. London: Routledge.

Fantasia, Rick. 1988. *Cultures of Solidarity: Consciousness, Action, and Contemporary American Workers*. Berkeley, CA: University of California Press.

Fairbank, John. 1992. *China: A New History*. Cambridge, MA: The Belknap Press.

Federation of Automobile Dealers Associations. 2006. "What has WTO Membership Brought to China's Auto Industry?" Retrieved September 21, 2009 (www.fadaweb.com/wto.htm).

Feng, Tongqing. 2002. *Zhongguo Gongren de Mingyun: Gaige Yilai Zhongguo Gongren de Shehui xingdong. (The Destiny of Chinese Workers: Social Action of Workers since the Reform)*. Beijing: Social Sciences Academic Press.

First Financial Daily, 2010. "Shoukun fenpei zhidu, qiche hangye gongren xinchou diwei paihuai" (Restricted by the Distribution System, Auto Industry Workers' Wages Remain Low). September 7. Retrieved July 7, 2011 (http://auto.ifeng.com/news/domesticindustry/20100907/415831.shtml).

Fishman, Ted. 2005. *China, Inc.: How the Rise of the Next Superpower Challenges America and the World*. New York, NY: Scribner.

Ford, Henry and Samuel Crowther. 1926. *Today and Tomorrow*. Garden City, NY: Doubleday, Page & Co.

Ford Motor Company. 2007. *Ford Motor Company: 2007 Annual Report*. Retrieved May 15, 2014 (http://corporate.ford.com/doc/2007_ar.pdf).

Frazier, Mark. 2002. *The Making of Chinese Industrial Workplace: State, Revolution, and Labor Management*. New York, NY: Cambridge University Press.

Friedman, Eli and Ching Kwan Lee. 2010. "Remaking the World of Chinese Labour: A 30-Year Retrospective." *British Journal of Industrial Relations* 48 (3): 507–33.

Friedman, Gerald. 2008. *Reigniting the Labor Movement: Restoring Means to Ends in a Democratic Labor Movement*. London, Routledge.

Gallagher, Mary. 2004. "'Time Is Money, Efficiency Is Life': The Transformation of Labor Relations in China." *Studies in Comparative International Development* 39 (2): 11–44.

2005a. *Contagious Capitalism: Globalization and the Politics of Labor in China*. Princeton, NJ: Princeton University Press.

2005b. "'Use the Law as Your Weapon!': Institutional Change and Legal Mobilization in China," pp. 54–83. In *Engaging the Law in China: State, Society, and Possibilities for Justice*, edited by N. Diamant, S. Lubman, and K. O'Brien. Stanford, CA: Stanford University Press.

Gallagher, Mary, and Baohua Dong. 2011. "Legislating Harmony: Labor Law Reform in Contemporary China ," pp. 36–60. In *From Iron Rice Bowl to Informalization: Markets, Workers, and the State in a Changing China*, edited by S. Kuruvilla, C. Lee, and M. Gallagher. Ithaca, NY: Cornell University Press.

Gao, Paul. 2002. "A Tune-up for China's Auto Industry." *The McKinsey Quarterly*, 1: 144–55.

Gartman, David. 1986. *Auto Slavery: The Labor Process in the American Automobile Industry, 1897–1950*. New Brunswick, NJ: Rutgers University Press.

Geng, Yanbing and Jiapeng Ji. 2012. "Quanzong zaitui laodongfa xiugai huo she laowu paiqian xianzhi" (ACFTU Proposed to Amend the Labor Contract Law or Set Up Restrictions on Labor Dispatch Again). *21st Century Business Herald*, February 9. Retrieved June 10, 2012 (www.21cbh.com/HTML/2012-2-9/yMMDY5XzQwMDYyMA.html).

Gereffi, Gary, and Miguel Korzeniewicz, eds. 1994. *Commodity Chains and Global Capitalism*. Westport, CT: Greenwood Press.

Global Labor Strategies (GLS). 2007. "The Battle for Labor Rights in China: New Developments." November. Accessed on August 27, 2008 (http://laborstrategies.blogs.com/global_labor_strategies/2007/11/the-battle-for-.html).

——— 2008. "Why China Matters: Labor Rights in the Era of Globalization." April. Retrieved on August 27, 2008 (http://laborstrategies.blogs.com/global_labor_strategies/files/why_china_matters_gls_report.pdf).

Gordon, Andrew. 1996. "Conditions for the Disappearance of the Japanese Working-Class Movement," pp.11–52. In *Putting Class in Its Place: Worker Identities in East Asia*, edited by E. Perry. Berkeley, CA: Institute of East Asian Studies, University of California, Berkeley.

Gordon, David, Richard Edwards, and Michael Reich. 1982. *Segmented Work, Divided Workers: The Historical Transformation of Labor in the United States*. Cambridge: Cambridge University Press.

Gouldner, Alvin. 1954. *Patterns of Industrial Bureaucracy*. Glencoe, IL: Free Press.

Graham, Laurie. 1995. *On the Line at Subaru-Isuzu: The Japanese Model and the American Worker*. Ithaca, NY: ILR Press/Cornell University Press.

Gramsci, Antonio. 1971. *Selections from the Prison Notebooks*. New York, NY: International Publishers.

Granick, David. 1991. "Multiple Labour Markets in the Industrial State Enterprise Sector." *The China Quarterly*, 126: 269–89.

Guo, Huaidi. 2010. "Naihai Bentian Gongren Daibiao Fachu Gongkaixin" (Nanhai Honda Worker Representatives Issued an Open Letter). *Caixin Online*, June 3. Retrieved June 5, 2010 (http://stock.sohu.com/20100603/n272552246.shtml).

Guthrie, Doug. 1999. *Dragon in a Three-piece Suit: The Emergence of Capitalism in China*. Princeton, NJ: Princeton University Press.

Habermas, Jurgen. 1973. *Legitimation Crisis*. Translated by T. McCarthy. Boston, MA: Beacon Press.

Haley, Usha. 2012. "Putting the Pedal to the Metal: Subsidies to China's Auto-parts Industry from 2001 to 2011." *Economic Policy Institute* Briefing Paper No. 316. Retrieved June 20, 2013 (www.epi.org/publication/bp316-china-auto-parts-industry/).

Han, Dongfang. 2013. "The fast emerging Labour Movement in China." Speech delivered at "Work, Employment and Society Conference," The British Sociological Association, University of Warwick, UK, September 3. Retrieved September 16, 2013 (www.clb.org.hk/en/content/han-dongfang-discusses-fast-emerging-labour-movement-china).

Harrison, Bennett. [1994] 1997. *Lean and Mean: Why Large Corporations Will Continue to Dominate the Global Economy*. (2nd ed.) New York, NY: The Guilford Press.

Harvey, David. 1989. *The Condition of Postmodernity: An Enquiry into the Origins of Cultural Change*. Cambridge, MA: Blackwell.

——— 1999. *The Limits to Capital*. Chicago, IL: University of Chicago Press.

2005. *A Brief History of Neoliberalism*. New York, NY: Oxford University Press.

Harwit, Eric. 1995. *China's Automobile Industry: Policies, Problems, and Prospects.* New York, NY: M.E. Sharpe.

2001. "The Impact of WTO Membership on the Automobile Industry in China." *The China Quarterly*, 167: 655–70.

Heilmann, Sebastian and Elizabeth J. Perry. 2011. "Embracing uncertainty: Guerrilla policy style and adaptive governance in China," pp.1–29. In *Mao's Invisible Hand: The Political Foundations of Adaptive Governance in China*, edited by S. Heilmann and E. Perry. Cambridge, MA: Harvard University Press.

Hirschman, Albert. 1970. *Exit, Voice, and Loyalty: Responses to Decline in Firms, Organizations, and States*. Cambridge, MA: Harvard University Press.

Hiraoka, L.S. 2001. "Foreign Development of China's Motor Vehicle Industry." *International Journal of Technology Management* 21 (5/6): 496–512.

Hodson, Randy. 1995a. "Cohesion or Conflict? Race, Solidarity, and Resistance in the Workplace." *Research in the Sociology of Work* 5: 135–59.

1995b. "Worker Resistance: An Underdeveloped Concept in the Sociology of Work." *Economic and Industrial Democracy* 16 (1):79–110.

2001. *Dignity at Work*. New York, NY: Cambridge University Press.

Hoffmann, Charles. 1974. *The Chinese Worker*. Albany, NY: State University of New York Press.

1977. "Worker Participation in Chinese Factories." *Modern China* 3 (3): 291–320.

Holliday, Ian and Paul Wilding. 2003. "Conclusion," pp.161–82. In *Welfare Capitalism in East Asia: Social Policy in the Tiger Economies*, edited by I. Holliday and P. Wilding. New York, NY: Palgrave Macmillan.

Howard, Pat. 1991. "Rice Bowls and Job Security: The Urban Contract Labour System." *The Australian Journal of Chinese Affairs* 25: 93–114.

Howell, Jude. 1998, "Trade unions in China: the challenge of foreign capital." Pp. 150–71 in *Adjusting to Capitalism: Chinese Workers and the State*, edited by Greg O'Leary. Armonk, NY: M.E. Sharpe.

Huang, Philip. 2009. "China's Neglected Informal Economy: Reality and Theory." *Modern China* 35 (4): 405–38.

Humphrey, John. 1982. *Capitalist Control and Workers' Struggle in the Brazilian Auto Industry*. Princeton, NJ: Princeton University Press.

Hung, Ho-fung. 2009, "America's Head Servant? The PRC's Dilemma in the Global Crisis." *New Left Review* 60 (Nov/Dec): 5–25.

Hurst, William. 2009. *The Chinese Worker after Socialism*. New York, NY: Cambridge University Press.

Hutton, Will and Meghnad Desai. 2007. "Does the future really belong to China?" *Prospect Magazine*, Issue 130, January 14. Retrieved June 13, 2011 (www.prospectmagazine.co.uk/2007/01/doesthefuturereallybelongtochina/).

IHLO. 2008, "New Labor Contract Law: Myth and Reality Six Months after Implementation." Retrieved October 2, 2008 (www.ihlo.org/LRC/WC/270608.html).

2010. "A Political Economic Analysis of the Strike in Honda and the Auto Parts Industry in China." July. Retrieved August 11, 2010 (www.ihlo.org/LRC/W/000710.pdf).

2012a. "ACFTU Pledges to Unionise Agency Workers." March. Retrieved June 28, 2012 (www.ihlo.org/LRC/ACFTU/000312.html).

2012b. "Local Governments Exploring Legal Frameworks to Regulate Agency Work." March. Retrieved June 28, 2012 (www.ihlo.org/LRC/W/000312.html).

ILO (International Labour Office). 2009. "Private Employment Agencies, Temporary Agency Workers and their Contribution to the Labour Market." Issues paper for discussion at the Workshop to promote ratification of the Private Employment Agencies Convention, 1997 (No. 181), October 20–21, Geneva.

Ishida, Mitsuo. 1997. "Japan: Beyond the Model for Lean Production," pp. 45–60. In *After Lean Production: Evolving Employment Practices in the World Auto Industry*, edited by T. Kochan, R. Lansbury, and J. P. MacDuffie. Ithaca, NY: Cornell University Press.

Jefferys, Steve. 1986. *Management and Managed: Fifty Years of Crisis at Chrysler*. New York, NY: Cambridge University Press.

1989. "'Matters of Mutual Interest': The Unionization Process at Dodge Main, 1933–1939," pp. 100–28. In *On the Line: Essays in the History of Auto Work*, edited by N. Lichtenstein and S. Meyer. Champaign, IL: University of Illinois Press.

Jones, Shannon. 2013. "General Motors in drive to cut skilled trades jobs in US plants." *World Socialist Web Site*, April 11. Retrieved May 17, 2013 (www.wsws.org/en/articles/2013/04/11/skil-a11.html).

Kalleberg, Arne. 2001. "Organizing Flexibility: The Flexible Firm in a New Century." *British Journal of Industrial Relations*, 39(4): 479–504.

2003. "Flexible Firms and Labor Market Segmentation: Effects of Workplace Restructuring on Jobs and Workers." *Work and Occupations*, 30 (2): 154–75.

Kamata, Satoshi. 1982. *Japan in the Passing Lane: An Insider's Account of Life in a Japanese Auto Factory*. Translated and edited by Tatsuru Akimoto. New York, NY: Pantheon Books.

Kaminski, Timothy. 2007. "Rank and File Resistance Haunts Auto Barons and UAW Bureaucrats." *Socialist Appeal*, December 14. Retrieved June 8, 2012 (www.socialistappeal.org/analysis/labor-movement-mainmenu-71/482-rank-and-file-resistance-haunts-auto-barons-and-uaw-bureaucrats).

Katznelson, Ira. 1986. "Working-class formation: Constructing cases and comparisons," pp. 3–41. In *Working-Class Formation: Nineteenth-Century Patterns in Western Europe and the United States*, edited by I. Katznelson and A. Zolberg. Princeton, NJ: Princeton University Press.

Kerkvliet, Benedict. 2011. "Workers' protests in contemporary Vietnam," pp. 160–210. In *Labour in Vietnam*, edited by A. Chan. Singapore: Institute of South East Asian Studies.

Kimeldorf, Howard. 1999. *Battling for American Labor: Wobblies, Craft Workers, and the Making of the Union Movement*. Berkeley, CA: University of California Press.

Kirpal, Simone. 2011. "Skills and Labour Markets in Germany and the UK," pp. 23–53. In *Labour-Market Flexibility and Individual Careers: A Comparative Study* (Technical and Vocational Education and Training: Issues, Concerns and Prospects 13), edited by S. Kirpal. Dordrecht: Springer.

Knight, John and Lina Song. 2005. *Towards a Labour Market in China*. New York, NY: Oxford University Press.

Knox, Angela. 2010. "'Lost in Translation': An Analysis of Temporary Work Agency Employment in Hotels." *Work, Employment and Society* 24 (3): 449–67.

Kochan, Thomas, Harry Katz, and Robert McKersie. [1986] 1994. *The Transformation of American Industrial Relations*. (2nd ed.) Ithaca, NY: ILR Press.

Kochan, Thomas A., Russell D. Lansbury, and John Paul MacDuffie, eds. 1997. *After Lean Production: Evolving Employment Practices in the World Auto Industry*. Ithaca, NY: Cornell University Press.

Koo, Hagen, 2001. *Korean Workers: The Culture and Politics of Class Formation.* Ithaca, NY: Cornell University Press.

Kume, Ikuo. 1998. *Disparaged Success: Labor Politics in Postwar Japan.* Ithaca, NY: Cornell University Press.

Kuruvilla, Sarosh, Ching Kwan Lee, and Mary Gallagher E., eds. 2011. *From Iron Rice Bowl to Informalization: Markets, Workers, and the State in a Changing China.* Ithaca, NY: Cornell University Press.

Landry, Pierre. 2008. *Decentralized Authoritarianism in China: The Communist Party's Control of Local Elites in the Post-Mao Era.* New York, NY: Cambridge University Press.

Lee, Byoung-hoon and Stephen J. Frenkel. 2004. "Divided Workers: Social Relations between Contract and Regular Workers in a Korean Auto Company." *Work, Employment and Society* 18 (3): 507–30.

Lee, Ching Kwan. 1998. "The Labor Politics of Market Socialism: Collective Inaction and Class Experiences among State Workers in Guangzhou". *Modern China* 24 (1): 3–33.

  1999. "From Organized Dependence to Disorganized Despotism: Changing Labour Regimes in Chinese Factories". *The China Quarterly* 157: 44–71.

  2000. "The 'Revenge of History': Collective Memories and Labor Protest in Northeastern China." *Ethnography* 1 (2): 217–37.

  2002. "From the Spector of Mao to the Spirit of the Law: Labor Insurgency in China". *Theory and Society* 31 (2): 189–228.

  2007. *Against the Law: Labor Protests in China's Rustbelt and Sunbelt.* Berkeley, CA: University of California Press.

Levi, Margaret. 2003. "Organizing power: The prospects for an American labor movement." *Perspectives on Politics* 1 (1): 45–68.

Li, Cheng. 2012. "The End of the CCP's Resilient Authoritarianism? A Tripartite Assessment of Shifting Power in China." *The China Quarterly* 211: 595–623.

Li, Tainguo, Dongliang Zheng, Manxue Yin. 2009. "Labor Dispatch Research Report." Labor Dispatch Research Group of Labor Science Research Institute. Retrieved March 2, 2012 (www.ilss.net.cn/n1196/n23277/n23391/6129416.html).

Lian, Yingting and Hongwei Chen. 2007. "laodong zhengyi anjian jingpen shier nian: shuliang zengjia 13.5 bei" (*Labor Dispute Cases Exploded over the Past Twelve Years: the Number Increased by 13.5 Times*). *Legal Daily*, August 19. Retrieved January 22, 2008 (http://news.xinhuanet.com/employment/2007-08/19/content_6563586_3.htm).

Liang, Zhiping, ed. 2002. *Fazhi zai Zhongguo: Zhidu, huayu yu shijian* (Rule of Law in China: Institutions, Discourse, and Practice). Beijing: China University of Political Science and Law Press.

Lichtenstein, Nelson. 1989. "'The Man in the Middle': A Social History of Automobile Industry Foreman," pp. 153–89. In *On the Line: Essays in the History of Auto Work*, edited by N. Lichtenstein and S. Meyer. Champaign, IL: University of Illinois Press.

  2002. *State of the Union: A Century of American Labor.* Princeton, NJ: Princeton University Press.

Lieberthal, Kenneth. [1995] 2004. *Governing China: From Revolution Through Reform.* (2nd ed.) New York, NY: W. W. Norton & Company, Inc.

Lin, Jia. 2013. "Guifan laowu paiqian, qieshi baozhang laodongzhe quanyi" (Regulating Labor Dispatch, Effectively Safeguarding Workers' Legitimate Rights and Interests).

People's Daily Online – Chinese Union News, January 14. Retrieved August 6, 2013 (http://acftu.people.com.cn/n/2013/0114/c67502-20193500-7.html).

Liu, Mingwei. 2010. "Union Organizing in China: Still a Monolithic Labor Movement?" *Industrial & Labor Relations Review* 64 (1): 30–52.

Liu, Xia. 2009. "The Chinese domestic car sales reached 9.38 million, increased by 6.7% in 2008," *The First Financial Daily*, January 13.

2010. "CBN Automobile Industry Income Survey." *First Financial Daily*, June 7, 2010. Retrieved July 10, 2011 (www.yicai.com/news/2010/06/358830.html).

Lorentzen, Peter. 2008. "Regularized Rioting: Permitting Public Protest in an Authoritarian Regime." *Quarterly Journal of Political Science* 8 (2): 127–58.

Lu, Feng. 2006. "Woguo gongzi yu laodong chengben biandong ji guoji bijiao" (China's wages and labor cost change and international comparison). Working Paper Series No C2006008, China Center for Economic Research. Beijing, China.

Lu, Xiaobo and Elizabeth J. Perry, eds. 1997. *Danwei: the Changing Chinese Workplace in Historical and Comparative Perspective*. Armonk, NY: M.E. Sharpe.

Ludlam, Janine. 1991. "Reform and the Redefinition of the Social Contract under Gorbachev." *World Politics* 43 (2): 284–312.

Martin, Andrew W. 2008. "The institutional logic of union organizing and the effectiveness of social movement repertoires." *American Journal of Sociology* 113: 1067–1103.

Marukawa, Tomoo. 1995. "Industrial Groups and Division of Labor in China's Automobile Industry." *The Developing Economies*, 33 (3): 330–54.

Meng, Xianglin. 2004. "Woguo sili xuexiao fazhan de lichen, moshi ji qianjing fenxi" (Analysis of the Development of China's Private Schools: Histories, Models and Prospects). *Journal of Jianghan University (Social Sciences)* 21(2): 97–100.

Meyer, Stephen, III. 1981. *The Five Dollar Day: Labor Management and Social Control in the Ford Motor Company, 1908–1921*. Albany, NY: State University of New York Press.

Meyerson, Harold. 2010. "China's Workers Learn to Speak Up -- But Carefully." *The Washington Post*, June 16, A17. Retrieved June 24, 2010 (www.washingtonpost.com/wp-dyn/content/article/2010/06/15/AR2010061503773.html?wpisrc=nl_cuzhead).

Michelson, Ethan. 2008. "Dear Lawyer Bao: Everyday Problems, Legal Advice, and State Power in China." *Social Problems* 55 (1): 43–71.

Milkman, Ruth. 1989. "Rosie the Riveter Revisited: Management's Postwar Purge of Women Automobile Workers," pp.129–52. In *On the Line: Essays in the History of Auto Work*, edited by N. Lichtenstein and S. Meyer. Champaign, IL: University of Illinois Press.

1997. *Farewell to the Factory: Auto Workers in the Twentieth Century*. Berkeley, CA: University of California Press.

2006. *L.A. Story: Immigrant Workers and the Future of the U.S. Labor Movement*. New York: Russell Sage Foundation.

Ministry of Education and Ministry of Finance. 2007. "Zhongdeng zhiye xuexiao xuesheng shixi guanli banfa"(Regulations on Secondary Vocational School Student Internship). Retrieved July 12, 2013 (www.moe.edu.cn/publicfiles/business/htmlfiles/moe/moe_1846/200711/28933.html).

Ministry of Human Resources and Social Security of P. R. China (MOHRSS). 2009. "Laodong zhengyi tiaojie zhongcai fa shishi yi zhounian zuotanhui zhaokai" (Annual Forum Held for Labor Dispute Mediation and Arbitration Law). May 9. Retrieved May 25, 2009 (www.gov.cn/gzdt/2009-05/09/content_1309305.htm).

Ministry of Machinery Industry. 1994. *Dangdai zhongguo guoji jiaoche gongye fazhan yu zhongguo jiaoche gongye fazhan zhanlue* (The development of the contemporary Chinese international auto sedan industry and the Chinese auto sedan development strategy). Beijing: Ministry of Machinery Industry.

MOHRSS of Jilin Province. 2011. "Jilin Sheng Laowu Paiqian Guanli Banfa" (Provisions on Administration of Labor Dispatch of Jilin Province). Printed and distributed on November 22.

Mitlacher, Lars. 2007. "The Role of Temporary Agency Work in Different Industrial Relations Systems — A Comparison between Germany and the USA." *British Journal of Industrial Relations* 45 (3): 581–606.

Montgomery, David. 1979. *Workers' Control in America: Studies in the History of Work, Technology, and Labor Struggles*. New York, NY: Cambridge University Press.

Moody, Kim. 1997. *Workers in a Lean World: Unions in the International Economy*. London: Verso.

Nag, Biswajit, Saikat Banerjee, and Rittwik Chatterjee. 2007. "Changing Features of the Automobile Industry in Asia: Comparison of Production, Trade and Market Structure in Selected Countries." Working Paper No. 3707 (www.unescap.org/tid/artnet/pub/wp3707.pdf).

Nair, Vipin and Jeff Green. 2009. "Indian Strike that Shut Ford Plant Said to Affect GM." *Bloomberg*, October 29. Retrieved December 5, 2009 (www.bloomberg.com/apps/news?pid=20601103&sid=av7vTfLPfc68).

National Business Daily. 2010. "Zhong zhengche qing bujian, zhongguo qiche chanye daijie zhikun." ("Emphasizing automobile assemblers and ignoring auto-parts manufacturing: The unresolved problem in the Chinese automobile industry.") May 28. Retrieved July 12, 2011 (http://business.sohu.com/20100528/n272400610.shtml).

Naughton, Barry. 2007. *The Chinese Economy: Transitions and Growth*. Cambridge, MA: The MIT Press.

National Bureau of Statistics (NBS). 2010. "2009 Monitoring Survey Report of migrant workers." March 19. Retrieved June 11, 2011 (www.stats.gov.cn/tjfx/fxbg/t20100319_402628281.htm).

National Bureau of Statistics (NBS) and Ministry of Human Resources and Social Security (MOHRSS). 1995–2010. *China Labour Statistical Yearbook*. Beijing: China Statistics Press.

Ngok, Kinglun. 2008. "The Changes of Chinese Labor Policy and Labor Legislation in the Context of Market Transition." *International Labor and Working Class History* 73 (1): 45–64.

Ni, Hui. 2010. "Bentian bagong shendu pouxi: zhongguo jingji taiguo yilai jiagong maoyi" (Deep analysis of Honda strike: the Chinese economy is too dependent on processing trade). *The NetEase Daily Economic News*, May 28. Retrieved June 5, 2010 (www.nbd.com.cn/newshtml/20100528/20100528173557940.html).

Nichols, Theo (et al). 2004. "Factory Regimes and the Dismantling of Established Labor in Asia: A Review of Cases from Large Manufacturing Plants in China, South Korea and Taiwan." *Work, Employment and Society* 18 (4): 663–85.

O'Brien, Kevin. 1996. "Rightful Resistance." *World Politics* 49 (1): 31–55.

O'Brien, Kevin, and Lianjiang Li. 2006. *Rightful Resistance in Rural China*. New York, NY: Cambridge University Press.

O'Conner, James. 1973. *The Fiscal Crisis of the State*. New York, NY: St. Martin's Press.

Oestreicher, Richard. 1986. *Solidarity and Fragmentation: Working People and Class Consciousness in Detroit, 1875–1900*. Champaign, IL: University of Illinois Press.

O'Leary, Greg (ed.). 1998. *Adjusting to Capitalism: Chinese Workers and the State*. Armonk, NY: M.E. Sharpe.

Palier, Bruno and Kathleen Thelen. 2010. "Institutionalizing Dualism: Complementarities and Change in France and Germany." *Politics & Society* 38 (1): 119–148.

Pan, Yi and Yunxue Deng. 2011. "Labor Dispatch System in Reform." ("laowu paiqian zhidu gaige jinxingshi") *South Wind (Nan Feng Chuang)*. March 17. Retrieved June 28, 2012 (http://news.sina.com.cn/c/sd/2011-03-17/173522133927.shtml).

Park, Albert and Fang Cai. 2011. "The Informalization of the Chinese Labor Market," pp.17–35. In *From Iron Rice Bowl to Informalization: Markets, Workers, and the State in a Changing China*, edited by S. Kuruvilla, C. K. Lee, and M. Gallagher, Ithaca, NY: Cornell University Press.

Parker, Mike and Jane Slaughter. 1995. "Unions and Management by Stress," pp. 41–53. In *Lean Work, Empowerment and Exploitation in the Global Auto Industry*, edited by S. Babson. Detroit, MI: Wayne State University Press.

Pearson, Margaret. 2003. "Mapping the Rise of China's Regulatory State: Economic Regulation and Network and Insurance Industries." Paper presented at the Annual Meeting of The Association of Asian Studies, New York, NY, March 27, 2003.

Peck, Jamie, 1996. *Work-Place: the Social Regulation of Labor Markets*. New York, NY: The Guilford Press.

Peck, Jamie and Nikolas Theodore. 1998. "The Business of Contingent Work: Growth and Restructuring in Chicago's Temporary Employment Industry." *Work, Employment and Society* 12 (4): 655–74.

2002. "Temped Out? Industry Rhetoric, Labor Regulation and Economic Restructuring in the Temporary Staffing Business." *Economic and Industrial Democracy* 23 (2): 143–75.

Peck, Jamie, Nikolas Theodore, and Kevin Ward. 2005. "Constructing Markets for Temporary Labour: Employment Liberalization and the Internationalization of the Staffing Industry." *Global Networks* 5 (1): 3–26.

People's Daily. 2005. "Building harmonious society crucial for China's progress: Hu." June 27. Retrieved September 18, 2009 (http://english.peopledaily.com.cn/200506/27/eng20050627_192495.html).

2010. "Hu Jintao: Speech at the 2010 National Model Workers and Advanced Workers Award Ceremony," April 28, A1.

Perry, Elizabeth. 1993. *Shanghai on Strike: The Politics of Chinese Labor*. Stanford, CA: Stanford University Press.

1994a. "Shanghai's Strike Wave of 1957." *The China Quarterly* 137: 1–27.

1994b. "Labor Divided: Sources of State Formation in Modern China," pp.143–73. In *State Power and Social Forces: Domination and Transformation in the Third World*, edited by J. Migdal, A. Kohli, and V. Shue. New York, NY: Cambridge University Press.

1994c. "Trends in the Study of Chinese Politics: State-Society Relations." *China Quarterly* 139: 704–13.

1997. "From Native-Place to Workplace: Labor Origins and Outcomes of China's Danwei System," pp.42–59. In *Danwei: The Changing Chinese Workplace in Historical and Comparative Perspective*, edited by X. Lu and E. Perry. Armonk, NY: M.E. Sharpe.

2002. *Challenging the Mandate of Heaven: Social Protest and State Power in China.* Armonk, NY: M.E. Sharpe.

2006. *Patrolling the Revolution: Worker Militias, Citizenship, and the Modern Chinese State.* Lanham, MD: Rowman & Littlefield Publishers.

2007. "Studying Chinese politics: Farewell to revolution?" *The China Journal* 57: 1–22.

2010. "Popular protest: Playing by the rules," pp.11–28. In *China Today, China Tomorrow: Domestic Politics, Economy, and Society*, edited by J. Fewsmith. Lanham, MD: Rowman & Littlefield Publishers.

Perry, Elizabeth J. and Li, Xun. 1997. *Proletarian Power: Shanghai in the Cultural Revolution.* Boulder, CO: Westview Press.

Pierson, David. 2010. "China's Factory Workers Finding, and Flexing, Their Muscle." *Los Angeles Times*, June 2. Retrieved June 4, 2010 (www.latimes.com/business/la-fi-china-labor-20100602,0,2573020.story).

Piore, Michael. 1979. *Birds of Passage: Migrant Labor and Industrial Societies.* New York, NY: Cambridge University Press.

Piven, Frances. 2008. "Can Power from Below Change the World?" *American Sociological Review* 73 (1): 1–14.

Piven, Frances and Richard Cloward. 1977. *Poor People's Movements: Why They Succeed, How They Fail.* New York, NY: Vintage Books.

2000. "Power Repertoires and Globalization." *Politics & Society* 28(3): 413–30.

Poulantzas, Nicos. [1968] 1975. *Political Power and Social Classes.* (2nd ed.) London: Verso.

Pravda, Alex and Blair Ruble. 1986. "Communist Trade Unions: Varieties of Dualism," pp. 1–22. In *Trade Unions in Communist States*, edited by A. Pravda and B. Ruble. Boston, MA: Allen & Unwin.

Price, John. 1995. "Lean Production at Suzuki and Toyota: A Historical Perspective," pp. 81–107. In *Lean Work: Empowerment and Exploitation in the Global Auto Industry*, edited by S. Babson. Detroit, MI: Wayne State University Press.

1997. *Japan Works: Power and Paradox in Postwar Industrial Relations.* Ithaca, NY: ILR Press.

Pun, Ngai. 2005. *Made in China: Women Factory Workers in a Global Workplace.* Durham, NC: Duke University Press.

Pun, Ngai and Jenny Chan. 2012. "Global Capital, the State, and Chinese Workers: The Foxconn Experience." *Modern China* 38 (4): 383–410.

Pun, Ngai and Chris Smith. 2007. "Putting Transnational Labour Process in its Place: The Dormitory Labour Regime in Post-Socialist China." *Work, Employment, and Society* 21 (1): 27–45.

Purcell, John, Kate Purcell, and Stephanie Tailby. 2004. "Temporary Work Agencies: Here Today, Gone Tomorrow?" *British Journal of Industrial Relations* 42 (4): 705–25.

Puxin Management Consulting Co., Ltd. 2012. "2011nian qiche zhizao hangye xinchou diaoyan baogao." ("2011 Automobile Manufacturing Industry Remuneration Survey Report.") August 18. Retrieved July 10, 2013 (www.puxinhr.com/content/1_20120401110606.shtml).

Qiancheng Wuyou (51job.com). 2011. "2011 Renli ziyuan dianfan qiye hangye baogao – qiche/lingpeijian hangye" (2011 Human Resources Management Model Enterprises Report – Automotive/Parts Industry). Retrieved July 24, 2013 (http://my.51job.com/careerpost/2010/mkt_awards10/FileDownload/2011hrmAUTO%20SurveyReport.pdf)

Ray, Carol. 1986. "Corporate Culture: The Last Frontier of Control?" *Journal of Management Studies* 23 (3): 287–97.

Rinehart, James, Chris Huxley, and David Robertson. 1995. "Team Concept at CAMI," pp.220–34. In *Lean Work: Empowerment and Exploitation in the Global Auto Industry*, edited by S. Babson. Detroit, MI: Wayne State University Press.

Roberts, Dexter, Moon Ihlwan, Ian Rowley, and Gail Edmondson. 2005. "GM And VW: How Not to Succeed in China" *Business Week*, May 8.

Rodgers, Ronald. 1996. "Industrial Relations in the Korean Auto Industry: The Implications of Industrial Sector Requirements and Societal Effects for International Competitiveness," pp. 87–135. In *Social Reconstructions of the World Automobile Industry: Competition, Power, and Industrial Flexibility*, edited by F. Deyo. New York, NY: St. Martin's Press.

Rogozhin, Alex, Michael Gallaher, and Walter McManus. 2009. "Automobile Industry Retail Price Equivalent and Indirect Cost Multipliers." Prepared for the U.S. Environmental Protection Agency by RTI International and Transportation Research Institute, University of Michigan. Washington, D.C.: Assessment and Standards Division, Office of Transportation and Air Quality, U.S. Environmental Protection Agency. Retrieved April 11, 2014 (http://www.epa.gov/otaq/ld-hwy/420r09003.pdf).

Rubin, Beth. 1995. "Flexible Accumulation: The Decline of Contract and Social Transformation." *Research in Social Stratification and Mobility* 14: 297–323.

Russo, Bill.2009. "China's Next Revolution: Transforming the Global Auto Industry." *China Talk*, July. (www.globalautoindustry.com/article.php?id=4193&jaar=2009&maand=7&target=China)

Sabel, Charles. 1982. *Work and Politics: The Division of Labor in Industry*. New York, NY: Cambridge University Press.

Sayer, R. Andrew and Richard Walker. 1992. *The New Social Economy: Reworking the Division of Labor*. Cambridge, MA: Blackwell.

Schumpeter, Joseph. 1954. *Capitalism, Socialism, and Democracy*. London: Allen and Unwin.

Scott, James. 1985. *Weapons of the Weak: Everyday Forms of Peasant Resistance*. New Haven, CT: Yale University Press.

Seidman, Gay. 1994. *Manufacturing Militance: Workers' Movements in Brazil and South Africa, 1970–1985*. Berkeley, CA: University of California Press.

Shanghai Information Center. 2002. "Special Report: Chinese SOEs Being Reborn after Reform." *Economic View*, 1092, September 16.

Shanghai Municipal Statistics Bureau. 1996–2010. *Shanghai Tongji Nianjian (Shanghai Statistical Yearbook)*. Beijing: China Statistics Press.

Shanghai SASAC. 2011. "Guanyu Jinyibu Guifan Shi Guoziwei Xitong Guoyou Qiye Laowu Paiqian Yonggong de Zhidao Yijian" (Directive on Further Regulating Labor Dispatch in State-Owned Enterprises that belong to the Municipal SASAC system). Issued on May 30.

Shapiro, Lila. 2011. "UAW Divided As Workers Seek Payback In Contract Negotiations." *The Huffington Post*, August 25. Retrieved December 28, 2011 (www.huffingtonpost.com/2011/08/25/uaw-contract-negotiations_n_936873.html?view=screen).

Sheehan, Jackie. 1998. *Chinese Workers: A New History*. London: Routledge.

Shenkar, Oded. 2006. *The Chinese Century: The Rising Chinese Economy and its Impact on the Global Economy, the Balance of Power, and Your Job*. Upper Saddle River, NJ: Wharton School Publishing.

Shirouzu, Norihiko. 2010. "*Chinese Workers Challenge Beijing's Authority.*" *The Wall Street Journal*, June 13. Retrieved June 13, 2010 (http://online.wsj.com/article/SB10001424052748704067504575304690307516072.html).

Shue, Vivienne. 2010. "Legitimacy crisis in China?" Pp. 41–68 in *Chinese Politics: State, Society and the Markets*, edited by Peter Gries and Stanley Rosen. London and New York: Routledge.

Silver, Beverly. 2003. *Forces of Labor: Workers' Movements and Globalization since 1870*. New York, NY: Cambridge University Press.

  2005. "Labor upsurges: From Detroit to Ulsan and beyond." *Critical Sociology* 31(3): 439–51.

Silver, Beverly and Lu Zhang. 2009. "China as an emerging epicenter of world labor unrest," pp. 174–87. In *China and the Transformation of Global Capitalism*, edited by H.-F. Hung. Baltimore, MD: Johns Hopkins University Press.

Sitrin, Marina. (Ed.) 2006. *Horizontalism: Voices of Popular Power in Argentina*. Oakland, CA: AK Press.

Skocpol, Theda. 1979. *States and Social Revolutions: A Comparative Analysis of France, Russia, and China*. New York, NY: Cambridge University Press.

Smith, Vicki. 1998. "The Fractured World of the Temporary Worker: Power, Participation, and Fragmentation in the Contemporary Workplace." *Social Problems* 45: 411–30.

Solinger, Dorothy. 1995. "The Chinese Work Unit and Transient Labor in the Transition from Socialism." *Modern China* 21(2): 155–83.

  1999. *Contesting Citizenship in Urban China: Peasant Migrants, the State, and the Logic of the Market*. Berkeley: University of California Press.

  2002. "Labour Market Reform and the Plight of the Laid-Off Proletariat." *The China Quarterly* 170: 304–26.

  2005. "Path Dependency Reexamined: Chinese Welfare Policy in the Transition to Unemployment." *Comparative Politics* 38 (1): 83–101.

Song, Jiyeoun. 2012. "Economic Distress, Labor Market Reforms, and Dualism in Japan and Korea." *Governance* 25 (3): 415–38.

Southern Metropolis Daily. 2010. "Zhongguo cheye lanling gongren xinchou diaocha: jiaban xiongmeng suode jihe?" ("Income survey among Chinese blue-collar auto workers: How much can they earn with so much overtime?") April 19. Retrieved June 24, 2012 (http://auto.sina.com.cn/news/2010-04-19/0814591318.shtml).

Standing Committee of the 8th National People's Congress of P. R. China. 1994. *Zhonghua Renmin Gongheguo Laodong Fa (The Labor Law of the People's Republic of China)*. Beijing: China Procuratorial Press.

Standing Committee of the 10th National People's Congress of P. R. China. 2007. *Zhonghua Renmin Gongheguo Laodong Hetong Fa (The Labor Contract Law of the People's Republic of China)*. Beijing: China Procuratorial Press.

Stark, David. 1986. "Rethinking Internal Labor Markets – New Insights from A Comparative Perspective." *American Sociological Review* 51 (4): 492–504.

Stone, Katherine. V. 2006. "Flexibilization, Globalization, and Privatization: Three Challenges to Labor Rights in Our Time." *Osgoode Hall Law Journal* 44 (1): 77–104.

Straughn, Jeremy. 2005. "'Taking the State at Its Word': The arts of consentful contention in the German Democratic Republic." *American Journal of Sociology* 110 (6): 1598–1650.

Su, Yang and Xin He. 2010. "Street as Courtroom: State Accommodation of Labor Protest in South China." *Law & Society Review* 44: 157–84.

Tang, Wenfang and William Parish. 2000. *Chinese Urban Life under Reform: The Changing Social Contract*. New York, NY: Cambridge University Press.

Taylor, Bill, Kai Chang, and Qi Li. 2003. *Industrial Relations in China*. Cheltenham, UK: Edward Elgar.

Taylor, M. 1986. "The product-cycle model: A critique." *Environment and Planning A* 18: 751–61.

Teets, Jessica, Stanley Rosen, and Peter Hays Gries. 2010. "Introduction: Political change, contestation, and pluralization in China Today," pp.1–21. In *Chinese Politics: State, Society and the Markets*, edited by P. Hays Gries and S. Rosen. London: Routledge.

The Foxconn Research Group. 2010. "Liang'an Sandi" Gaoxiao Fushikang Diaoyan Zong Baogao" (The Foxconn Research Report by the Mainland, Taiwan, and Hong Kong Universities). October.

   2011. "Xijin: Fushikang Nei Qian Diaoyan Baogao" (Go West: Research Report on Foxconn Relocation to Inland China). May.

The New York Times. 2010. "China's Labor Tests Its Muscle." June 17. Retrieved June 19, 2010 (http://topics.nytimes.com/top/news/international/countriesandterritories/china/labor-issues/index.html).

The State Council. 2005. "The Decision of the State Council on Vigorously Developing Vocational Education." October 28. Retrieved June 29, 2012 (www.gov.cn/zwgk/2005-11/09/content_94296.htm).

   2009. "Qiche chanye tiaozheng he zhenxing guihua" (Plan on Adjusting and Revitalizing the Automotive Industry). March 20. Retrieved October 12, 2009 (www.gov.cn/zwgk/2009-03/20/content_1264324.htm).

The State Development and Reform Commission (SDRC). 2004. "Qiche gongye fazhan zhengce." ("Automotive Industry Development Policy"). May 21, 2004. Beijing: SDRC.

The State Planning Commission (SPC). 1994. "Qiche gongye chanye zhengce" ("Industrial Policy of Automotive Industry"). February 19, 1994.

Thelen, Kathleen and Ikuo Kume. 1999. "The Effects of Globalization on Labor Revisited: Lessons from Germany and Japan." *Politics & Society* 27(4): 477–505.

Therborn, Goran. 1978. *What Does the Ruling Class Do When it Rules? State Apparatuses and State Power under Feudalism, Capitalism, and Socialism*. London: Verso.

Thun, Eric. 2004. "Industrial Policy, Chinese-Style: FDI, Regulation, and Dreams of National Champions in the Auto Sector." *Journal of East Asian Studies* 4 (3): 453–89.

   2006. *Changing Lanes in China: Foreign Direct Investment, Local Government, and Auto Sector Development*. New York, NY: Cambridge University Press.

Townsend, R. James. 1967. *Political Participation in Communist China*. Berkeley and Los Angeles, CA: University of California Press.

Treece, James. 1997. "China Takes Hard Road to a Market Economy." *Automotive News*. July 14, p. 1+.

Tsang, Eric. 1994. "Human Resource Management Problems in Sino-foreign Joint Ventures." *International Journal of Manpower*, 15 (9): 4–21.

Tu, Guoming. 2007. "Shanghai Shi Qiye Laowu Yonggong de Xianzhuang, Wenti yu Duice," (Agency Employment at Enterprises in Shanghai: Current Situations, Problems, and Countermeasures), pp.14–22. In *Laodong Paiqian de Fazhan yu Falv Guizhi (The Development and Legal Regulation of Labor Dispatch)*, edited by Zhou Changzheng. Beijing, China Labor and Social Security Press.

U.S. Bureau of Labor Statistics (BLS). 2013a. *International Labor Comparisons*. April. Retrieved April 15, 2014 (www.bls.gov/fls/ichccindustry.htm#29–30).

2013b. *Manufacturing in China.* June 7. Retrieved April 15, 2014 (www.bls.gov/fls/china.htm).

U.S. Department of Education, National Center for Education Statistics. 2012. *Digest of Education Statistics, 2011* (NCES 2012–001). Retrieved September 16, 2013 (http://nces.ed.gov/fastfacts/display.asp?id=98).

Vallas, Steven. 1999. "Rethinking Post Fordism: The Meaning of Workplace Flexibility." *Sociological Theory* 17 (1): 68–101.

2003. "Why Teamwork Fails: Obstacles to Workplace Change in Four Manufacturing Plants." *American Sociological Review* 68 (2): 223–50.

2006. "Empowerment Redux: Structure, Agency, and the Remaking of Managerial Authority." *American Journal of Sociology* 111 (6): 1677–1717.

Vernon, Raymond. 1966. "International investment and international trade in the product cycle." *Quarterly Journal of Economics* 80 (2): 190–207.

Walder, Andrew. 1986. *Communist Neo-Traditionalism: Work and Authority in Chinese Industry.* Berkeley, CA: University of California Press.

Wallerstein, Immanuel. 1995. "Response: Declining States, Declining rights?" *International Labor and Working Class History* 47: 24–7.

2004. *World-Systems Analysis: An Introduction.* Durham, NC: Duke University Press.

Wang, Aileen, and Simon Rabinovitch. 2010. "Why Labor Unrest is good for China and the World." June 2. Retrieved June 4, 2010 (www.reuters.com/article/idUSTRE6511TT20100602).

Wang, Bixue. 2006. "Labor Dispatching Encounters Legal Difficulty" (*laowu paiqian zaoyu falv nanti*). *People's Daily,* January 4, p14.

Wang, Canshan. 2010. "Zhongguo Qiche Jituan Lirunlv Paihang Bang, Biyadi Ba Touchu" (BYD Claimed the Top Spot on the China Auto Groups Profitability Ranking List). *Guangzhou Daily.* April 19.

Wang, Hua. 2003. "Policy Reforms and Foreign Direct Investment: the Case of the Chinese Automobile Industry." *Journal of Economics and Business* 6 (1): 287–314.

Warner, Malcolm. 1995. "Human Resources in the People's Republic of China: The 'Three Systems' Reforms." *Human Resource Management Journal* 6 (2): 32–43.

2000. *Changing Workplace Relations in the Chinese Economy.* New York, NY: St. Martin's Press.

Wasserstrom, Jeffrey. 2010. "Strike Out: What the Foreign Media Misses in Covering China's Labor Unrest." *Foreign Policy,* June 18. Retrieved June 19, 2010 (www.foreignpolicy.com/articles/2010/06/18/strike_out).

Weber, Max. 1968. *Economy and Society: An Outline of Interpretive Sociology,* edited by G. Roth and C. Wittich, 3 vols. New York, NY: Bedminister Press.

1978. "The Nature of Social Action," pp.7–32. In *Max Weber: Selections in translation,* edited by W. Runciman. Translated by E. Mathews. New York, NY: Cambridge University Press.

Welch, David. 2011. "The UAW's Bargaining Dilemma: Wages or Jobs?" *Bloomberg Businessweek,* Companies & Industries. September 15. Retrieved April 26, 2012 (www.businessweek.com/magazine/the-uaws-bargaining-dilemma-wages-or-jobs-09152011.html).

Weng, Shiyou. 2009. "Labor Dispatching Regulations are to Get Tighter, Labor Cost is Expected to Rise at Large Enterprises" (Laowu paiqian guiding congjin zhiding, da qiye yonggong chengben keneng shangsheng). *Economic Observations,* October 24.

White, Gordon. 1987. "The Politics of Economic Reform in Chinese Industry: The Introduction of the Labour Contract System." *The China Quarterly* 111: 365–89.

White, Lynn. 1976. "Workers' Politics in Shanghai." *The Journal of Asian Studies* 36 (1): 99–116.

White, Stephen. 1986. "Economic Performance and Communist Legitimacy." *World Politics* 38(3): 462–82.

Whyte, Martin King and William L. Parish. 1984. *Urban Life in Contemporary China*. Chicago, IL: University of Chicago Press.

Widick, B. J. Eli (Ed.). 1976. *Auto Work and Its Discontents*. Baltimore, MD: Johns Hopkins University Press.

Williams, Karel, Colin Haslam, Sukhdev Johal, John Williams, Andy Adoroff, and Robert Willis. 1995. "Management Practice or Structural Factors: The Case of America Versus Japan in the Car Industry." *Economic and Industrial Democracy* 16 (1): 9–37.

Willis, Paul. 1977. *Learning to Labour: How Working Class Kids get Working Class Jobs*. Farmborough: Saxon House.

Wilson, Jeanne. 1990. "The Polish lesson: China and Poland 1980–1990," *Studies in Comparative Communism* 23 (3–4): pp. 259–280.

Womack, James, Johns, Daniel, and Roos, Daniel. 1990. *The Machine that Changed the World*. New York, NY: Rawson Associates.

Wonacott, Peter and Krishna Pokharel. 2009. "Strikes Roil India Auto Sector: Protests Threaten Industry that Helps Drive Nation's Economy." *Wall Street Journal*, October 21. Retrieved October 28, 2009 (http://online.wsj.com/article/SB125604570010196419.html).

Wong, Edward. 2010. "As China Aids Labor, Unrest is still Rising." *The New York Times*, June 20. Retrieved June 30, 2010 (www.nytimes.com/2010/06/21/world/asia/21chinalabor.html?pagewanted=1&ei=5099&partner=TOPIXNEWS).

Wright, Erik Olin. 1997. *Class Counts: Comparative Studies in Class Analysis*. New York, NY: Cambridge University Press.

 2000. "Working-Class Power, Capitalist-Class Interests, and Class Compromise." *American Journal of Sociology* 105 (4): 957–1002.

Wright, Teresa. 2010. *Accepting Authoritarianism: State-Society Relations in China's Reform Era*. Stanford, CA: Stanford University Press.

Xia, Dawei, Shi Donghui, and Zhang Lei. 2002. *Qiche Gongye: Jishu Jinbu yu Chanye Zuzhi (Automobile Industry: Technology Advancement and Industry Organization). Shanghai*, China: Shanghai Finance and Economic University Press.

Xiang, Yunzhang. 2011a. "Quanwei Baogao Cheng Laowu Paiqian Da Liu Qian Wan Ren, Quanzong Jianyi Xiugai Laodong Hetong Fa" (Authoritative Report Says Agency Workers have Reached 60 million, ACFTU Urges to Revise Labor Contract Law). *The Economic Observer*. March 3. Retrieved November 2, 2011 (http://finance.ifeng.com/news/20110225/3503356.shtml).

 2011b. "Laowu Paiqian Liuyue Zhengdun, Weigui Yangqi Shou Dang Qi Chong" (Non-Compliant Central SOEs Bear the Brunt of Rectification of Labor Dispatch Starting in June). *The Economic Observer*. April 23. Retrieved November 2, 2011 (www.eeo.com.cn/Politics/beijing_news/2011/04/23/199740.shtml).

Xiao, Hua and Jiang Qiang. 2007. "New Policy of Labor relationship: Hua Wei's Scandal," *China's Corner*, November 22 (www.rednet.cn).

Xiao, Qiang. 2008. Speech at Congressional Executive Commission on China (CECC) Hearing on "What Will Drive China's Future Legal Development? Reports from the Field." Washington, D.C., June 18.

Xinhua. 2003. "Developing Corporate Culture is Key to Global Strategy." November 30. Retrieved June 7, 2013 (www.chinadaily.com.cn/en/doc/2003-11/30/content_285962.htm).

2005a. "Hu: Speech at the Conference of Honoring National Laborer Models and Advanced Workers." May 2.

2005b. "Laowu paiqiangong weiquan zaoyu falv nanti" (*Protections for Agency Workers' Rights Meet Legal Difficulties*) June 20. Retrieved April 10, 2009 (http://news.xinhuanet.com/legal/2005-06/20/content_3108717.htm).

2007. "Hu: Address to representatives of the ACFTU, the Communist Youth League, the Youth Union, and the Women's Federation at the Annual Sessions of the National Committee of the Chinese People's Political Consultative Conference." March 7.

2008a. "Hu Jintao: Attended and Addressed the 2008 Economic Globalization and Trade Unions International Forum Opening Ceremony," January 7. Retrieved June 30, 2013 (http://news.xinhuanet.com/newscenter/2008-01/07/content_7378124.htm).

2008b. "China Expands Its Social Security System." July 31.

2008c. "Ministry of Human Resources and Social Security will develop specific measures to regulate the labor dispatch." September 27 (http://news.xinhuanet.com/legal/2008-09/27/content_10121294.htm).

2008d. "China seeks smooth communication with citizens." October 14 (http://news.xinhuanet.com/english/2008-10/14/content_10195062.html).

2010a. "China's GDP expands 8.7% in 2009." January 21 (http://news.xinhuanet.com/english2010/business/2010-01/21/c_13145167.htm).

2010b. "Hu Jintao: zai 2010 nian quanguo laodong mofan he xianjin gongzuozhe biaozhang dahui shang de jianghua" (Hu Jintao: Speech at the Awards Ceremony of the 2010 National Model Workers and Advanced Workers). April 27. Retrieved May 1, 2010 (http://news.xinhuanet.com/politics/2010-04/27/c_1259809.htm).

2010c. "Qiushi zazhi fabiao Li Keqiang tongzhi wenzhang qiangdiao tiaozheng jingji jiegou dui cujin chixu fazhan juyou guanjianxing zuoyong" (*Qiushi* Magazine Published Li Keqiang's Article Emphasizing Adjustment of Economic Structure is Critical to Promote Sustainable Development). May 31. Retrieved June 4, 2010 (http://news.xinhuanet.com/politics/2010-05/31/c_12163253.htm).

2012. "China's motor vehicles top 233 mln." July 17. Retrieved August 31, 2013 (http://news.xinhuanet.com/english/china/2012-07/17/c_131721176.htm).

2013. "Xi Jinping xinnian zai shi shenhua gaige xinhao" (Xi Jinping Released the Deepening Reform Signals in the New Year). January 3. Retrieved January 6, 2013 (http://news.xinhuanet.com/world/2013-01/03/c_124177028.htm).

Xu, Yi, Qi He, Wang Weilie, and Wang Yu'nan. 2011. "Dui laowu paiqian yonggong wenti de sikao" (Reflection on the Problems of Labor Dispatch). *Chinese Workers.* March 15. Retrieved September 5, 2011 (www.chineseworkers.com.cn/_d271368532.htm).

Yardley, J. 2006. "China Unveils Plan to Aid Farmers, but Avoids Land Issue." *The New York Times*, February 23.

Ye, Hua and Jing Meng. 2008. "Gongxue jiehe zhiye jiaoyu moshi de tantao" (Discussions on the work-study model). *China Electric Power Education* 104: 48–49.

Young, Edward. 2001. "Foreign makers untroubled by China industry shakeup." *Automotive News* 75, July 9.

Yu, Min 2007. "lun paiqian laodongzhe yu zhengshigong de daiyu chabie" (*On Treatment Differences of Dispatched Workers and Formal Workers*). *Journal of China Institute of Industrial Relations* 121 (14): 28–31.

Zetka, James. 1995. *Militancy, Market Dynamics, and Workplace Authority: The Struggle over Labor Process Outcomes in the U.S. Automobile Industry, 1946 to 1973.* Albany, NY: State University of New York Press.

Zeng, Jinsheng. 2007. "Tizhiwai yuangong shi erdeng gongmin ma?" ("Are Employees Outside the System Second-Class Citizens?") *People's Forum*, May 15. Retrieved July 17 2013 (http://cpc.people.com.cn/GB/68742/68758/68847/5759132.html).

Zhang, Da, 2010. "China's automobile production output is expected to reach 15 million in 2010," *Xinhua News*, January 12. (http://news.xinhuanet.com/fortune/2010-01/12/content_12794755.htm)

Zhang, Guifeng. 2010. "Bentian Bagong de laodong quanli qishi" (The Revelation of the Honda Strike for Labor Rights). *Youth Times*, May 28, A02. Retrieved June 5, 2010 (www.qnsb.com/fzepaper/site1/qnsb/html/2010-05/28/content_259479.htm).

Zhang, Lu. 2008. "Lean Production and Labor Controls in the Chinese Automobile Industry in an Age of Globalization." *International Labor and Working Class History* 73 (1):24–44.

2010. "Do Spreading Auto Strikes Mean Hope for a Workers" Movement in China?" *Labor Notes Magazine*, July 13, No. 376.

2011. "The Paradox of Labor Force Dualism and State-Labor-Capital Relations in the Chinese Automobile Industry," pp.107–137. In *From Iron Rice Bowl to Informalization: Markets, Workers, and the State in a Changing China*, edited by S. Kuruvilla, C. K. Lee, and M. Gallagher. Ithaca, NY: Cornell University Press.

Zhang, Wei and Robert Taylor, 2001. "EU Technology Transfer to China: The automotive Industry as a case study," *Journal of the Asia-pacific Economy* 6 (2): 261–74.

Zhang, Weijie. 2006. "laowu paiqian, ruhe burang laodongzhe chikui" (How not to Disadvantage Workers in Labor Dispatch). *Worker's Daily*, March 15: 7.

Zhang, Xiaodan. 2005. *"Bargaining without Union: Paternalist Labor Relations in China's Reform Era."* PhD Dissertation, Department of Sociology, Columbia University, New York, NY.

Zhang, Zhijin. 2005. "laodong paiqian jigou yingdang quid" (*Labor Dispatch Organizations Should be Banned*). *Economic Information Daily*, August 20.

Zheng, Meng. 2010. "Nanhai tinggong yangben" (Nanhai Strike Exampler). *Caijing Magazine*, 2010 (7), June 7. Retrieved June 10, 2010 (http://magazine.caijing.com.cn/2010-06-06/110453979.html).

Zheng, Shangyuan. 2008. "budang laowu paiqian jiqi guanzhi" (Wrongful Labor Dispatch and Regulation on It). *Jurists Review* 2: 8–13.

Zhongguo tongji nianjian (China Statistical Yearbook). 2007. Beijing: Zhongguo tongji chubanshe.

Zhou, Changzheng, ed. 2007. *Laodong Paiqian de Fazhan yu Falv Guizhi (The Development and Legal Regulation of Labor Dispatch)*. Beijing, China Labor and Social Security Press.

Zhou, Qiong. 2010. "Guangdong sheng laodong baozhang bumen guanyuan: xiwang bentian bagong shijian tuidong shouru fengpei gaige" (Guangdong Provincial Labor and Social Security Department Official: Hope Honda Strike Promote Income Distribution Reform). *Caixin Online*, June 2. Retrieved June 5, 2010 (http://business.sohu.com/20100602/n272524217.shtml).

Zhou, Zhenghua and Ziqian Liu. 2010. "Zhiji Nanhai Bentian 'Tinggongmeng' Shijian" (Direct Investigation of Nanhai Honda "Strike" Incident).*China Newsweek*, June 2. Retrieved June 12, 2010 (www.inewsweek.cn/cnw/news/info/society/2010-06-02/6279.shtml).

Zhuang, Qinghong. 2012. "Xu jingti 'shitou mo shang le yin, lian he ye bu xiang guo le'" ("We must be alert to 'becoming addicted to touching the stones, to the point where we don't want to cross the river anymore'"). *China Youth Daily*, January 9, A03.

Zolberg, Aristide. 1972. "Moments of Madness." *Politics & Society* 2 (2): 183–207.

Index

ACFTU. *See* All-China Federation of Trade Unions

activism. *See* cellular activism

All-China Federation of Trade Unions (ACFTU), 2, 56, 98–9, 194
  Labor Contract Law (LCL) and, 175, 180

American Motor Corporation (AMC), 27, 29–30

An Gang Constitution, 24–5
  departure from the "one-man rule" management, 25
  as socialist experiment of democratic management, 25

Andreas, Joel, 25

aspirations of younger formal workers, 116

assembly line production. *See also* shop floor, production organization on
  body shop, 83–4
  composition of workforce in, 60–2
  factory autoworkers and, 7, 10
  formal workers and, 63–4
  labor force dualism and, 45
  minimum efficient scale standards, 27
  modular, 84
  optimum efficient scale standards, 27
  paint shop, 84
  in press shop, 83
  restrictions on foreign ownership, 8
  skill level of workers with, 62–5
  student workers and, 70–1
  Taylorist/Fordist influences on, 21, 24–5, 39, 82
  temporary workers and, 69–70, 153
  wages in, range of, 75–6
  working hours with, 91–2

associational bargaining power, for autoworkers, 10

automation, in Chinese automobile industry. *See also* automobile industry, in China, mechanization of; just-in-time mass production; shop floor, production organization on
  capital-intensive industry, 89–92
  changing demand for worker skills, due to, 64–6, 89–90
  human wave tactics, 91
  lean production and, 93, 131–2
  mechanization, distinction from, 88
  standardized operations, 89–90
  technique control, 89–90
  technology upgrading, 88–9
  workers' marketplace bargaining power, affected by, 65–6, 89–90
  workers' workplace bargaining power, affected by, 89–91

automobile factories
  ethnography inside, 4–8
  factory regimes, 12–13
  labor force dualism in, 76

automobile industry, in China. *See also* development strategies, during the economic reform era; production, in Chinese automobile industry
  annual growth rates for, 73–4
  auto-assembly sector, 7–8, 28–33, 35, 42, 59–60, 74, 76, 80, 82, 90–1, 125
  automation in, 90–1
  auto-parts sector, 59–60, 76, 189
  blue-collar production in, 60–1
  central government intervention and policy for, 8
  consolidation in, 27, 36
  during Cultural Revolution, 25
  demographics of, 26
  development strategy, from 1986–2006, 26–8
  domestic private enterprises in, 8
  dominant ownership types in, 8
  early innovators in, 14
  expansion of, 40–2, 191
  exponential growth of, 3, 79

228

Japan (cont.)
as influence on corporate culture, 103,
129–30
as influence on HRM practice, 94
job classifications in, 99–100
lean production systems in, 83, 93
lean-and-dual model, 40
performance appraisals in, 105
production statistics in, 26
satei system in, 104
Toyota Production System in, 26, 140
Jeely, 8
Jintao, Hu, 56, 194
JIT mass production. *See* just-in-time mass
production
job classifications
in Chinese automobile industry, 99–100
in comparison to US automakers, 99–100
as different from skilled trade classifications,
64, 100
distinctions between blue-collar and
white-collar workers, 103
factory social order and, 103, 113
performance appraisals and, 100
at plant level, 100
at USA-1, 100–4
job insecurity
for formal workers, 123–5
labor contracts and, 53–4
for temporary workers, 151
job security
for formal workers, 122–6
in SOEs, 123–5
joint ventures (JVs)
in auto assembly sector, 8, 29–30, 32
auto market share, 30
Beijing Jeep, 33
in Chinese automobile industry, 3
under *danwei* system, 33
FDI through, 29
government approval of, 29
hegemonic consent in, 128–9
historical development of, 23
innovation in, 32
interventionism in, 42
layoffs in, 33
profitability of, 32–3
restructuring of auto industry and,
42, 48
Sino-American, 43, 76, 84, 92, 99, 140
Sino-German, 6, 43, 69, 79, 89, 117, 123–5,
128–9, 147
Sino-Japanese, 43, 67, 88–9, 91, 123, 140

SOEs and, 29, 31
SVW, 32–3, 38
in triple alliance, 28–30
wages for workers in, 33
wages in, range of, 75–6
worker benefits, 33
JPN-1, 37–45, 75–7, 88–9, 91, 103, 110, 123,
129–30, 132
June Strike, 154–7
just-in-time (JIT) mass production, 83–5
assembly shop, 85
body shop, 83–4
kanban method, 84–5
paint shop, 84
press shop, 83
temporary workers and, 153
JVs. *See* joint ventures

kanban method, 84–5
Kia, 30
Koo, Hagen, 103

labor agencies, 57
JPN-1, 123
Labor Contract Law (LCL), 13–14, 53–5
ACFTU and, 175, 180
agency employment regulation under, 162
amendments to, 179
employer's responses to, 176
labor dispatch under, 57, 174–5
making of, 174–7
National Labor Relations Act and, 181
objectives of, 173–4
open-term contracts under, 177
pro-capital/pro-labor negotiations under,
177
resistance of temporary workers and, 159–60
state boundary-drawing strategy, 177–80, 185
temporary agency workers under, 161–3, 169
unintended consequences of, 174–7
labor contracts, 53–4
at GER-2, 102
job insecurity with, 53–4
non-fixed *See* open-term contracts
open-term, 177
short-term, 54
at SOE-2, 124–5
at USA-1, 101, 130
labor dispatch, 55–7
in China, 56
expansion of, 56
FESCO, 56
flexibilization of labor, 57

Printed in the United States
By Bookmasters